The Japanese Police System Today

The Japanese Police System Today

A Comparative Study

L. Craig Parker, Jr.

An East Gate Book

M.E. Sharpe

Armonk, New York
London, England

An East Gate Book

Library of Congress Cataloging-in-Publication Data

Parker, L. Craig.

    The Japanese police system today : a comparative study / by L. Craig Parker, Jr.
      p. cm.
    "An East gate book"
    Includes index.
    ISBN 0-7656-0761-1 (alk. paper) — ISBN 0-7656-0762-X (pbk. : alk. paper)
    1. Police—Japan. 2. Police-community relations—Japan. I. Title.

HV8257.A2 P36 2001   2001020723
363.2′0952—dc21   CIP

Contents

List of Tables and Figures	ix
Preface	xi
1. Overview: Crime in Japan and the United States	3
2. The Historical and Legal Framework	12
Dispute Resolution	12
Historical Trends	18
Neighborhood Associations	25
The Suppression of Radicals	26
Policing after World War II	29
3. Overview of Police	32
Introduction	32
4. *Kōban* Police	38
The Tokyo Metropolitan Police Department	38
The Tsukiji Police Station	43
Guns in Japan and the United States	44
Emergency Calls	45
The Role of Women	52
Interview Tactics at Police Boxes	56

Policing Tokyo's Outlying Areas: Shitaya, Seijo,
  Akabane, Motofuji, and Sanya   58
The Shitaya Police Station   58
The Seijo Police Station   60
The Akabane Police Station   64
The Motofuji Police Station   65
Policing Sanya   66

5. Attitudes of the Police toward Their Work   69
Street Police   70
How They Become Interested   70
Police Crimes   78
Problems and Future Prospects   78
Police Administrators   80

6. The Hokkaido and Okayama Prefectural Police Forces   91
The Hokkaido Setting   91
Policing Hokkaido   92
The *Chūzai-san*   97
Profile of a *Chūzai-san*   100
Visits to Other *Chūzaisho* in Hokkaido   103
The Okayama Prefectural Police   105
The Ikayama-Higashi Police Station   109
The Okayama-Nishi Police Station   112
Visit to an Okayama *Chūzaisho*   119
The Railway Police   121

7. The Investigation of Crime   122
Financial and Computer Related Crime   129
Violence   130
The Role of the Public Prosecutor   134

8. Courts, Corrections, and Probation   146
Courts and the Trial Process   146
Imprisonment   149
Probation, Parole, and Community-based Treatment   154

9. Crime by Foreigners   158
Overview and Role of the Media   158

10. Crisis with Youth   174
    Overview   174
    Bōsōzoku   180
    The Kobe Murders   182
    Violence against Teachers and Authority Figures   184
    Dropping Out and Truancy   185
    Juvenile Counseling Centers   186
    Alcohol and Drug Abuse among Teens   190
    The Family Court   194
    Conclusion   195

11. The Police and the Community   197
    Family Counseling   197
    Suicide   201
    Living on the Edge—Day Workers, the Homeless,
      Prostitutes, and Social Welfare Recipients   207
    Crime Prevention   209
    Private Security   213
    Changes in Public Opinion toward the Police   214
    Comments from Scholars and Criminal Justice
      Professionals   217
    Public Opinion and Survey Data 1970s and 1980s   219
    Comments and Survey Data in 2000   221
    Dissidents, Radicals, and the Police   223
    The *Aum Shinrikyo* Sect   227
    Organized Crime   231

12. Conclusion   237
    Lessons from Japan   238

References   247
Index   255

List of Tables and Figures

Tables

1.1 International Comparison of Homicides, Homicide Rates,
and Homicides Cleared   6

5.1 Reasons Given for Joining the Police in Okayama
Prefecture   72

7.1 Financial and Bad Loan–Related Offenses Cleared,
1993–1997   130

7.2 Breakdown of High-Tech Crimes Known to Police and
Cleared in 1997   130

7.3 Cases Disposed of by Public Prosecutors by Offense and
Disposition, 1988–1997   138

7.4 Courts of First Instance, Adjudicated by Offense, 1996   142

8.1 Average Length of Trials and Number of Trial Dates,
1988–1992   150

8.2 Judgments by All Criminal Courts, 1989–1993   152

9.1 Foreign Residents in Japan   160

9.2 Number of Foreigners Arrested in Japan, 1988–1997   166

9.3 Foreigners Arrested by Country and Region, 1992–1997   168

9.4a Number of Foreigners Legally Entering Japan, 1980–1998   170

9.4b Number of Foreigners Illegally "Overstaying" in Japan,
January 1, 1999   170

9.4c Number of Foreigners Arrested by Tokyo Metropolitan
Police for Penal Code Offenses, 1994–1998   170

9.4d Number of All Foreign Offenders Compared to Chinese
Offenders, 1998   171

9.5a Foreign Offenders Arrested by Continent, 1998—
Tokyo M.P.D.   172
9.5b Foreign Offenses in Tokyo by Visa Status, 1998—
Tokyo M.P.D.   172
9.5c Felony Offenses (murder, robbery, rape, arson) with
Weapons, Foreign Offenders and All Offenders, 1988   173
9.5d Foreign Drug Offenses by Nationality, 1998   173
10.1 Police Arrests for Various Drug Law Violations,
1955–1997   193
11.1 Types of Problems and Disposition of Counseling Cases
by Police, 1997   202
11.2 Suicide by Age, 1997   205
11.3 Causes and Motives for Suicides, 1997   206
11.4 Leading Causes of Death in Japan, 1998   207
11.5 *Boryokudan* Membership in Japan, 1997   233
11.6 Arrests of Regular and Associate *Boryokudan* Members,
1988–1997   234

Figures

4.1a, 4.1b The Residence Information Card (for alien
residents)   47–48
4.2 Suggestions for Police Recruits   50
4.3 *Kōban* Officer Log   53
5.1 Organizational Chart of National Police Agency   90
6.1 Prefectural Police Organizational Structure   93
6.2 Police Station Organizational Structure   94
6.3 Organization of Okayama Police   107
6.4, 6.5, 6.6, 6.7 Examples of crime prevention leaflets
distributed by the Okayama police.   115–118
8.1 Proceedings in a Criminal Trial   148
8.2 Instructions and Regulations (Excerpts) Given to Prisoners
of Fuchu Prison   155
10.1 Teenagers Arrested for Murder, Robbery, Rape, and
Arson, 1988–1998   178
10.2 Rate of Serious Juvenile Crimes Cleared (per 100,000)
by Police for Germany, United Kingdom, United States,
France, Japan, and South Korea, 1987–1996   179
10.3 Juvenile Violators of the Stimulant Drugs Control Law
and Those Cleared by Police, 1970–1997   192
11.1 Suicide Rates among Japanese Citizens, 1950–1998   204

Preface

I anticipated an interesting year in Japan when I was informed that I had received a Fulbright Research Fellowship for 1980–81, but I had no idea that my plan to study police–community relations would lead me to such a challenging and rewarding experience. At the outset, less than twenty-four hours after my arrival in Tokyo, I was informed that the National Police Agency could give me "about one week in September" for my research. However, soon after this news, which had been relayed by the Ministry of Foreign Affairs to the Fulbright office, I had the good fortune to meet a prestigious Japanese legal scholar who immediately contacted members of the Tokyo Public Safety Commission and set in motion a series of introductions that proved invaluable in my efforts to gain support for my research program.

As I learned quickly, without personal introductions many projects are doomed in Japan. This problem is not peculiar to foreigners: the Japanese face it as well. A Japanese businessman will not approach a fellow businessman or a bureaucrat without a proper introduction if he expects to be successful in his endeavors. Often the initiating party will ask a former classmate or an acquaintance to arrange the meeting. This "go-between" may be able to lay the groundwork or actually arrange an introduction. The Japanese have a word for this: *nemawashi*, "to lay the groundwork for obtaining one's objective." I was fortunate that despite the initial unresponsiveness of the police bureaucracy, with some timely *nemawashi* I was able to obtain their full cooperation. Once they agreed to help, I was denied nothing.

Over the last twenty-five years or so, various Western researchers have penetrated the Japanese police bureaucracy and have conducted extensive studies (e.g., see David H. Bayley, *Forces of Order: Policing Modern Japan*, and Walter L. Ames, *Police and Community in Japan*). Despite the fact that these studies convey a complimentary view of Japanese police services, conversations I had with legal scholars and officials convinced me that the Japanese police in the early 1980s were reluctant to accommodate further research. One may ask, however, whether there is a police agency anywhere in the world that would be eager to receive researchers. By the very nature of police work, administrators shy away from exposing the inner mechanisms of their agencies. However, in this instance there may have been an advantage to being an outsider. A legal scholar at Sophia University in Tokyo pointed out that just as it might be easier for a Japanese researcher to gain access to the police community in America, likewise a Japanese police department might be more willing to receive a foreign official or scholar than his Japanese counterpart.

There are advantages to approaching a country with an open mind free from bias and preconceived notions, but I must admit that on more than one occasion I would have gladly traded my newcomer status for that of a seasoned scholar familiar with the language and customs of Japan. Not being a Japanologist placed a burden on me as a researcher, but my Japanese friends and colleagues were invaluable in assisting me in getting acquainted with the country and its customs. Fellow scholars and criminal justice professionals were particularly helpful; I felt that there were any number of them upon whom I could rely for assistance.

This continued to be true in the follow-up research I conducted in 1999 for this new edition of my earlier book, published in 1984 by Kodansha (*The Japanese Police System Today: An American Perspective*). Also, there were many occasions when my status as an outsider worked to my advantage. For the uninitiated foreigner the simplest daily encounter can be a learning experience, whether asking directions—in which police are frequently very helpful—or trying to get on the right subway for Shinjuku. Occasionally my requests for assistance from an ordinary citizen on a mundane matter such as locating the proper train in a busy subway station went unheeded, but my Japanese friends pointed out that frequently this was because of the embarrassment that some Japanese feel because of their inability to answer in English. Since English is taught beginning in junior high school, there is an expectation that most Japanese are able to speak at least a little. The inability to do so in such a situation is usually due to shyness or a lack of self-confidence. In the majority of cases, however, I encountered a willingness to help, and indeed many times Japanese people went out of their way to assist me. This was true in the early 1980s and was equally true in 1999.

My research relied on an observational approach. To conduct my original research I spent five months in Tokyo, two months in Hokkaido, and an additional month in a variety of other locations throughout Japan. I made numerous visits to police boxes and conducted many interviews with police officers, public prosecutors, social scientists, legal scholars, judges, probation offices, and citizens. I was able to cross-check sensitive information that emerged from the field study of police behavior with individual police officers and scholars who became my friends. The follow-up research, conducted during the summer of 1999, included observations of police operations and interviews with police and justice officials in Tokyo and Okayama City (Okayama Prefecture). The latter opportunity developed because my colleague Senior Superintendent Mitsuo Uehara had been the Chief of Okayama Prefectural Police. My extensive background as a criminal justice scholar and consulting psychologist also provided a valuable framework for evaluating observations of the Japanese system.

For the most part I found the police to be candid and forthright. Japanese officials are naturally interested in making a favorable impression, so one is usually treated with respect at police boxes and in interviews with administrators. This is preferable to having to contend with hostility or total indifference, but this politeness, for which the Japanese are known, can also be a hindrance to the researcher. It is necessary for the foreigner to have associates he can rely upon and with whom he can cross-check matters such as the disciplining of officers and weaknesses within the system. In the United States, precinct-level police might or might not cooperate with a researcher, regardless of whether or not they had the support of the police administration. In Japan, once the police administration agrees to assist you, there is full compliance at all levels. This is just one example of the vertical hierarchical structure of Japanese society that Chie Nakane described so accurately (1970). As in the Japanese industrial sector, teamwork and support are very much in evidence among the police. Loyalty is also highly valued, and commands from superiors are typically executed to the letter by lower-ranking officers. In the United States, a research project involving street-level police personnel would need the approval of both the administration and the union leadership, whereas in Japan no such complication arises. Moreover, a job action by sick calls, such as occasionally takes place in the United States, would be unimaginable in Japan. Japanese police are not unionized.

Several people were particularly helpful, and I would like to take this opportunity to thank them. My colleague, Isshu Takahashi, a law professor at Hosei University, was of immeasurable assistance in familiarizing me with Japanese customs and behavior. In 1980 my biggest handicap was my inability to speak Japanese, and I was extremely fortunate in being able to obtain the services of such a bright and versatile translator as Mari Kanai, who played a critical role in helping me cope with the language problem. She is the daughter of a Japanese diplomat and had traveled widely during her twenty-six years. She graduated from Keio University and spoke excellent English. Her extensive exposure to Western culture allowed her to be sensitive to my research concerns. As a friend noted, an interpreter does much more than change English phrases into Japanese ones and vice versa: she or he also acts as an intermediary between the researcher and the subjects of the study. Mari was able to relate to police officers and other officials in a candid, friendly manner, which greatly facilitated my dialogue with them. With her family background and experience, she was at ease with high-ranking officials as well as with working police. In the Japanese language, knowing the appropriate level of politeness to use in a given situation is essential. Mari was able to aid me in interpreting the various nuances of interpersonal relationships expressed in the language itself.

While initially I had been concerned about using a female interpreter in Japan's masculine police world, I came to realize that the sex of the interpreter was far less important than the personality of the individual. I consulted any number of Japanese colleagues on this subject, and the general consensus was that a well-qualified woman interpreter would be perfectly acceptable. Since interpreters tend to be women in Japan, I believe there was nothing unusual in an American professor arriving at a police box accompanied by a woman interpreter.

I would be remiss were I not to mention the fine assistance offered by Susumu Kitaidai, a former student at International Christian University. Kitaidai was fluent in English. Like Mari Kanai he had spent a number of years outside of Japan. He had, in fact, lived almost half his life in White Plains, New York, and Washington, D.C. Periodically he filled in for Mari Kanai when she was not available.

During the period of my research in Japan in the 1980s many people assisted me by arranging contacts, offering suggestions, and gathering data. They were properly identified in the earlier edition.

For the new edition, I wish to thank the following persons for reading it and consulting with me. They include Lisa Carter, Mitsuo Uehara, and Ken Hattori. Also, Doug Merwin, Patricia Loo, Angela Piliouras, and the staff of M.E. Sharpe did a wonderful job in preparing the revised manuscript for publication.

L. Craig Parker
Professor of Criminal Justice
University of New Haven
April 2001

The Japanese Police System Today

1

Overview: Crime in Japan and the United States

In the United States awareness of Japan has increased rapidly in recent decades, largely due to what was perceived as a growing economic threat. With economic anxiety, however, came a certain amount of cross-cultural curiosity. Among the points of interest is Japan's surprisingly low crime rate. Though less dazzling than the economic achievements of "Japan Inc.," facts such as this low level of crime have continued to draw our attention to a national phenomenon that is far more complex and, I feel, far more interesting than the simple ability to produce good, small cars. Although Japan was mired in a deep recession in the 1990s, with bankruptcies and suicides being linked to the economic despair, it was not long ago that Americans were apprehensive that the Japanese were out to buy up some of the most prestigious properties—including Rockefeller Center in New York City—in the United States. Michael Crichton's best-selling novel *Rising Sun* (1992), in which powerful Japanese business interests attempt to thwart a murder investigation in Los Angeles, only added fuel to the fire.

During my first visit to Japan in 1980–81, I strolled the streets of Tokyo, Kyoto, Yokohama, Kobe, Sapporo, and a number of other Japanese cities and towns without once feeling threatened or menaced by an individual or a group. I rode subways that were not defaced with graffiti, and I wandered through parks at midnight in the heart of Tokyo without apprehension. I concede that this state of mind took a while to acquire, since I had become accustomed to the streets of New York and

Boston long before arriving in Tokyo. Though not altogether crime free, by any yardstick one wishes to use, Japan continues to provide a relatively tranquil and safe social environment. This remarkable feature of Japanese society deserves attention from the United States, which is in the midst of a crime crisis. One way to illustrate the success of the Japanese in this area is by comparison with the United States, and while this work is not intended to be systematic, point-by-point comparison of each country's approach to law enforcement, I would like to begin with a comparative perspective. The primary purpose of this book, however, is to explore the role of the police in community relations in Japan, as seen through the eyes of a psychologist.

It is difficult to draw comparisons between crime data reports from Japan and the United States because the different levels of public confidence in police effectiveness in these countries result in different rates of reporting crime. In addition, descriptive terms for crimes—even after making allowances for possible inaccuracy of translation—may have different connotations in each country, further confounding comparisons.

It appears that the Japanese report a larger percentage of crime than Americans do. This is evidenced by the discrepancies between their various crime indices and our own. Because of the unreliability of statistical data issued in the *Uniform Crime Reports* of the Federal Bureau of Investigation (FBI), the U.S. Department of Justice began direct household surveys of crime a number of years ago. This approach revealed, not surprisingly, a significantly higher incidence of actual crime than that reported by citizens to police.

The FBI, as the clearinghouse or coordinating agency, must contend not only with the outright manipulation of data as reported by many police departments, but also with their varying systems of crime classification. Admittedly, there have been attempts to standardize police reporting of crime, but these appear to have enjoyed only modest success. Pressure to report certain types of crime has political implications for local police chiefs. A police analyst eager to obtain federal funds for a pet project may "stack the deck" in a certain category. Thus, ultimately, the FBI must rely on the veracity of the reports issued by the hundreds of police agencies throughout the nation, even though error and bias are known to exist.

The National Police Agency in Japan coordinates policy-making and standards for the forty-seven prefectural police organizations throughout the country and thus has an advantage when it comes to the standardization of police practices and the compilation of data. The reporting system and classification of crime data are therefore more accurate. Because high-ranking police officials are insulated from the whims of local politicians, and because they are rotated in their assignments approximately every two years, they are not likely to be vulnerable to pressures to tamper with the raw data in their possession. This subject will be discussed later in detail.

Notwithstanding the problems inherent in reporting and compiling statistical data, what do some of the comparisons between Japan and the United States indicate for a recent year? Although the Japanese population was 126 million in 1996 and the United States population was 265 million (a bit more than double), the incidence of crime was much greater in the United States (U.S. Department of Justice 1997; National Police Agency of Japan 1998). For example, the total number of homicides in Japan was 1,257 in 1996 compared to 19,650 in the United States. In the case of robbery, there were 535,590 reported to the police in the United States compared to just 2,463 robberies reported to the police in Japan. The numbers for rape were also dramatically different—in the United States 96,250 rapes were reported, while in Japan the comparable number was just 1,483. The usual caveat applies here, that although law enforcement authorities in both countries have used various means to encourage the reporting of the crime of rape, it continues to be underreported in both nations. An inspection of the category larceny– theft (including auto theft) shows that in the United States there were 9,298,900, while in Japan during 1996 there were 1,588,698 offenses reported to the police (U.S. Department of Justice 1997; National Police Agency of Japan 1998). Thus, there are staggering differences in the numbers of crimes committed in both countries, with the number of robberies representing a particularly dramatic difference—approximately 220 times as many robberies in the United States as in Japan. Interestingly, this is a roughly similar ratio to the one reported in the 1984 edition of this book.

Table 1.1 provides comparisons with four other nations on homicides, homicide clearance rates, and homicide rates per 100,000 population as reported by the Japanese Ministry of Justice (1998). The data are consistent with the above-mentioned crime statistics in revealing not only the large discrepancies between homicide rates in the United States and the other developed countries, but in clearance rates as well. Here Japan is superior not only to the United States, but also to the other Western European countries. All five countries showed modest declines in actual

Table 1.1

International Comparison of Homicides, Homicide Rates, and Homicides Cleared (rates are per 100,000 population)

No. homicides reported by police	United States	United Kingdom	Germany	France	Japan
1994	23,326	1,377	3,751	2,696	1,321
Crime rate	9.0	2.7	4.6	4.7	1.1
Clearance rate	64.4	89.5	87.2	72.6	96.1
1995	21,606	1,379	3,960	2,563	1,312
Crime rate	8.2	2.7	4.9	4.4	1.0
Clearance rate	64.8	90.8	88.2	75.1	96.3
1996	19,645	1,355	3,531	2,385	1,257
Crime rate	7.4	2.6	4.3	4.1	1.0
Clearance rate	66.9	91.0	92.1	74.9	98.5

Source: Ministry of Justice 1998.

numbers of homicides between 1994 and 1996. In the comparison on rate of homicide between the United States and Japan, the rates of 1.0 for Japan and 7.4 for the United States for 1996 reveal a slight improvement in the U.S. rate that the author reported back in 1980. Then the numbers were 1.6 Japan and 9.0 United States. European countries do not have the glaringly high crime rates of the United States, but even in comparison with them, Japan still has impressively low crime rates. How can this be accounted for, considering that Japan's population is as urbanized, industrialized, and sophisticated as those of the most advanced Western nations? This is not an elusive matter that defies understanding. Moreover, by understanding it, we can gain a greater appreciation of our own crime problems.

For years, the Japanese seemed to accept without question the difference between their society and others' on the subject of crime control. Over the years, however, the publication of various books by David Bayley, Walter Ames, and William Clifford has helped to awaken Westerners to what is occurring in the Japanese system of justice, and in turn the Japanese have become more conscious of their own success. Alvin Toffler, the author of *Future Shock*, collaborated with his wife, Heidi, on a series of articles that focused on the strengths and weaknesses of Japanese society. The Tofflers expressed concern that the media bombardment of the early eighties, which emphasized Japanese successes, would result in a "backlash." In their view, a caricature had been emerging in which "we see 115,000,000 docile, dedicated and highly motivated workers smoothly managed by a few giant, paternalistic corporations whose top leaders work hand-in-glove with an understanding government" (Toffler and Toffler 1981). In their opinion, that picture was far from the truth. The notion of *Japan As Number One,* the title of Ezra Vogel's 1980 book, grossly oversimplified a nation that had real weaknesses and vulnerabilities in addition to its highly advertised strengths. As one example, they cite Japan's energy problems. While in the United States we rely upon other nations for just 22.4 percent of our energy requirements, Japan must import 86.3 percent of its energy. Concerning food supplies, the Tofflers reminded us that while Americans were among the top food exporters in the world, the European Economic Community must import 25 percent of its food and the Japanese are required to import over 50 percent of their food to meet demand. In short, while Japanese fuel-efficient automobiles, technologically sophisticated radios and television sets, and other quality products attracted wide attention, there was a vulnerability acknowledged by few at the time. The so-called economic miracle or the "bubble economy" of the early 1990s burst in a major recession, with extensive bankruptcies and a major decline in real estate values. Thus, the Tofflers' assessment proved prophetic.

The issues related to the low crime rate in Japan that will be explored in this book include the following: first, the homogeneous makeup of Japanese society, which is a powerful factor in exerting social controls on illegal, and in many instances, deviant behavior. There are very few minorities in Japan, with Koreans representing the largest group, but they number only approximately 700,000 in a total population of 126 million. However, by the late 1990s, increasing numbers of foreigners, particularly Chinese, were causing concern for Japanese justice officials. A chapter on this subject addresses this problem of the "internationalization of crime."

A second issue, which is not easily separated from the overall social fabric of Japanese life, is the large network of both formal and informal groups. Membership in a group or one's role in the group appears to be far more important than individuality, which is so highly prized in the United States. The emphasis on teamwork and the support Japanese offer one another clearly has implications for the low crime rate. Japanese family relationships are important in any discussion of the role of the group. Family members have a sense of responsibility for one another. The nature of this responsibility and the part played by family and larger community groups will be examined at length.

As a corollary to the closeness that develops through group life, the

Japanese attempt to solve interpersonal conflict and seek harmony wherever possible. Japanese are fond of attributing their ability to get along with one another at least in part to the fact that they are living in a small island country. As I noted in an article for the *Japan Times:* "Japanese rarely act on feelings of hostility in public. A shove will not bring retaliation in a physical way, or probably even a verbal way. In Chicago, an obscene gesture could possibly result in your summary execution by the offended party. A shove in a New York subway might conceivably result in a knife between your ribs" (Parker 1981).

The Japanese also help to discipline one another through informal assistance and intervention. While occasionally police have to assist drunks, fellow workers are far more likely to come to their assistance. In contrast, Americans tend not to associate in groups as often, and a drunk is more likely to have to rely on public officials for help than on a colleague or friend.

Related to these other social values is the powerful role of conformity. Despite the westernization that has taken place in Japan since World War II, the pressure to conform is still very strong. The Japanese have a saying: "The nail that sticks up will get hammered down." American Fulbright lecturers, often unacquainted with Japanese society, express dismay that their students demonstrate little willingness to speak out and engage in energetic debate in class sessions. The Japanese student is afraid to stand out from the rest of his or her classmates. It is not unusual to hear of Japanese businessmen who have worked abroad for a number of years struggling to find their place in their companies upon returning to Japan. They may lose out on their promotions or advance at a different rate from their colleagues because they are suspected of having been tainted by their exposure to foreign ways. Similarly, students who receive their college education in the United States or other Western nations are sometimes handicapped when they have to compete with their Japanese-educated fellows for jobs. This sort of conformity, as will be seen, carries over into the realms of crime and crime prevention.

The legal system reflects the value of conflict resolution through nonadversarial methods. There is considerably less litigation in Japan than in other industrialized nations. The first response to coping with a neighborhood problem is not to consult one's lawyer for advice, but to attempt to work out a compromise with one's potential adversary. There are only 3 percent as many lawyers in Japan as in the United States—a figure that reflects this lesser demand for litigation.

The Japanese generally have much greater respect for legal and governmental institutions than do Americans, and the police benefit from this attitude. Unlike the situation in the United States, where police, particularly in larger cities, are beleaguered and viewed with suspicion, Japanese police are generally trusted and respected. The development of the legal system and the historical evolution of police services will be discussed later in this book.

In outlining some of the reasons for the low crime rate in Japan, one cannot ignore the strict gun control laws. In 1996, just 128 crimes were committed with guns. Strict regulations contribute to a low incidence of firearms-related crimes in Japan, and in 1996 there were just forty-three firearms-related murders and attempted murders (National Police Agency of Japan 1998). Below is the policy concerning firearms and swords in Japan:

> In Japan, in principle, possession of firearms and swords is prohibited under the Firearms and Swords Control Law. The Law's intent is to prevent danger and to secure the public safety.
>
> To possess firearms, one must obtain a license from the Prefectural Public Safety Commission. No firearms license is granted to persons under age 18 (or under 20 for a hunting gun), persons suffering from mental disorder, persons addicted to drugs, persons with no fixed residence, persons having a criminal record (particularly in violation of the Firearms and Swords Control Law), and persons, like *Boryokudan* members, who are justifiably feared as a threat to public safety.
>
> Gun licenses must be renewed every three years. As of 1996, approximately 440,000 hunting guns and air guns were licensed.
>
> Handgun regulations are the most restrictive. Handgun possession is almost totally banned, except for legally permitted police officers and Self-Defense Forces personnel only while on duty, and a limited number of sport pistol shooters permitted by the prefectural Public Safety Commission.
>
> Possession of a toy gun is also prohibited as long as the gun falls under the category of "imitation gun." Whether a toy gun is regarded as an "imitation gun" depends on its resemblance to a genuine one in appearance, mechanism, or function. (p. 35)

This policy is clearly one of the major reasons for the low rate of violent crime in Japan, and Americans could take a lesson from the Japanese in this respect. My Japanese colleagues indicated that they could not understand the obsession many Americans have with gun ownership.

Economic considerations are also important in accounting for Japan's comparatively low crime rate, notwithstanding the recession of the late 1990s. Examining averages in Japan and the United States for income, production, and other economic factors is misleading because although the figures often parallel each other in a general way, they do not disclose important underlying variations. Particularly important in the case of Japan is the generally high standard of living and the broad distribution of wealth among all social strata. Unemployment, although higher in the 1990s, is still lower than in the United States. For 1997, the unemployment rate in Japan was just 3.4 percent, while in the United States it was 4.9 percent (Foreign Press Center 1999). Most Japanese consider themselves members of the middle class. Still, the postwar Japanese policies such as lifetime employment and seniority-based salaries have changed dramatically as the economic recession has taken its toll. Gradually firms are beginning to lay off employees in economically distressed industries or those engaged in restructurings to avoid bankruptcies. In late 1999, Nissan's new, tough-minded, appointed foreign boss, Carlos Ghosn, announced plans to cut 16,500 jobs, which on the surface seemed to represent a radical departure from Japan's lifetime employment system (Gordon 1999). However, a closer look at the policy revealed that cost-cutting would take place over three years and many of the adjustments would come through attrition, hiring freezes, voluntary retirements, and reassignments of employees to subsidiaries. Still the policy from a Japanese perspective must seem like radical surgery. These social and economic changes have proven to be not only painful but embarrassing for many Japanese, as "outsiders" rarely have had an economic foothold in Japanese society. Also, there are more and more cases of Japanese changing jobs, and employers are beginning to promote individuals based on merit and not seniority. These are very significant changes in Japan because lifetime employment and promotions (along with salary increases) based on seniority have been part of the bedrock of the Japanese culture.

On the other hand, notwithstanding the economic recession, there is little outward evidence of the Japanese consumer cutting back on purchases such as clothing and entertainment. Tokyo seemed little different to the visitor in 1999 compared to 1980. Entertainment and shopping districts such as Shinjuku and the Ginza flourished with the usual bright lights and pounding music.

Skiing on some of Japan's winter slopes offered a glimpse of the affluence that is widespread. Rarely did one encounter a Japanese who was not dressed in a fashionable outfit. At the ski lodges of Hokkaido, waitresses on vacation are indistinguishable from wealthy matrons. In city areas where one might expect to find poverty and decay, such as near railway stations, one rarely comes upon derelicts that are more often seen in American cities. In the late 1990s, this problem has been particularly evident in downtown San Francisco. Walking with police during their regular patrols in all types of neighborhoods in Tokyo and elsewhere, I rarely saw an entire section of a city bereft of resources, deteriorating, and run-down, as is so often the case in the inner cities in the United States.

Finally, in exploring the various reasons for Japan's low crime rate, a brief discussion of justice agencies and institutions—other than the police—will also be offered.

2

The Historical and Legal Framework

Dispute Resolution

Japan has traditionally been described as a nation in which the formal system of justice, so eagerly embraced in the United States, is shunned, and extrajudicial informal procedures are sought. Historically, the whole concept of "dispute" has been an anathema to the Japanese, who prefer to see disagreements or conflicts between parties in a less aggressive light. As Kawashima (1963) suggests:

> Litigation presupposes and admits the existence of a dispute and leads to a decision which makes clear who is right or wrong in accordance with standards that are independent of the wills of the disputants. Furthermore, judicial decisions emphasize the conflict between the parties, deprive them of participation in the settlement, and assign a moral fault which can be avoided in a compromise solution. (p. 43)

While Meiji government leaders near the end of the nineteenth century moved rapidly to introduce a European-style legal system in Japan, the deeply rooted feudalism of the Tokugawa period was not to be immediately overcome. Early innovations, such as the Penal Code of 1880 and the Criminal Procedure Code of 1890, reflected influence from the French system. Later, the Meiji legal system tended to show the Germanic (Prussian) influence that can be seen in many of the social and political reforms of the time. Tanabe comments on the reluctance of

Japanese to engage in litigation in the wake of the implementation of these codes and statutes:

> Under the long tradition of unusually strong governmental control and community pressure, the rights consciousness of the Japanese people was very low. Strong social and psychological pressures discouraged the filing of lawsuits, and manifold out-of-court resolution, techniques and mechanisms, such as mediation by relatives, court marshals, or local leaders, were commonly used. The compromise of civil disputes was generally regarded as the most desirable solution. In farming villages and small towns, suit against a neighbor was even a moral wrong. (1963, p. 77)

Even today, some contracts and agreements are still concluded orally without relying on lawyers. In other cases, a simple, written agreement might be drawn up by the parties themselves. Despite this historical reluctance to engage in litigation, change has been creeping in since World War II. My discussions with a wide variety of legal scholars, police officers, court personnel, and private citizens suggest that legal consciousness is growing in Japan. The number of cases brought to court has increased since World War II.

An interesting feature of the Japanese system of policing is that the availability of neighborhood police boxes allows citizens to seek out officers as informal arbiters of conflict. Citizens still rely on police for this type of counseling (known as *komarigoto sodan*) and problem resolution to a far greater degree than do Americans. In general, the Japanese prefer a moral norm as opposed to a legal one for conflict resolution. Turning to a lawyer is admitting failure. According to Gibney:

> To the Japanese, the law is not a norm but a framework for discussion. The good Japanese judge is the man who can arrange and settle the most compromises out of court. When an American calls his lawyer, he is confident and happy to rely on the strength of his whole social system, the rule of law. When a Japanese calls his lawyer, he is sadly admitting that, in this case, his social system has broken down. (1975, p. 82)

Kawashima (1963) noted that there are two characteristics of the traditional social groups in Japan that have influenced the nonadversarial and extrajudicial approach to dispute resolution. First, there is the hierarchical characteristic, that is, social status is clearly defined in terms of deference and authority. Family, community, and even contractual relationships are hierarchical. A contract of employment implies the deference of the employee to the employer; according to a contract of apprenticeship, the apprentice defers to the master; from a contract of sale, the seller defers to the buyer. Furthermore, Kawashima was quick to point out, the status of the master or employer is "patriarchal" and not "despotic." The implication is that the master or employer, while dominating in the relationship, will also give in and compromise on requests from the subordinate. This delicate balance of socially prescribed roles in Japan is alien to the American system of law and justice, which has been based on fixed, universal standards.

A second characteristic of traditional social groups in Japan is that between individuals of equal status, relationships have been both "particularistic" and "functionally diffuse." That is to say, for members of the same village community who are equal in social status, relationships are supposed to be "intimate" (a somewhat weakened version of the term as defined by Westerners), and their roles are defined vaguely and flexibly so that they lend themselves to adjustment whenever circumstances dictate. Thus, relationships are imbedded in a tradition that urges compromise, adjustment, and fluidity. Disputes are not supposed to arise, and the drawing up of formal, legal contracts only anticipates the breakdown of agreements between parties.

Private citizens are reluctant to invoke the law, but business firms are no more eager to engage in litigation.

> Japanese companies rarely sue each other, for example, over breach of contract; indeed, their written contracts usually aren't very specific in the first place. Executives from squabbling companies prefer to work their problems out through personal trust and understanding. (Meyerson 1981, 4)

Japanese businessmen do not arrive armed with lawyers at important conferences with government officials. There is a reluctance to sue because financial incentives are lacking. In antitrust suits, for example, plaintiffs are not awarded "treble damages."

Kitagawa's (1974) discussion of field research on the lack of desire of Japanese to engage in litigation indicates similar findings: The motivation for the small number of proceedings is connected with the traditional social-ordering structures. "From 65–75 percent of those questioned favored the extralegal methods of conciliation for resolution of legal disputes." Large businesses in Japan have solved about 70 to 99 percent of their legal disputes through private reconciliation, while about 1 to 30 percent of such disputes have been brought to trial.

While the Japanese tradition has discouraged litigation, the United States has increasingly relied upon formal legal proceedings to resolve conflicts. Articles appear in American journals and magazines decrying the increase in the number of lawyers and litigation. In Auerbach's (1976) attack on the growth of law and the number of lawyers in the United States in his article "A Plague of Lawyers," he notes that the ratio of lawyers to the general population had grown from one lawyer for every 1,100 Americans at the beginning of the twentieth century to one for every 530 Americans by 1976. As McKay (1978) observed, "Americans typically insist on more, not less, law as corrective." He offered the efforts of Ralph Nader and his associates in the field of public interest law as one example of how social change has been accomplished through litigation in America. While I disagree with the notion that Americans, given the choice, would opt for more law, it is clear that the open marketplace and the diversity of U.S. society have created an atmosphere in which law and litigation have grown without constraint. As we enter a new millennium, we see that there has been a gradual growth in the numbers of mediators and other forms of dispute resolution, but the massive scale of the legal profession tends to crowd out these other dispute resolution approaches.

The survey, "Japanese Legal Consciousness," conducted by the Japan Culture Council (*Nihon Bunka Kaigi*), which sampled 1,500 people living in Tokyo in 1971, further documented the feelings of the Japanese about legal matters. Ames (1981), in reporting on this survey, observed that both the form (*tatemae*) and deeper gut-level feeling (*honne*) are revealed in the responses to three questions. Eighty-nine percent of the subjects stated that it was best to write up a contract no matter how much the two parties trusted each other, and 90 percent felt that the contract should be very detailed in order to avoid misinterpretations—these attitudes might be termed *tatemae*. However, interestingly enough (and in apparent contradiction to the earlier responses), 65 percent felt that the contract could be abrogated by simply renegotiating with the other party when circumstances dictated; this view represents the *honne,* or underlying intention. While the first two responses are consistent with the westernization of Japan, the latter one appears to stem from a more traditional Japanese view.

Another factor contributing to the apparent lack of litigation in Japan is that many matters normally reserved for licensed attorneys in the

United States are handled by nonlicensed lawyers in Japan. These nonlicensed "lawyers" are usually graduates of law programs offered by Japanese colleges and universities at a level equivalent to undergraduate education in the United States. If one wishes to become a practicing lawyer, judge, or public prosecutor, one must apply for admission to the two-year course at the Judicial and Legal Training Institute, where admission standards are extremely high. Competition has been so severe, in recent decades, that even a graduate of Tokyo University's elite law faculty was far from being assured a place in what was a typical class of 500 out of 30,000 yearly applicants. That process is now easing a bit as we move to the year 2002. In an interview with the author on August 28, 1999, practicing attorney Yamakawa stated that 1,000 openings currently exist in the two-year program and that a high-level governmental commission is studying the possibility of expanding the number to 2,000 or even 3,000 openings in the future. This would mean a larger pool of lawyers, prosecutors, and judges, but still small numbers of legal functionaries in comparison with the United States.

Japanese universities, like the rest of the society, are hierarchically ranked, with Tokyo University coming first in most fields, and the prestige of graduating from such an institution assures a variety of options, even for those not admitted to the Judicial and Legal Training Institute. For example, a majority of the members of the elite class of bureaucrats at the National Police Agency are Tokyo University law faculty graduates. Only ten to twenty of those who successfully pass the National Public Service Examination each year are admitted to this special class—hereafter referred to as the "elite" program—as assistant inspectors. The majority of these young officers eventually become chiefs of the forty-seven prefectural police agencies or assume other top posts. In general, national governmental positions that carry responsibility are considered prestigious choices in Japan and are open primarily to graduates of the upper-ranked universities.

Most of the twenty or more high-ranking officers I interviewed or worked with at the headquarters of the National Police Agency in Tokyo in both 1980 and 1999, were graduates of the law faculty at Tokyo University. While these graduates frequently seek employment in the various national ministries and bureaucracies, they also find their way into positions of prominence in business and elsewhere, and thus their work may not be legal in nature, despite their having completed an undergraduate degree in law.

A law course at a university in Japan is similar to most undergraduate majors in the United States; the first one and a half years are quite general, while the last two and a half years are more specialized. Graduates of these programs, while not designated as lawyers, are able to draft wills, litigate small claims, offer tax advice, and write contracts. Most of these same functions are performed in the United States by lawyers who have passed state bar examinations. Japan now has approximately 14,500 lawyers serving a population of 126 million, compared to the 985,000 lawyers practicing in the United States, with a population just a little more than twice Japan's. The ratios are 1 to 9,200 in Japan and 1 to 350 in the United States.

The Japanese concept of rights also has a bearing on the national attitude toward litigation. The expectation that agreements will be kept and obligations met makes the notion of "demanding one's rights" something of an anomaly. Historically, the individual's rights have been subservient to the needs of the group in Japan. Kawashima (1963) explained that the individual's desires are "absorbed in the interest of the collectivity to which he belongs, and the interest of the collectivity is recognized as having primary importance, while the interest of the individual has merely a secondary importance." In his study of police in Japan, Walter Ames noted that the previously mentioned survey of legal consciousness suggested a greater awareness of rights now than before the Occupation. He continued:

> In a question about the priority of individual rights or the priority of the public welfare, the answers were almost equally divided (48 percent felt the public welfare should take precedence over individual rights, while 42 percent felt the opposite). (1963, p. 239)

During interviews with police officers who were working out of the mini–police stations and in administrative offices in various cities, I frequently asked both in the early 1980s and in 1999, "What has changed the most during your career?" Numerous responses were received on the theme of "citizens' awareness of their rights." Not surprisingly, the police viewed this growth in the number of people citing their rights as making their job more difficult. Younger citizens, in particular, are less compliant than they used to be. Human rights commissions have flourished all over Japan since the end of World War II, and a "Human Rights Protection Commission" exists in every prefecture.

The erosion of traditional values, which provided a braking effect on the growth of criminal behavior, and the increased reliance on law were evident to Hirano more than thirty-five years ago:

> The role of criminal law as an agency of social control will become more pervasive, since nonlegal forms of control such as the family and community will surely become less and less powerful. At the same time, criminal law will become more functional and less moralistic. (1963, p. 290)

Historical Trends

While a detailed history of Japan's judicial system is beyond the scope of this work, some observations concerning the beginnings of the police system seem appropriate. During the feudal period of the Tokugawa Shogunate, from 1603 to 1867, there were four clearly defined classes. At the top were the *samurai*, who were the warriors and the military arm of the feudal lords, or *daimyo*. They were followed by the peasants, the artisans, and the merchants. The class system of this time was very strict and upward movement was difficult—you were born into a class and you stayed there throughout your lifetime. Loyalty to the government and to one's family characterized this period, and there was little reliance on formal law. Hirano noted that throughout Japanese history,

> It is not the awareness of punishment which serves to deter a Japanese so much as the awareness of the impact which the fact of his involvement in criminal proceedings would have on himself and, more important, on his family. (1963, p. 291)

Westney (1982) noted that formalized police services as we know them today did not appear until the Meiji period. Instead, *samurai* attached to government agencies acted as police. Their activities were overseen by magistrates assigned to cities and towns. *Samurai* alone were entitled to wear weapons during this period, and wore two swords in their belts, one, three, or four feet long, and the other two feet long, which served both as weapons and as symbols of rank. Attached to *samurai* status was not only the power but the obligation to act as a kind of policeman. At least officially a *samurai* had the right to draw his sword and kill a commoner who deviated in any way from the proper social role. *Samurai,* particularly lower-ranking *samurai,* were sensitive about this status prerogative and tended to draw their swords at the slightest provocation. Examples of behavior that deviated from the norm included not bowing low enough or not kneeling when the feudal lord's procession was passing by. A number of international incidents occurred during the 1850s and 1860s in which *samurai* retainers cut down Westerners who did not kneel when the procession of a feudal lord was passing.

Japanese society during this period resembled fifteenth-century Europe in some respects. The country was divided into 245 feudal domains, each controlled by the *shogun,* or overlord. The well-ordered system of social relationships was based on Confucian principles that had been imported from China. In some respects Japan is still a Confucian society, the vertical and hierarchical structure being perhaps its most salient feature. But the society of the Tokugawa period was even more hierarchical, with an elaborate system of social obligations that were used as an indirect, but nonetheless powerful, means of suppression.

To the Meiji emperor and his government fell the difficult task of rapidly modernizing a nation that had been in seclusion for centuries. The apparatus of the feudal empire was dismantled within a few years after the Meiji Restoration, and a program of modernization, that is, westernization, was begun by the new government. Many scholars, both Western and Japanese, have noted that the changes were in no small measure brought about to improve upon the treaties that have been foisted upon the Japanese by Western governments. A particular irritant was the fact that Westerners had refused to permit their own people to be prosecuted under native law for criminal offenses but insisted instead on administering their own justice. To alleviate this situation and provide Japan with a legal system acceptable to Westerners, as noted earlier, codes of criminal law were adopted, first on the French model and later on the German.

The concept of human rights in Japan cannot be fully understood without exploring the relationship of the emperor to his subjects. One description of the role of the emperor dating from the early Meiji period states that

> [He] possessed both political power and spiritual authority, [and] embodied the prerequisites of both the German emperor and the Pope. The people were not only the emperor's subjects politically but his followers spiritually. In addition to enacting laws, the emperor issued imperial rescripts on education, national esprit and morality. The people were required to observe the law in their overt behavior and were also obliged to order

their consciences in accord with imperial rescripts. A portrait of the emperor was enshrined in every school, and the principal often read rescripts aloud. Moreover, all subjects were required to stand in awed attention when facing the emperor's portrait or when listening to rescripts. Insofar as the arbiter of spiritual values and political authority were one, ethics and power, public and private [oyake and watakushi], were completely fused together. (Kuno 1978, p. 61)

A different perspective on the role of the individual in the Meiji state is offered in the government's "The Way of the Subject" (Shimin no michi):

What we call our private life amounts, in the final analysis, to the practice of the Way of the Subject, and takes on public significance as we carry out our duty to assist in imperial rule. . . . Thus even while engaged in private activities, we must never forget our duty to devote ourselves to the emperor and serve the state. In our country everything one does—whether he is in government or in private business, whether he is a parent raising children or a son studying in school—is in fulfillment of his particular duty as an imperial subject. (Kuno 1978, p. 62)

The obligations to the state are abundantly clear. Basing their power on this kind of obedience, the Meiji leaders established an authoritarian regime that was intolerant of opposition to its policies. Early champions of civil rights movements were suppressed by direct police intervention or through more devious methods.

Most social scientists agree that the authoritarian spirit, like its philosophical version, Confucianism, survives to some extent in modern Japan. Ishida (1968) notes that while protest activity in Japan has become more common, nonetheless "the tradition of saying no is very weak among Japanese." Ike (1972) cites a "reference for paternalism," and Koschmann, commenting on Japan's history, says of the Japanese that "Never conquered by or directly confronted with external forms of political rule, they remained unaware of the potentially relative, fallible nature of all authority. Authority was a 'given,' taken for granted as an unalienable part of the natural order" (Koschmann 1978).

Matsumoto, a professor of Japanese political thought at Tokyo University, has observed that

There is an assumption that the state is a prior and self-justifying entity, sufficient in itself. This results in the belief that political functions, and the existence, maintenance and development of the state should take precedence over the goals of other individuals and associations, or at least, that the former are more important than the latter. (Koschmann 1978, p. 38)

The structural outline and character of Japan's present-day police force were already visible in the Meiji era. Features inherited from that period include the "routine family visits" to households by police officers and the widely scattered distribution of police boxes—*kōban* and *chūzaisho*—throughout the country. (*Kōban* are police boxes or mini-stations in cities, while *chūzaisho* are rural police boxes that are residential in character, typically with a staff of one officer and accommodation for the officer's family in the rear of the building.)

During the early days of the Meiji era, the nation was in a state of turbulence and the new government found it difficult to maintain order. Uprisings and bloodshed occurred in many places; people felt apprehensive and fearful. According to Kanetake-Oura,

There was not lacking a rough element which, dissatisfied with the new Government, watched for an opportunity to rise against it. Moreover, many ruffians at large constituted a danger to the people. The main object of the police at that time was to arrest these malcontents and bravadoes. (1910, p. 283)

Clearly, the task required a strong police force.

The structure of the force that was established was highly centralized and powerful, and police duties embraced a variety of activities that would be foreign to most modern forces. For example, public health, sanitation, construction, and fire-fighting activities were all under police jurisdiction. Despite having control of these public services, police in the Meiji period, unlike today, were not considered public servants. Instead, their principal functions were surveillance and political control. As a police bureau chief of the time put it, "There would be no household in Japan into which the eyes of the police would not see and the ears would not hear" (Sugai 1957, p. 4).

This task of surveillance and control was carried out by a force of 3,000 former *samurai,* a fact that soon proved to be a problem in itself. Individuals who were used to functioning on the basis of their social status had to be taught to function within an organizational structure. Sugai comments on the pluses and minuses of a police force made up of former *samurai*:

This method of choosing men was singularly effective in guaranteeing their staunchness and relative immunity from corruption because of a system of morality peculiar to the former warrior class. On the other hand, this practice had certain drawbacks in that it tended to develop in the police an attitude of disrespect and superciliousness toward the people. (1957)

Anticipating the potential problems, the Meiji government hit upon one idea to facilitate control of the police force: two-thirds of the men selected came from just one province in Kyushu. This practice of selecting police for the Tokyo Metropolitan Police Department from other regions of Japan is still prevalent. It is believed that police officers working in areas away from their place of birth avoid the problems of enforcing the law with relatives and friends.

Westney (1982) explained that the police department was patterned after a combination of the Paris Prefecture of Police and the Yokohama Police Department. While it was the Tokyo Police Department that eventually emerged as the model for other Japanese police departments, it was Yokohama—partly because of the large number of foreigners who lived there—that actually had the first police department in Japan. Westerners residing in Yokohama were familiar with effective policing and pressed for its development. Prior to 1868, the foreign community itself was responsible for policing, and because Englishmen were predominant, the Yokohama police reflected "the English model of organization, drill, patrolling system, and weaponry."

While the Tokyo police initially retained the flavor of the English-style Yokohama force, with the transfer of the police operation from the Tokyo Prefectural Government to the Ministry of Justice, the organization was revised. A group of officials was sent abroad to study police departments in a number of countries—France, Belgium, Germany, Russia, Austria, and Italy. The French approach, however, was apparently favored from the outset, and it was French influence that eventually shaped the Tokyo Police Department. The French model, under which the police had wide-ranging administrative functions and a high degree of political involvement, was particularly appealing to the Japanese. The police department that was created in Tokyo controlled other services, such as fire-fighting, prisons, and health, and became a "powerful and virtually autonomous organization that like its model played a central role in the life of the national capital and had close ties to the central government" (Westney 1982, p. 19).

The biannual "routine family visits" that police conduct today in Japan had their origin at this time. Again, Westney's account is most useful. She explains that during the Meiji period, police gathered information that included the name, occupation, age, and social status of each resident. While today all households are supposed to be visited twice annually, during this earlier period the frequency was contingent upon one's social status. Property owners and people of high reputation were visited just once a year. People of lesser status—including those who did not own property—were visited twice annually. Finally, those who were unemployed or had criminal records were subjected to three visits annually. Later, in the period leading up to World War II, the repressive element of the police was in evidence with the household visits. As Tipton stated, "they established a system of household investigation to keep track of residents and such matters as their occupations and trends in thought, which the Tokyo (State Police) used for information gathering" (1990, p. 58).

The police function was moved in 1874 from the Ministry of Justice to the Ministry of Home Affairs. The new police agency was named the Police Bureau and it continued under the Home Ministry until it was abolished in 1947. The Metropolitan Police Department was established in Tokyo, and prefectural governors were given jurisdiction over their respective police forces:

> Salaries, travel allowances, etc. of police officers above inspector's rank were paid from the national treasury; other expenses, such as maintaining policemen in lower ranks and providing and keeping up office buildings, were mainly met by local taxes but partially subsidized by the national government—the ratio of subsidies being four-tenths of all expenses for the Metropolitan Police Board and one-sixth for other prefectures. (Sugai 1957, p. 4)

The cooperation in the Meiji period between the national and prefectural governments for the support of police services is roughly similar to the organizational breakdown that presently exists between the National Police Agency and prefectural police agencies (for example, the National Police Agency currently pays the salaries of all officers at the rank of senior superintendent or above).

As noted above, the system of *kōban* and *chūzaisho* also had its inception during the Meiji period, and there were more than four hundred police boxes throughout the city of Tokyo in 1877. In addition to the buildings themselves, the method of staffing them has also been preserved, especially in the high ratio of supervisors to patrolmen. During the Meiji period, one officer supervised three patrolmen at a *kōban;* one walked the beat, one was stationed outside, and one was on duty inside processing paperwork. The pattern is strikingly similar today.

Kōban were placed at transportation centers, major intersections, shopping areas, at entrances to public parks, near the entrances to temple areas, and at other locations where people congregated and where crime might be expected to occur. The term *kōban* had originally been used to identify the dormitory-like buildings in Tokyo in which police lived, but was later applied to nonresidential urban police boxes. Police boxes have officially been called *hashutsujo* since 1888, but the term *kōban* persists.

One of the early legal statements on the role of police during the Meiji era was described by Kanetake-Oura in 1910:

1. Fundamental Laws Relating to the Police system
    (a) The Constitution of the Empire of Japan—1889. Art. 9. The Emperor issues, or causes to be issued, the ordinances necessary for the carrying out of the laws, or for the maintenance of the public peace and order, and for the promotion of the welfare of the subjects.
    (b) Regulations relating to the Administrative Police (drawn up in 1875).

These regulations defined for the first time in Japan the sphere and aim of police authority, and indicated the functions of police administration. We mention here some important articles of these regulations:

Art. 1. The object of the administrative police is to anticipate evils threatening the people and so to preserve the latter's safety.

Art. 2. The local governor (except in the prefecture of Tokyo) superintends the police affairs of the locality, appoints police sergeants to their respective duties, and dispatches them, whenever necessary, to different places, to overlook policemen in the discharge of their duties.

The business of the police is divided into the following four parts:
(1) Protecting the people from wrongdoers.
(2) Acting as sanitary inspectors.
(3) Checking lewdness and profligacy.
(4) Detecting and proving against persons who contemplate acts contrary to the established laws of the land.

Art. 5. The police shall aim at preserving public welfare, and in no case shall one pry into petty incidents of family affairs, nor use his position to gain profit for himself. (Kanetake-Oura 1910, p. 282)

Neighborhood Associations

Associations in which neighbors assisted each other in a variety of activities, such as planting rice, building houses, and other aspects of daily living, were an integral part of the social fabric during the Meiji era. The general term for these groups is *tonari-gumi*. In rural areas they were called *burakukai* and in urban areas *chonaikai*. Approximately ten to twenty families formed one *tonari-gumi*.

The neighborhood associations are important in considering crime control because they were the forerunners of crime-prevention associations. *Tonari-gumi* existed up to the time of the Occupation, when they were forced to disband by the Allied Forces. They have since re-formed, though their influence is much weaker. Since the leaders of these groups were reputed to have been extremely loyal to the emperor and the government, Western authorities suspected them of being part of the prewar authoritarian apparatus, with leaders using coercive and autocratic tactics in dealings with group members, and it was not uncommon for members and leaders to report secretly on citizens who departed from government policy. In the early period of their existence, the heads of the neighborhood associations were appointed by the city government chiefs, but later they were elected.

In the prewar period, these government-appointed heads of the neighborhood associations had close working relationships with the police officials in their area. The *burakukai* and *chonaikai* maintained their own meeting halls, and these served as centers of community activity. The *tonari-gumi* were semiofficial arms of the police and were used in the general task of keeping order.

In postwar Japan, the status of these groups and their relations with the police are somewhat different. In place of the disbanded neighborhood associations, local crime-prevention groups have formed with a narrower framework. To some extent the ties with the police remain close, but the associations' leadership is now elected, and some friction with the authorities has been known to occur, especially around election time, when it is not uncommon to have *chonaikai* members arrested for campaign violations.

Today, the *burakukai* and *chonaikai* continue to function in outlying areas, but Japanese authorities claim that their strength has dwindled in the cities due to the unwillingness of unmarried residents of apartments and condominiums to join. Conversely, residents of very small apartments were sometimes excluded from *chonaikai* because they are perceived to be short-term residents of the area. The perception is not unjustified, since occupants of these units move, on the average, once every two years.

Historically, the neighborhood *tonari-gumi* were involved in a variety of social and civic activities. For example, on the occasion of a birth or wedding, a sum of money was collected by the head of the group, who likewise organized assistance for the families of deceased persons. A variety of obligations and rituals was involved with participation in such neighborhood groups, and individuals who were able to engage in these forms of social intercourse with skill and confidence felt a sense of accomplishment and self-esteem. The network of social and neighborhood obligations involves the complex notion of *giri*, literally "duty," which is considered a basic principle of social interaction in Japan, though most scholars agree that its influence has decreased in recent years. While the traditional *tonari-gumi* were broken up by the Occupation forces, many of their functions were adopted by newly formed neighborhood groups.

It is not difficult to imagine the ways in which the network of relationships established through the *tonari-gumi* and their modern counterparts lent itself to crime prevention activity. Among the wide variety of neighborhood obligations, crime prevention was just one more aspect of community life. The modern-day crime-prevention associations will be discussed at greater length in a later chapter.

The Suppression of Radicals

The strong repressive measures taken by the government against radical leftists during the pre–World War II period have been described by Mitchell (1976), Okudaira (1973), Tipton (1990), and others. Their descriptions of the atmosphere surrounding the promulgation of the Peace Preservation Law and related laws, along with the sweeping enforcement of it by police and prosecutors, paint an ugly picture. The general turbulence of the times, combined with the rising influence of left-wing radicals, resulted in the passing of the Peace Preservation Law in

1925. The office of the Police Bureau in the Home Ministry was particularly active at this time. Okudaira, in particular, captures the mood of the period:

> The dangerous thoughts, which the Peace Preservation Law raised as the subject of control, implied, in the beginning, Communism and anarchism, and later the implication of the term "dangerous" became more and more stretched, and finally every anti-government thought—the identifications were made by the administration of each period—was regarded to be under the application of the law. The victims of the Peace Preservation Law were not only those who attempted to reform the then-existing Buddhism, the believers in Shintoism or in the numerous newly risen religions but also those belonging to "Jehovah's Witnesses," "Seventh-day Adventists," and the "No-church Independent Sect." On the other hand, the controlling authorities attached great importance to cultural movements along with labor and political movements. Consequently, students' researches in the social sciences or the liberal arts were the most important subjects of restraint. (1973, p. 49)

An earlier law that was also repressive in nature was the Public Police Law of 1900. This law was aimed at antigovernment political groups, but it also restricted organized labor. These political groups were required to register their programs with the police, and they needed permission to meet. Their meetings could be dissolved by the police and their organizations disbanded, and membership in secret organizations was prohibited. Violators of the Public Police Law could be punished by fines and up to one year in prison.

It was left primarily to the Home Ministry's Police Bureau to suppress radicals and control protest movements, and unlike the situation in Western countries, where political organization and publications were regulated through the courts, in Japan police used administrative techniques to maintain public order. Faced with increasing left-wing radicalism, in 1902 the government created a Higher Police Unit and a second unit, the Special Higher Police. The repressive machinery of the Japanese justice system of the prewar period appears to have emerged for a variety of reasons in addition to those already mentioned. Mitchell explains:

> The reasons for thought control in Japan were complex and not confined to flaws in the Meiji Constitution, a tradition of authoritarianism, and the

weakness of liberalism. Other factors less subject to direct manipulation by Japan's leaders must be considered: the rapidity with which the whole world's economic system collapsed and the more uncompromising attitudes of China and the United States. These problems, together with the rise of communism, signified the weakening of the old economic and political order. (1976, p. 192)

Mitchell explains that prosecutors were powerful during the 1920s. They dressed like judges and identified themselves closely with the judiciary. They helped in the drafting of court documents and handling of cases and frequently played the role of preliminary judges. One of the tools of the prosecutors' wide-ranging power was the designation "charges withheld." Under this classification an individual was neither prosecuted nor totally absolved of charges. He was cast into a probationary limbo under the jurisdiction of the prosecutor. Any further violations on his part were sure to result in vigorous prosecution.

The control and suppression that characterized the political climate of the early Meiji period is reflected in Okudaira's remarks on the role of censorship in enforcing government policy. He noted that the control of newspapers shifted from prepublication censorship to a less direct postpublication censorship, in which heavy penalties were exacted from writers and editors who affronted the government censors. Legislation enacted in 1875 placed the seat of censorship within the Police Bureau of the Home Ministry, and books regarded as detrimental to the public peace could be seized and the presses that printed them destroyed. Publications were scrutinized by justice officials, and the head of the Book Section of the Special Higher Police stated: "We prohibited things which were against public order and good morals" (Okudaira, 1962).

This same era of interwar Japan has been studied by Tipton (1990) in reviewing the role of police. Her book, *Japanese Police State* provided an extensive review of the repressive nature of the governmental apparatus that wielded power against both left-wing and right-wing movements in Japan.

In general, it should be noted that while the authoritarian nature of the crackdown on perceived dissidents created apprehension and fear among the ranks of the citizens of Japan during the pre–World War II period, the size of the police force was not overly large. The ratio of police to citizens was comparable to that in Europe and the United States according to Tipton: "Tokyo in the late 1920s had about 12,700 police officers for a population of about 4.5 million (28.2 police officials per 10,000 population); New York, with a population of 5.6 million in 1920, maintained a force of 12,000 police officials (21.4 per 10,000 population). In 1931 county districts in England averaged 10.2 police officials per 10,000 population" (1990, p. 30).

But, of course, the size of a police force is not the critical element per se in its role in society. The Administrative Enabling Law and the repressive Peace Preservation Law provided the vehicles for terror and detention inflicted on citizens during the 1920s and 1930s. For example, in 1929 there were 269,000 detentions and in 1931, 473,000, but that number expanded to 1.2 million by 1933. As Tipton (1990) noted, "police frequently pressured suspects by detaining them over and over, in effect holding them in custody without formal charges." Some individuals were held for as long as two years. Furthermore, the actions of the police were not subject to any formal legal appeal. A citizen had no place to turn for relief. At the present time, Japanese prosecutors and law enforcement authorities still legally detain suspects for questioning for longer periods than do their counterparts in the United States and Europe. The roots of this modern-day practice can be seen in the police practices of this early period of the twentieth century. The entire political context of the 1920s and 1930s was leading up to the full-blown fascism of the World War II period, variously referred to as "imperial fascism" and the "absolutist emperor system."

Those who worked against the intent of the law of that time were subject to that arrogance with which public officials generally treated average citizens, and it is not surprising that some older Japanese still have a bitter, resentful feeling toward the police. This anger, mixed with anxiety, occasionally emerged in my interviews with older citizens.

Policing after World War II

Research by Chwialkowski (1998) stresses that much of Japan's present-day highly acclaimed police system had its foundation in the roles played by Americans—particularly General Robert Eichenberger. The American Occupation Force had inherited a police force that had engaged in a vaguely defined role, in which they "openly stated that it was within the scope of their duties to stifle dissent, harass political meetings and interfere in elections, and arbitrarily arrest and imprison a political disturber of the peace" (Perry 1980, p. 148).

One of the police specialists brought in from the United States, Lewis Valentine, suggested a major revamping of the Japanese police force after observing police abuses of private citizens, and General Douglas MacArthur supported the changes. The emphasis was on making the police force less authoritarian, more responsive to public opinion, restrained by a democratically structured constitution, and accountable to local communities (Bayley 1976). In addition, paramilitary organizations were eliminated and various neighborhood associations that had allowed Japanese to spy on one another were also removed. The American authorities sought to cleanse the police force of individuals who were antidemocratic, and police were not permitted to be members of labor organizations (Cohen 1987). The constitution that was put into place in Japan resembled, at least in broad outline, the American one— it included right to counsel, guarantee of a speedy trial, right to cross-examine witnesses, protection from forced confessions, and so forth (Chwialkowski 1998). Earlier responsibilities such as sanitation, fire, health, and "thought control" were no longer part of the scope of activities of police. The responsibilities of the police were limited to maintaining peace and order in Japan, investigating crimes, and protecting the life and property of the citizens. To assume some of the functions removed from police work, the Public Safety Commission system was introduced at both national and prefectural levels. The police were to concentrate on standards, identification, communication, training, scientific crime detection, and statistics. By 1946 a second wave of reform focused on decentralizing police forces; the philosophy behind the reform was that in addition to democratizing law enforcement, the decentralizing of police would return greater control to local communities (Chwialkowski 1998). The decentralized system required that all citizens and towns with more than 5,000 residents be required to maintain their own police departments.

While Chwialkowski (1998), Perry (1980), and others maintain that the basic reforms of protection of rights, community ties, and the police image as friends of the citizenry have been retained to the present day, the decentralized structure was dismantled for the more traditional nationalistic approach. The National Police Agency's publication, *The Police of Japan,* (1998) politely refers to the deep dismay of Japanese government authorities at the decentralization of police by describing "organizational defects" and "heavy financial burdens" of the new structure. Those "inefficiencies" were corrected when the Police Law of

1954 was adopted, and the national character of the police services was restored. The Public Safety Commissions were retained, and all municipal and rural police agencies were integrated under the framework of the forty-seven prefectural police departments.

In summary, this historical view of Japanese justice is necessary to understand today's system of policing. A number of specific features such as the "routine family visits" of the Meiji era have been carried over virtually intact. The attitudes of present-day citizens toward the police have been shaped by the police behavior of the Meiji and pre–World War II periods. Legal concepts rooted in Confucian doctrine continue to affect dispute resolution in Japan, and the attempt at democratization of the Japanese justice apparatus has resulted in, among other things, a greater concern for human rights.

3

Overview of Police

Japan has a national police system, with a decentralized structure of prefectural police agencies throughout the nation and a national police agency at the top of the hierarchy. The National Police Agency is where the policies and standards are created and implemented. It operates under the guidance of the National Public Safety Commission. In 1998, Japan employed around 263,483 police personnel, of whom 8,100 were female officers, and 7,661 members of the total worked directly for the national police Agency (Foreign Press Center 1999). In the United States there were 531,496 full-time local police, including 420,000 sworn personnel (U.S. Department of Justice 1999). On average, there is one police officer responsible for a population of 553 throughout Japan.

Appreciating police services in Japan requires some understanding of the organizational structure behind the police on the beat. In descending order the rank structure of police in Japan is

- Police superintendent supervisor
- Chief police superintendent
- Senior police superintendent
- Police superintendent
- Police inspector
- Assistant police inspector
- Police sergeant
- Senior policeman
- Policeman

Americans have historically been wary of vesting too much power in a centralized police agency, notwithstanding the specialized and limited role of federal law enforcement agencies such as the FBI, the Secret Service, and the Drug Enforcement Agency. But in Japan the cultural and political history has contributed to a post–World War II rebirth of a police force that operates through a national system. It is undeniable that there are advantages to a well-oiled and carefully crafted national system of law enforcement, and the Japanese approach reveals the strengths of a unified system.

One of the most notable of these is the high level of professionalism among police officers. A professional is one who emphasizes public service, has high standards of performance, has a broad knowledge of his or her field, and participates in professional conferences and associations. When measured by the standards set by law and medicine, the police in both Japan and the United States fall short of the mark, primarily because independence of judgment and action is lost in the demands of the organization. Japanese police, however, with the advantage of being unfettered by the demands of labor unions, come closer to meeting the classic sociological criteria for professionalism.

In her discussion of the history of the Japanese police during the Meiji period, Westney suggested that encouraging professionalism was

> a means of reducing turnover in the force and of improving police standards of performance without a marked increase in expenditures, and it facilitated the standardization of police practice throughout the country. However, it had other, unanticipated consequences: It increased the autonomy of the police force, it reduced its responsiveness to its social environment, and it reinforced the social distance between the policeman and the public. (1982, p. 35)

The foundation for contemporary policing was set during this Meiji era, and the continuity of certain features is remarkable. An extremely important question raised by Westney has to do with the price of police professionalism in Japan: Are police less responsive to the social environment, and has the social distance between the police and the public been reinforced? Whether the benefits outweigh the disadvantages is open to question, but it is certain that dedication and commitment to the job run high among Japanese police. An American legal-affairs officer assigned to the U.S. Embassy in Tokyo who had worked with the police over a number of years remarked, "They're not wondering if they can step out of police work and find a better-paying job like American police."

Entrance standards and training are rigorously controlled by the National Police Agency. Undoubtedly major economic savings are also obtained as a result of this coordinated national system. An increasing number of college graduates have been attracted to police work, and by the mid-1990s, 68 percent of those selected were college graduates, while 32 percent had completed high school (National Police Agency of Japan 1998).

Though the United States cannot claim such figures for entering police personnel, it does have a significant number of police officers who possess some college or university education. The U.S. Department of Justice (1999) reported that overall in 1997, 14 percent of departments, employing 31 percent of all police officers, required new recruits to have completed at least some college, up from 15 percent in 1993.

The American system is clearly ahead of the Japanese in offering college-level courses for officers once they have joined. Japan has no academic degree programs intended for working justice personnel. Thus, while a larger percentage of entering police personnel possess college degrees in Japan, there are fewer opportunities for the average police officer to obtain a degree once he or she is on the job. Criminology programs or criminal justice academic programs are not available; nor, apparently, has there been much demand for them.

College-level degree programs for police in America started increasing only after the riots of the 1960s. The Law Enforcement Assistance Administration of the Justice Department provided grants so that public justice employees could pursue degrees. However, the quality of education varied greatly, and some colleges offered very inferior education for police and other justice personnel.

The recruiting process in Japan varies depending on whether an applicant is being considered for the National Police Agency (a higher calling) or a Prefectural Police Agency. The NPA recruits from those who have passed the National Public Service Category I or II examination conducted by the National Personnel Authority. It also considers candidates from among those recommended by Prefectural Police Agencies as particularly talented based on their police careers, job performance, and work history. Often these applicants enter at the sergeant or assistant inspector level.

Prefectural police applicants also take a rigorous examination, and in 1997 there were 133,000 applicants nationwide. About 8,300 passed the exam, although it should be noted that different exams are given to high school and college graduates. University graduates now represent about 68 percent of successful applicants (National Police Agency 1998). The National Police Agency describes recruit training as follows:

> Newly recruited prefectural police officers undergo an initial training program consisting of pre-service, on-the-job, and comprehensive training courses. They first attend a ten month pre-service training course at their prefectural police school. During this course, they acquire the basic attitude toward readiness and alertness essential to police duties. They also learn basic community policing knowledge and skills.
>
> Following graduation, they are assigned to a front-line police station for eight-months of on-the-job training at a police box. As a police cadet, they practice actual community policing under the one-to-one instruction of a senior officer.
>
> Finally, they return to the police school for a three-month comprehensive training program to build self-control, acquire professional legal knowledge, and hone their community policing knowledge and skills. This training also enhances their physical and mental strength. (1998, p. 14)

Training periods for American police vary from several weeks to six months or more, but the average was twenty-seven weeks in 1997 (U.S. Department of Justice 1999). In Japan, candidates who are high school graduates must complete a ten-month period of training, while college graduates are trained for six months. Japanese trainees are in residence, or in a boarding environment with rigorous demands placed upon them in a tightly scheduled atmosphere. The training curriculum includes general education subjects, firearms training, and first aid. Subject matter includes law, police studies, computer science, and martial arts training. The latter includes judo and kendo (i.e., Japanese swordsmanship).

Japanese generally have a great interest in martial arts, and the police are no exception. The police are proud of their skill in this area and the National Police Agency boasts of their skills and accomplishments:

> When a police officer is attacked or resisted by a suspect, he must suppress the resistance and apprehend the suspect with minimum effective force. To do this, police officers eagerly practice judo, kendo [Japanese fencing], arrest techniques, and marksmanship. Their proficiency in mar-

tial arts and marksmanship is so excellent that Japanese police officers often achieve outstanding records in domestic and international competitions. All-Japan annual police championships are held in judo, kendo, arrest techniques, marksmanship, and long-distance running to develop police proficiency in martial arts. These competitions also engender esprit de corps and build morale. (1998, p. 16)

Many specialized and advance courses are offered to police officers such as evidence collection, international criminal investigation, foreign languages, traffic investigation, police dog training, bookkeeping, and other courses (Tokyo Metropolitan Police Department 1998).

Following graduation, they are assigned to a police station for eight months of on-the-job training at a mini–police station or *kōban*. There they practice their community policing skills before returning to the police training facility for a final three months.

Training by National Police Agency personnel is vastly different than that for entering police recruits who will be employed by the various towns and cities under the auspices of the Prefectual Police Agencies. After all, the NPA Training Academy is primary concerned with training the future corps of police managers. Here is how the NPA describes this supervisory and management training:

Assistant police inspectors receive five weeks of training and then are assigned as a sub-section chief at a police station.

Police officers promoted to police inspector enter the National Police Academy in Tokyo for a two-month training program. They master management and leadership skills, and develop the practical skills for duties as the section chief of a police station.

Further, the National Police Academy provides supervisory training for superintendents designated the given assignments as either a chief of a police station or section chief of a prefectural police headquarters. This is the highest-level training course available for police officers.

The Highest Training Institute for Investigation Leaders, at the National Police Academy, trains police inspectors and above in leadership, management, and advanced techniques and technologies concerning criminal investigation.

As a training institution for transnational criminal investigation, the National Police Academy's International Research and Training Institute for Criminal Investigation provides both foreign language training for Japanese police officers and training to police officers from other countries. (National Police Agency 1998, p. 15)

For 1999, the basic starting salary for a police officer who is a university graduate was 2,872,800 yen ($27,645). But, like other government and private-sector employees, police personnel receive bonuses. Therefore, police receive the equivalent of approximately 5.25 months' salary, this represents an additional 1,206,575 yen ($11,491). Add in a housing allowance of 104,400 yen annually ($994) and total compensation for a starting officer is around $40,130 (National Police Agency 1999). With extremely inexpensive dormitory-style housing—for single personnel—made available, along with a broad medical plan, the new police officer's financial status compares quite favorably with that of entry-level workers in other fields. For instance, the National Police Agency is quick to point out that probation officers, along with other public-sector employees, start at a lower salary.

In 1997 the average annual entrance salary for full-time police officers in the United States ranged from $28,400 in the smallest jurisdictions to $30,600 in the largest (U.S. Department of Justice 1999). Also, salaries for officers with five years of service for the following cities were reported for 1997: San Jose, $60,000 (total compensation including pensions, health benefits, etc., $82,806); New York City, $43,593 (total compensation $75,176); Los Angeles, $61,282 (total compensation $72,713); and Chicago, $47,177 (total compensation $69,092) (Kennedy 1997).

4

Kōban Police

The Tokyo Metropolitan Police Department

This study of police behavior is based upon visits to, interviews with, and observations of police at work in a variety of locations, including Tokyo, Chiba, Kobe, Sapporo, Yokohama, Kyoto, and Okayama. Some of the interviews and visits were conducted in 1980–81 and some in 1999. During 1980, I concentrated initially on the Tokyo Metropolitan Police Department (M.P.D.), and I revisited it in 1999.

A glossy piece of public relations literature published by the Tokyo Metropolitan Police Department proudly described the agency in the following fashion: "Tokyo is the center of government, business, culture and transportation of Japan, with a population of some 12 million in an area of 2,171 square kilometers (828 square miles). The total personnel of the M.P.D. was 50,613, which included 2,901 civilians as of 1998. There were approximately 1,330 police boxes which included 237 residential *kōbans*" (Tokyo Metropolitan Police Department 1998).

While the plans for my study were coordinated with officials of the National Police Agency during 1980 and 1999, a direct personal introduction by a Tokyo Public Safety Commission member to a police administrator at the Tokyo Metropolitan Police Department provided the key to initially studying the police in the Tokyo M.P.D. As noted previously, personal introductions are of critical importance in paving the way for any project in Japan. The series of planning sessions that ensued required visits to the Tokyo Metropolitan Police Department's headquarters and offered a glimpse of police activities that are in marked contrast with the service-oriented work of the patrol officer on the beat. (The Japanese refer to the patrol officer as *omawari-san*, meaning something close to "Mr. Walk-around.")

The headquarters loomed like a fortress near the Imperial Palace grounds. The atmosphere inside was very formal and a bit startling if one is unprepared for the military demeanor of the police personnel on duty. Officers guarded the entrance and inside the building uniformed women await visitors behind a desk. Arriving officials were greeted with the equivalent of a snap to attention and were crisply saluted. Impeccably dressed officers issued identifying badges to visitors, who were required to wait for an escort before proceeding to a particular conference area or office in the eighteen-story building.

In 1980, the administrative head of the Patrol Division and three of his assistants were assigned to assist in my research. In addition to the patrol head's three assistants, the planning sessions included my interpreter and the M.P.D.'s interpreter. One officer kept careful note of all discussions—he even made a written note of the fact that my interpreter had graduated from Keio University. Plans for the ensuing three months were worked out over cups of green tea. Generally the atmosphere was cordial and friendly and we even managed to share a bit of humor. I was eager to allay any anxiety on their part about my intentions by clearly defining the scope of the study. I requested permission to visit police boxes, interview police officers, observe officer–citizen contact, and observe certain programs (for example, the counseling centers for juvenile offenders and pre-delinquent youth). In addition, I wanted flexibility to pursue other interests that might develop during my research. I realized that in all of this it was important to have the support of these administrators.

One of my main objectives has been to learn about police-community relations and how it has evolved over the twenty-year period between 1980 and 1999. Originally, I began at the grass-roots level, that is, with the daily work of police at *kōban* and *chūzaisho*, and requested permission to spend time in a variety of locations within the Tokyo Metropolitan Police Department's jurisdiction—areas that would reflect different socioeconomic conditions and offer a wide exposure to Japanese urban life. With this in mind, the following stations were mutually agreed upon: Tsukiji/Ginza (an entertainment and shopping center); Shitaya (an older commercial and working-class residential section);

Kōban in Tokyo, 1996 (signs often included English in the 1990s)

Source: Tokyo Metropolitan Police Department 1997.

Seijō (a quiet, upper-class residential section some distance from downtown); Akabane (a somewhat commercial, lower-middle-class area in the north, which includes large housing projects); and Motofuji (a region that encompasses a campus of Tokyo University).

In order to understand the *kōban* system, it is useful to see it (and most other Japanese police activities) as an outgrowth of the well-known Japanese penchant for order. The most salient feature of this orderly system is a national standardization that would be both foreign and enviable to an American policeman accustomed to the varied behavior of the thousands of different police agencies in the United States. In America, with most towns, municipalities, and states operating their own autonomous police departments, the differences in patterns and styles

Kōban Police Officer Offering Directions

Source: Tokyo Metropolitan Police Department 1997.

of policing are taken for granted; for example, some departments are service-oriented, while others may emphasize keeping order.

The working hours of officers within the M.P.D. are quite unlike the shift patterns of American police. Typically, American police work rotating shifts. For example, they might work several weeks on the "graveyard" shift (night work: 11:00 P.M. to 7:00 A.M.), followed by either several weeks of a 7:00 A.M. to 3:00 P.M. shift or a 3:00 P.M. to 11:00 P.M. shift. In some departments, newly recruited officers will be on the "graveyard" shift for an extended period due to their lack of seniority. Because of the large number of departments it is impossible to generalize about nationwide patterns in the United States. The aforementioned schedules are just examples from departments I have become familiar with in the eastern section of the country.

The pattern in Japan is very different. Police stationed at *kōban* and assigned to patrol typically work the following schedule:

1st day: Full-day duty (a twenty-four-hour period, from morning to morning)
2nd day: Off day (that follows the "Full day," which included overnight)
3rd day: Normal day (morning to evening)

The hours for detectives and other personnel assigned to specialized duties vary from this, but approximately forty-four to forty-eight hours per week are standard for M.P.D. personnel. Overtime is common, and this adds to the total hours accumulated.

Kōban usually have several small rooms. The glass-enclosed room in front has a desk. The rear rooms, or occasionally an upstairs room, provide a *tatami* mat area for sleeping and sometimes a separate room for preparing modest meals. (*Tatami* mats are approximately three feet by six feet and consist of a thick base of straw, covered with woven rushes.) A concealed safe is available for locking up weapons while the officer is asleep. *Kōban* vary tremendously in size and shape, but they tend to be crowded, a condition typical of Japanese housing as well.

Though the police have few complaints, the dilapidated condition of some *kōban* is the frequent cause of some grumbles. An M.P.D. regulation requires that the front door remain open at all times, and during the summer months the oppressive heat—temperatures in Tokyo are comparable to those in Washington, D.C.—renders the air conditioning units in some *kōban* useless.

Outside *kōban* and *chūzaisho* there are often billboards on which posters of "wanted" persons are pinned up. The drab gray cement of most police boxes is sometimes brightened by flowers or bowls of fruit, though this is more characteristic of the residential police boxes. Quite often food is delivered to the *kōban* by a local restaurant; otherwise, officers may bring something from home. When officers go out for a meal, they do not wear uniforms as it is against police regulations to do so, and most officers, sensitive to citizens who have not forgotten the arrogance of officers prior to World War II, prefer not to appear in uniform except in an official capacity.

At the M.P.D., a superintendent general is in charge. This is the only such position in the entire country, reflecting the "queen bee" status of this department. Only the commissioner general of the National Police Agency ranks above the chief of the M.P.D., and he, of course, is in charge of all police services for the nation. One key fact of the national system is that all officers at the rank of senior police superintendent and above are considered to be national public servants in the employ of the National Police Agency. They are appointed by the National public Safety Commission. At the M.P.D., police officials of the rank of superintendent and below are local public officials who are appointed and dismissed by the superintendent general in consultation with the Tokyo Public Safety Commission. In addition to the National Public Safety Commission, each prefecture has its own Public Safety Commission.

The Tsukiji Police Station

Before visiting the mini-police station, or kōban, in a particular area, I met with the chief who had jurisdiction over that district. The chief of the Tsukiji station was an affable, older, graying man who wore single stars on his lapels that indicated his rank of senior superintendent. The ninety-five police stations of the M.P.D. are headed by either superintendents or senior superintendents. He was courteous and seemed eager to accommodate me. Within moments of my arrival, tea was served, as is customary, and we were joined by several assistants, including the station's full-time interpreter. Officially the station is known as the Tsukiji station, but the area it encompasses is popularly known as the Ginza. The Ginza, unlike most other districts, has thousands of foreign tourists daily, and it is necessary to have a full-time police interpreter available.

These visits with station chiefs were not merely courtesies, but provided opportunities for them to brief me on the characteristics of their operations and for me to ask questions. What was particularly intriguing about the Ginza was the fact that within these 2.5 square kilometers (about 1 square mile) over 3,000 pubs, restaurants, and other "public morals businesses," as the chief called them, plied their trade. Only 9,877 households with 23,358 residents exist in this area, a reflection of its commercial character. While the number of 23,358 residents is low, some 200,000 individuals work here and 500,000 people, including visi-

The Tsukiji Fish Market

Photo by Jen and Rob Frost

tors and shoppers, flow in and out on any given day. Ten police boxes operate under the Tsukiji station, and total personnel number around 400. The gigantic Tsukiji fish market (see photo above) is visited by around 70,000 persons daily, mostly buyers and sellers (Foreign Press Center 1999). A private security force is employed in the market area, but the M.P.D. patrols the perimeter and the rest of the Tsukiji/Ginza area.

During the early stages of my study, I asked foot patrolmen as well as supervisors about the types of situations they encountered in routine police work. I was particularly interested in the frequency and severity of violent crime. The Tsukiji police chief stated that "citizens rarely use weapons. While they may punch or strike out, it's almost unheard of for guns to be used—even the use of knives is unusual."

Guns in Japan and the United States

Guns, and handguns in particular, are rarely used in Japan. First some numbers on Japan: for Tokyo, in 1997 there were just twenty-six handgun "firing incidents," resulting in two deaths and eight injuries. One case involved a hostage taken in the Tokyo Stock Exchange, while another involved a dispute between two *boryokudan* (organized crime) members (Tokyo Metropolitan Police Department 1998). More generally, Herbert (1999), citing Handgun Control (a U.S. lobbying organization in Washington, D.C.), stated that for 1996 the following statistics on handgun homicides applied: New Zealand 2, Japan 15, Great Britain 30, Canada 106, Germany 213, and the United States 9,390. While American citizens have applauded the significant drop in overall crime rates during the past ten years, the sense of euphoria and that "we've got a handle on crime" is a widely held view and a mistake according to Elliott Currie (1998) in his highly acclaimed book, *Crime and Punishment in America*. His analysis, while acknowledging the reduction of crime, takes note of the fact that crime rates are still very high in the United States and that the high-flying economy has helped to mask the lack of real structural changes (including gun control) in both society and the criminal justice system that are required to get to long-term lower crime rates.

The FBI's *Uniform Crime Report* issued in October 1999 (Butterfield 1999b) proudly noted that there had been a 7 percent drop in homicides in 1998 due entirely to a decrease in killings committed with guns. Furthermore, a 10 percent reduction in robberies in the previous year was also linked to the reduced use of guns. Robberies committed with guns fell to 38 percent of all robberies in 1998 from 40 percent in 1997. For homicides, handguns accounted for 52 percent of murders, whereas rifles and shotguns accounted for only 4 percent (Butterfield 1999a). Prominent criminologist Alfred Blumstein (Butterfield 1999a) observed that gun control efforts, including the Brady Law of 1994, appeared to be having some impact, especially in keeping guns out of the hands of young people. The Federal Bureau of Alcohol, Tobacco, and Firearms has increased efforts to track firearms, and various states have passed gun control laws that limit purchases to one handgun per individual per month.

Emergency Calls

Domestic violence or, more specifically, husband–wife fights, whatever their actual incidence, are rarely reported to police. When pressed on this subject, officers, including several who became personal friends, conceded that there are such disputes but went on to explain that both the husbands and the wives are too embarrassed to report them. They maintain that there is little physical violence among couples. More common are complaints about excessive noise from a neighbor or unpaid loans to a friend or acquaintance. Domestic disputes, of course, are common in police work in the United States in smaller communities as well as larger ones. While officers on small town forces in the United States sometimes handle mundane matters such as noise or a problem of an unpaid loan, it would be rare in large cities. In the case of Tsukiji, this personal and financial counseling was rare at the main station, with only forty cases reported, but it was more common at the several *kōban* in the district.

As in the United States, in Japan police have an emergency telephone number (110). At the Communications Command Center, in the headquarters of the Tokyo Metropolitan Police Department, 842,529 calls were received for the entire city during 1997. Operators sitting at large video consoles refer many calls to the different police stations, including the Tsukiji station. As with emergency numbers in the United States, many calls have little to do with law enforcement, for instance, calls from emotionally disturbed persons or simple routine requests for general information.

Nationally, one "110" call was received every 5.1 seconds, and a total of 6,198,980 calls were received during 1996. Emergency calls automatically go through the Communications Center of each prefectural headquarters. Calls peak during the 10:00 P.M. to midnight period. The National Police Agency (1998) reported the following frequency ranking for emergency calls:

1. Traffic accidents (33.67%)
2. People offering information of different types, e.g., calls to give information on a "wanted" person (9.79%)
3. Demands and complaints (8.57%)
4. Inquiries to the police for some type of information (18.8%)
5. Reports on criminal matters (6.27%)
6. Sick or injured people, stray children (4.17%)
7. Reports on quarrels and disputes (3.5%)
8. Misinformation and false reports (1.49%)
9. Disasters (0.8%)
10. Unnatural deaths (0.5%)
11. Miscellaneous (2.8%)

Tokyo M.P.D. headquarters officials explained that during a year each patrol officer is responsible on the average for routine visits to 450 house-

Figure 4.1a The Residence Information Card (for alien residents)

様式第7（その3）

Residence Information Card
（巡回連絡カード－F）

従警主
氏　名

Dear Sir :

This is to inform you that as a patrolman assigned to this area, I am responsible for occasionally visiting every household in the area. The purpose of this visit is to get better acquainted with the residents in the area to promote understanding between the citizens and the police and for the police to offer better service to the community. We would like to request your cooperation in this respect by filling out the attached form. The police equipped with this information can insure speedy dispatch of police officers to your home in an emergency, efficient investigation thereof, efficient aid in case of disaster, efficient assistance to persons looking for your home and improved work procedures, etc.

Thank you.

(Please fill out the boxes bordered with a thick line. The information furnished will be kept confidential.)

HOME ADDRESS (現 住 所)								
	FULL NAME (氏　名)	TEL ( )	RELATION- SHIP (続 柄)	SEX (性 別)	NATION- ALITY (国 籍)	OCCUPATION OR SCHOOL (職 業, 学 年)	DATE OF BIRTH (生 年 月 日)	TERM OF RESIDENCE (居 住 期 間)
			HOUSE- HOLDER (世 帯 主)					ALIEN REG. CARD NO. (登 録 証 番 号)
FAMILY MEMBERS (家　族)								

Figure 4.1b The Reverse of the Residence Information Card

CONTACT IN CASE OF EMERGENCY (非常の場合の連絡先)	HOUSEHOLDER'S BUSINESS ADDRESS (世帯主の勤め先)	TEL (　　)			
	NAME AND ADDRESS OF FRIEND OR NEXT OF KIN TO BE CONTACTED (友人等の住所氏名)	TEL (　　)			
EMPLOYEES (使用人がおりましたら記入してください。)	FULL NAME (氏　名)	DATE OF BIRTH (生 年 月 日)	SEX (性別)	JOB (職　業)	ADDRESS OF FAMILY (家族の所在地)
LICENSEPLATE NUMBER OF AUTOMOBILE (自動車の番号、その他)	CAR (乗用)	TRUCK (貨物)			
COMMENTS OR SUGGESTIONS TO THE POLICE (警察に対する要望連絡等記入してください。)				報告 昭 . . 印	[illegible] 昭 . . 印

作成依頼年月日	. .	連絡 年 月・日	.	.	.	.	.	.	.	.	.	.	.	.	.	.
受理年月日	. .	連絡者印														
		連絡 年 月・日	.	.	.	.	.	.	.	.	.	.	.	.	.	.
代筆年月日 警察官 ㊞	. .	連絡者印														

holds or commercial establishments. For my first such visit I accompanied a middle-aged sergeant to interview the manager of a new ten-story commercial building, just three blocks from the Sukiyabashi police box. Asked about crime or vandalism, he said there were none to report for the first ten months of operation. His only complaint was that drunks occasionally slept at night under the overhanging roof of the building. The officer fills out a card on each of the residences or businesses visited and files it at the police box (see Figures 4.1a and 4.1b).

A two-page pamphlet has been prepared to tell police recruits how to approach these routine visits. Entitled "Guidance on Home Visits," it provides specific suggestions on etiquette, conversational ploys, and a variety of dos and don'ts (see Figure 4.2):

Officers have varying levels of interest in making the routine visits, and older officers who are more experienced and have more poise seem to enjoy it more than younger officers. Increasingly, there are instances in which these visits—not authorized by law but sustained by tradition—result in rejection by the resident, and younger officers are occasionally made uncomfortable, if not intimidated, by these encounters.

One is struck by the very low-keyed nature of police patrol work in Japan. Generally patrol police in Japan present a lower profile and engage in less "muscle flexing" with the public than do American officers. In Ginza, at the Sukiyabashi police box, which is perhaps the busiest in all of Japan, one does not sense an air of emergency that typifies so many United States inner-city police stations. While on some Friday nights there are drunken fights, generally there is no bloodshed of the type Americans have become familiar with. Accordingly, the police on the beat, or in their *kōban*, seem more relaxed than their American counterparts.

At Sukiyabashi, several officers remain inside, engaged in administrative work and processing complaints, while one or two officers stand alertly outside the *kōban*, demonstrating their receptiveness to inquiries and other matters. By far the most common request is for directions. Because most Japanese streets have no names and are numbered in a confusing way, giving directions to those unfamiliar with the area is a common task for Japanese police. In a central area of a large city, it is often the major task.

Surprisingly, during my interviews with *kōban* police in 1980 I rarely encountered an officer who had ever drawn his gun. After approximately a month of the field study, having asked the question perhaps fifty times,

Figure 4.2 **Suggestions for Police Recruits**

I.   Etiquette

1. Dress properly and neatly.
2. Knock on the door or ring doorbell before entering.
3. Do not peep in windows or touch articles such as decorations at the entrance.
4. When offered a chair or *zabuton* (cushion), sit down and greet the person properly.
5. If a woman receives you, keep the door open unless she asks you to close it.

II.   Communication

1. Offer appropriate greetings, indicating why you have come. If you are visiting the house for the first time, introduce yourself. For those who are not familiar with routine visits, explain and ask for their cooperation.
2. Select appropriate words. Make your speech clear with a choice of language appropriate to the person you are addressing. You may use the local dialect if there is one in your area.

III.   Note the Occasion

1. Avoid ceremonial occasions, when there are guests or when people are occupied with work.
2. When there is no one at home and contact is difficult, ask the neighbors when the family might be at home in order to carry out the routine visit.

IV.   Note the Content of the Conversation

1. Speak of familiar, interesting matters and make the conversation easy to understand.
2. Do not say things that may hurt the feelings of the residents.
3. Avoid rumors concerning neighbors and political topics.

I stopped inquiring directly about police use of firearms. One officer stated that he had been called to a bank robbery in progress, in which the robber was suspected of being armed; the officer drew his weapon but did not fire it. An officer's response at the Sukiyabashi police box was typical. He said that he had never drawn his weapon and, as far as he knew, not one officer stationed at his police box had drawn a weapon during the two years he had been assigned to that location. A follow-up with police officials in 1999 indicated no change in the frequency with which officers draw their weapons. Despite the bright lights, noise, and huge crowds that remind one of many American cities, police in Japan confront only a fraction of the violent crime that American officers encounter. Henry Kamm (1981), in an article for the *New York Times,* described several evenings spent with police in the Ikebukuro section of

The Sukiyabashi Police Box, One of the Busiest in Downtown Tokyo

Photo by Jen and Rob Frost

Tokyo. He observed that the area was a "teeming district of bars, cheap eating places, porno shops, Turkish baths that serve as a cover for prostitution, and two dozen love hotels where rooms can be rented by the hour." Despite this picture of a Japanese-style Times Square, he said,

> No crime was reported, no complaints were lodged, and no arrests were made. The only suspects questioned were men pushing bicycles that, despite arousing patrolmen's suspicion, proved to be owned and registered by the suspects. The only harsh treatment meted out was by an angry mother coming to reclaim her two small daughters who, instead of doing their homework, went in search of their father at a game parlor but lost sight of him.

The first problem encountered by police during the afternoon of my first *kōban* visit involved the report of a bicycle theft. A man who appeared to be a businessman in his thirties claimed that his bicycle had been locked but nonetheless had been stolen. It is a popular myth that Japanese do not lock the doors to their homes or attempt to secure other articles, such as bicycles, but in Tokyo, despite its low crime rates, many people do take such precautions. I was told, however, that people in rural areas still do not bother to lock their doors. Even if they lock their front doors, they often will not have made the rest of the house secure by locking the windows. Owners of new bicycles in rural areas usually lock them up, but older bikes are often not secured. A *kōban* officer's log for a particular day (see Figure 4.3) gives the flavor of an overnight tour of duty (National Police Academy 1998).

Visits and observation of police activities at various *kōban* in the Ginza were informative in a number of ways. A visit to the Odawaracho police box brought to light one aspect of the supervisory process. On that occasion I happened to meet the assistant police inspector who was making a routine visit as part of his circuit. He informed me that he traveled by bicycle to all ten police boxes in the Ginza offering guidance to recruits or newly assigned personnel. In addition, he was responsible for overseeing the activity of each police box in the district, and, in case of a robbery or other emergency, he had to be available to coordinate the various police boxes. In short, he functioned as a liaison between the police station and the *kōban*. For each of the shifts, a different officer assumed these liaison and supervisory functions.

The Role of Women

During 1980 one male police administrator offered this explanation as to why more women were not employed in police work, "It would be difficult, lots of walking, a lot of physical strain, working alone at night." This remark was not offered in a critical tone, but it reflected a general stereotype regarding the role of women. However, by 2000 some modest changes in the role of women in police work were very much in evidence. While twenty years earlier they were involved with juvenile matters, traffic, and restricted roles within local police agencies, they are now more and more in the mainstream of police work. They were visible in 1999 on Tokyo streets during patrol work and staffing police boxes. In 1980 I had been told that an old Japanese law prevented women from working overnight in a government agency—effectively banning women from the overnight police duty required at most *kōban* and thereby denying them opportunities to do the bread-and-butter police work of the Japanese system.

Figure 4.3 *Kōban* **Officer Log**

8:30	Work starts at police station	• Receives instruction from police chief and community section chief. • Gets uniform and equipment checkups.
9:00	Desk work	• Instructed by *kōban* chief to pay special attention to sneak-thief as they have many reports reported recently. • Receives a report from citizen that he left his bag behind in a public phone booth.
10:00	Patrol	• Gives crime prevention guidance focusing on residential areas frequently targeted by sneak-thieves. • Receives a command from police radio and rushes to the house of the resident who made an emergency call to police for being troubled by a peddler not leaving a house.
11:00	Desk work	• Upon a report, conducts traffic control for a traffic accident in the neighborhood until handing over the duties to traffic officers from the police station (11:10–12:00).
12:00	Lunch	
13:00	Desk work	• Receives a report finding a bag left in the telephone booth and takes contact to its owner after confirming what it contains. • Gives geographical guidance.
14:00	Routine visit to home and work places	• Gets a hearsay information that a suspicious looking man haunts a nearby park at night. • Visits ten households on the beat (two of them were absent) and tells them to watch out for sneak-thief. • Visits a home which previously had a thief sneak in and asks if there is anything unusual after that. • A resident seeks advice about his son frequently being tempted by a group of delinquents to go out after dark. • Officer notes physical features of the son and tells he would visit his home again for the further discussion.
16:00	Desk work	• Persons who consulted before claiming and being claimed for making noise by playing Karaoke; visit *kōban*. • Officer mediates between the two and presents a solution (16:30–18:00).
19:00	Supper	
20:00	Desk work	
21:00	Joint patrol	• Cracks down on drunken driving, with other *kōban* officers in the same precinct.
1:00	Night patrol	• Detects a few youngsters in a park and advises them to return home.
2:00	Nap	• Upon a fire report, rushes to the scene and rescues people (2:30–3:30).
7:30	Traffic control for school-children	• Controls traffic for schoolchildren on their way to school in cooperation with community residents.
8:30	Desk work	• Files a document.
9:00	Handing over duty	

As of April 1998, there were 8,100 women officers in Japan. The *White Paper on Police* (National Police Agency of Japan 1999) reported that women were employed in "criminal investigation, criminal identification, anti-*boryokudan* measures, guard/escort duties, rescue operations, helicopter patrols, traffic guidance, detention of female suspects, and public relations.

Concerning the role of women generally in Japan, by mid-1999 the Japanese had passed the Gender Equality Law. But as the *Japan Times* (August 28, 1999) noted, the legislation was "woefully lacking in specific compliance measures." According to this editorial, most companies still had two categories of employment, "fast track" for those who are headed toward management jobs and "non-career opening" for those (the majority of women) who were expected to leave employment because of marriage, pregnancy, or some other circumstance. The Tokyo Metropolitan Government found that while women made up 39.9 percent of the workforce in 1997, only 14.1 percent were in management posts (*Japan Times,* August 28, 1999). Also, due to the increasing unemployment in Japan linked to the ten years of recession, women college graduates were having a far tougher time obtaining jobs and particularly jobs commensurate with their abilities. As of October 1995, the female population of Japan numbered 64.2 million or 51.1 percent of the total population (Bando 1996).

At the World Conference on Women, held in Beijing, China, in 1995, Japan showed the least improvement among ten industrialized nations in terms of women's participation in government and corporate decision making (*Japan Times,* August 28, 1999). Furthermore, Japan's rigid seniority system also worked against the upward mobility of women to management positions. One plus has been the Parental Leave Law of 1992, which allowed a parent to take off up to one year to care for a child. The age of marriage now averages 26.3 years and the birth rate has declined so that it is lower than that in most industrialized nations. For 1990–95, the rate in Japan was 1.5 children per family, while in the United States it was 2.1 children (Bando 1996). Therefore, understandably, Japanese demographers anticipate a variety of problems by 2050.

One other development linked to the Gender Equality Law was the statement incorporating sexual harassment. The government claims that the law outlaws workplace discrimination and puts companies on notice that their behavior will be monitored (Magnier 1999). But a different interpretation is offered by city officials who claim that it was cosmetic.

They cite the fact that the law is still too vague, calls on companies only to "endeavor" to change, and includes no punishment for those who flagrantly violate the provisions.

One high-profile case in 1999 helps shed light on the problems of workplace equality for women (French October 27, 1999). A Tokyo morning television anchor resigned under pressure apparently linked to her having concealed her divorce. The woman, Ayumi Kurdoa, was one of Japan's most popular television personalities, and her departure created a furor. According to the report, feminists and sympathetic viewers were united in "the most bitter polemics" in years over women's rights. Acknowledging the double standard, the director of the Office of Gender Equality of the Prime Minister's Office noted, "After the war, Japan established a system of basic equality of the sexes under the law. But in actual life, the differences persisted in our customs, that women should stay at home and that men should work" (French October 27, 1999).

Astonishingly, Japan's unemployment rate remained below 2 percent until the mid-1970s, but then gradually increased to 2.8 percent by 1987. After the speculative "bubble economy" burst, the unemployment rate rose to 4.1 percent (high by Japanese standards) by 1998. This is the official rate with the unofficial rate being somewhat higher, as in most countries. This development has impacted Japanese society in a number of ways—for example, it has stimulated a vast wave of underemployment, as well as increased suicide rates (see later discussion on this topic) linked to loss of jobs and loss of face. Sakamoto (1999), in an extensive article for the *Asahi Evening News*, offered a series of poignant case studies of young Japanese university graduates who had paid the price of being underemployed and faced boring dead-end jobs that had contributed to depression and a sense of hopelessness about future career prospects.

Many salaried workers, who were in their thirties by 2000, had graduated at the height of the "asset-inflated" economy when it had been common for businesses to hire new employees en masse. As the economy shrank, these companies increasingly cut back middle managers in an attempt to restructure. Therefore, those hired in the 1980s had become fair game themselves for further downsizing by 2000. Prospects for promotion had become severely reduced. As Sakamoto noted,

> This has the potential to produce a vicious spiral in the fortunes not only of individual employees but of companies as a whole. Traditionally, Japanese companies do not discharge employees easily, so an increase in the number of discontented employees bodes ill for business. (1999, p. 5)

One specific example offered by the author identified a thirty-three-year-old man who worked for a Tokyo securities firm. He had no career prospects and did not have the faintest idea what to do about it. He had been seduced by a high initial salary, but got caught in the plummeting economy. He worked at the research division of his firm, but that unit appeared headed for restructuring. He felt hopeless and despondent about the future. Since he was still employed, along with being a young father, he felt unwilling to risk employment elsewhere (Sakamoto 1999). While there had been a gradual move away from the lifetime-employment system by 2000, there was still only a small percentage of workers willing to shift jobs in midstream because traditional employers often viewed job hoppers as tainted goods.

Interview Tactics at Police Boxes

My experiences at these first police boxes taught me some things about the general structure of the force that might have been difficult to learn from direct questions. In fact, who would and who would not answer my questions was in itself instructive. Lower-ranking officers questioned on general policy matters occasionally appeared perplexed by the inquiries. Initially, I wondered whether they were attempting to deflect controversy by giving short, superficial responses. However, somewhat later an alternative hypothesis emerged, namely that they had not concerned themselves with the subject; it was a matter for higher-ups to decide. For example, I asked a senior policeman at the Shintomicho Ekimae *kōban* if he thought it was necessary to visit all residential and commercial buildings twice a year. He replied, "They've decided it," "they" being the police administration.

To counter this reluctance to give clear answers, whether due to anxiety over the prying of a foreigner or to deference to superiors, I tried to create a low-keyed, relaxed atmosphere at the police boxes. At the outset of a visit to a new *kōban*, I mentioned that I was willing to talk with them about any aspect of American life that might be of interest. In addition, I had pictures of my family with me and frequently produced them, particularly in conversations with older officers who were often family men themselves. By indicating openness to their concerns, they understood that my research interests did not preclude discussions of other subjects.

On the whole these tactics succeeded, perhaps largely because the atmosphere at the *kōban* was naturally relaxed. Years earlier this task might have been more difficult: the atmosphere at some of these police boxes was more tense in the late sixties when radical student groups were aggressive. Many confrontations took place between police and students, and the police were called in to quell riots at the prestigious Tokyo University and elsewhere. One officer recounted that they were required systematically to search the immediate premises of the *kōban* every fifteen minutes for explosives.

Interviews at *kōban* were not the only means of learning about the grassroots police. I also spent some time on patrol with officers. One evening around midnight, when I was accompanying a motorized patrol, the officers checked a huge underground garage. On the three levels, over seventy men were loitering. Some were drunks, others were just down and out. One fellow, despite his unshaven, skid row appearance, claimed he made 150,000 (U.S.$1,442) a month by playing *pachinko*, a popular Japanese pinball game, the prizes of which are often surreptitiously exchanged for cash. Gambling for money is prohibited in Japan, but the sergeant explained that prosecution takes place only when the offense is directly observed by police. There were brief, amiable exchanges between the sergeant and several men, and no attempt was made to roust any of them from their overnight lodging.

The visit to the Tsukiji fish market police box was a fascinating and enjoyable experience despite the fact that it started before sunrise. It is necessary to arrive very early in order to capture the spirit of the market bargaining, which is in full swing by 4:00 A.M. The police box is located at the entrance to the market area. The older officer on duty reported that the area, which includes over two thousand shops, is relatively crime free, with only occasional reports of pickpockets. Two or three complaints a day are received. In earlier years, there were problems with "toughs" who occasionally got into knife fights, but the shop owners banded together to get rid of these undesirables. The main job of officers assigned to this *kōban* is providing crime-prevention information and making routine visits to the shop owners.

This seasoned officer, like many others, reported a reduction in the level of citizen cooperation over the years. He felt that young people, in particular, were less responsive to police officer contacts, and sometimes did not even answer when an officer asked a question. He said, "Before and right after World War II, the police were both respected and feared, but today some people are tempted to abolish the *kōban* system because of the decreased level of cooperation. I believe it should be maintained, but patience is required." The changing nature of citizen attitudes toward the police proved to be a recurrent theme, and often *kōban* officers raised the issue themselves, demonstrating that it was a problem.

Much later, an officer patrolling the Hongo area of Tokyo found a good way of summarizing the changes he had witnessed over the ten years of his service: "They used to treat us like members of the family and invite us in for coffee or tea; today that would be unthinkable." This problem of the weakening of ties between citizens and police in urban areas is of concern to police administrators, but to some it seems the inevitable product of modern industrialization. No clear-cut official strategy to attack this problem appears to have been formulated; officers are left to find their own solutions.

Policing Tokyo's Outlying Areas: Shitaya, Seijo, Akabane, Motofuji, and Sanya

The outlying police station areas I studied are for the most part very urban in character. Though unlike the Ginza, with its tourist attractions, high-priced restaurants, glittering shops, and smart nightclubs, among these "suburban" urban areas there is a certain similarity. On average, they are forty to sixty minutes by train from the heart of the city, each is quite commercial, and all blend readily into the seemingly endless bustling sea of metropolitan Tokyo. The one exception is the district served by the Seijo police station, where one finds the homes of middle-income and wealthy citizens—a kind of Japanese Westchester or Westport, with the qualification that houses and yards are considerably smaller.

The Shitaya Police Station

The demands of police administrators are quite different in this older section of Tokyo, which has approximately 240 personnel assigned to it. In the early days of the city, when it was still called Edo, a considerable number of politicians lived in this district. Many families can trace their ancestry back several generations, and traditional festivals are still enthusiastically celebrated. Craftsmen and intellectuals also live in Shitaya, and they have contributed to continuing economic stability, according to officials. While there is a great deal of commercial activity, relationships between police and citizens are closer here than in the Ginza or in the areas of Tokyo with a more transient population. Police chiefs are in an excellent position to comment on variations within the city because superintendents and senior superintendents are rotated approximately every two years. The chief at this station in Shitaya mentioned that, "Notwithstanding the fact that this is a city, people here do have an affection for their neighborhood." One consequence of the closer relationship between police and citizens is the increased activity of crime-prevention associations. These are organized according to district and include housewife associations, according to Shitaya police personnel. A social scientist at the National Research Institute of Police Science, the research arm of the National Police Agency, mentioned that the more conservative elements in the community, including shopkeepers and others who have much to gain from a closer relationship with police, provide the backbone of crime-prevention activity.

These relationships and associations seem to pay off with impressively low crime rates. The chief and his staff noted that while there are occasional burglaries in Shitaya, these tend to target houses and occur when the occupants are out. Armed robbery is extraordinarily rare, and these officials said that there had been no bank robberies in their district in the previous five-year period. Moreover, there were only two or three homicides per year for this entire station area.

These results notwithstanding, interviews with *kōban* police personnel in a variety of Japanese cities indicated that officers do not know their neighborhoods thoroughly, despite aid from the neighborhood associations. At one *kōban* in Shitaya, officers said it is possible to know a neighborhood thoroughly only when residents move very infrequently. Police record basic information—the names of residents, current employment, and so forth—on cards filed in the *kōban*, but in many neighborhoods people move too frequently for officers to keep accurate records from the routine visits. For instance, at this *kōban*, whose jurisdiction included approximately thirty-five hundred households and businesses, the two officers on duty stated that the turnover was around one thousand every two years or so. Most of those who moved were families living in the apartment complexes that had recently proliferated in a number of areas of the city.

Despite the crowded living conditions in Tokyo, the officers claimed that only about five calls a year about family quarrels had been received at their police boxes, and inevitably the dispute had subsided by the time the officers arrived. As noted earlier, the Japanese are reluctant to call the police about domestic disputes, and when the police are called, embarrassment seems to put an end to the quarrel before officers arrive.

The Shitaya police station had the following specialists assigned to it: five detectives, three crime-prevention officers, five "public safety" officers (who handled prostitution, drug enforcement, and firearms violations), and five juvenile officers.

During my visits to Shitaya, I learned of another difference between the work of Japanese and American police, namely, that the Japanese police rarely go to court. Information they gather on a criminal case is turned over to a prosecutor, and the court does not require their personal appearance. The prosecutor's written statement is usually sufficient. In the United States police officers often spend a significant amount of time going to court and waiting for a case to be heard.

One of the highlights of the field study conducted at Shitaya was the visit to the "Single Men's Kendo and Judo Tournament." Kendo is a form of fencing with a bamboo sword. Officers, outfitted in medieval-looking robes and wearing face shields, utter war cries as combat is joined. The contestants received a rousing send-off by the chief at an early morning ceremonial gathering in the upstairs gym of the Shitaya police station. This included the beating of a huge drum, a sake toast, and a pep talk by the chief. The contestants then traveled twenty minutes to the site of the tournament, where they met teams from eight other police stations. After a brief warm-up period, there was another short ceremony for all the participants. One of the reasons one rarely encounters an overweight Japanese police officer is that, as mentioned earlier, all officers are required to take either judo or kendo, and promotions at the lower levels require proficiency in these sports. Physical exercise is continued by most police long after the required years of training are over. Moreover, foot and bicycle patrols are still far more common than motorized patrols, and this contributes to the trim appearance of most personnel. By 2000, in the United States, as a result of the popularity of community policing there were a lot more officers on foot and bicycle patrol than in the early 1980s.

The Seijo Police Station

While the problem of eyewitness testimony was not peculiar to the Seijo station, I have included it at this point because the subject was raised at this station for the first time. The problems of eyewitness testimony are

Waseda University Area Police Box

Police Box—Tokyo Area

Tokyo Police Cyclist

Police Box at Edge of Tokyo

due, in general, to the inherent unreliability of eyewitnesses, but the problem is compounded by poorly developed police procedures for conducting lineups and photo arrays. In the United States the issue has received an increasing amount of attention from the courts and social scientists over the years (see Loftus 1979 and Parker 1980), but a great deal of work remains to be done.

The situation is worse in Japan, where relatively few precautions are taken in this delicate matter. Photo arrays are conducted far more often than corporeal, or "in person," identifications, which experts have regarded as being superior (see Wall 1965). Research into the administration of photo arrays has demonstrated that it is such a subtle process that officers who administer them can easily and unwittingly bias the witness. Many cases are on record (e.g., see Borchard 1932) in both Britain and the United States in which innocent parties have been convicted by confident but mistaken witnesses. Potentially even more prejudicial than the use of photo arrays is the use of "show-ups"—an arrangement in which a witness encounters a suspect in a one-on-one situation (sometimes face-to-face and sometimes through a one-way window). The U.S. Supreme Court has ruled against these and other circumstances that generate prejudice against the suspect. Nevertheless, "show-ups" and other similar techniques are apparently common in Japan.

Ministry of Justice officials and police administrators indicated that lineups are rarely employed in Japan. A lineup involves inserting a suspect into a group of individuals who are not so unlike the suspect as to draw the attention of the witness to him, and the witness is usually offered the opportunity to view the lineup through a one-way window. In 1980, one official at the Seijo police station explained that "photos are used first, before the confrontation between witness and suspect is arranged, and then the witness is allowed to observe the suspect through a type of one-way window. If you have to arrest the criminal quickly (for example, if a series of thefts has occurred), then the witnesses are allowed to observe the suspect directly . . . while their memories are fresh." These "show-ups" present serious problems since, among other things, the witness may be recalling the photo of the person he identified previously rather than the actual image of the person. (See, for example, my discussion in *Legal Psychology: Eyewitness Testimony, Jury Behavior* 1980). Japanese procedures seem to reflect a lower level of concern for the rights of the accused.

On several occasions I asked public prosecutors and police officials how a judge—there are no jury trials in Japan—would be able to determine whether the eyewitness identification process has been tainted. The consistent answer was that it is entirely up to the judge to make a determination of the accuracy and reliability of the eyewitness identification. Obviously, there is no way for even the most conscientious judge to obtain a complete and exact idea of procedures undertaken by the police and prosecutors.

For years a "montage" device—which allowed a technician to create a composite facial likeness of a suspect with the help of a witness—was employed by the Tokyo Metropolitan Police Department headquarters personnel. Now, however, more sophisticated devices are on the market to assist in the identification of suspects. Japan continues to be in the forefront of technological applications in law enforcement, and a Canadian software application called FACES was being seriously considered by the Tokyo Metropolitan Police Department in September 1999 (Asakura 1999). The highly touted product contained 4,000 facial features, including eyes, eyebrows, chins, and hair. This software device, in which a composite picture can be produced on a laptop computer, can create billions of different faces within minutes. The Quebec company Interquest claimed that one of its images, which had appeared on the popular American television program *America's Most Wanted,* had successfully led to the arrest of a child rapist.

The primarily residential area covered by the Seijo police station is ten times larger than that covered by the Shitaya station, and the main problems confronting police are somewhat different. The network of community groups and crime prevention associations was weaker due to the lifestyles of these upper-income families, and house burglaries were the main criminal activity that had been recorded for this area.

Police patrols and visits to *kōban* revealed typical minor problems: resident complaints of large trucks using a quiet, narrow, noncommercial street; an annoying peeping Tom; and several bicycle thefts.

I was fortunate that I became personal friends with several officers. I visited their homes, ate with them, played tennis with them, and visited nightclubs and jazz coffee shops with them in the Ginza, Shinjuku, Harajuku, and other places. This was not only a very pleasant experience in its own right but offered an opportunity to check on various matters and confirm or refute certain points raised in the course of the field research. One patrol sergeant was particularly helpful. He was a college graduate, exceptionally bright and personable, and was familiar with the work of a number of American criminologists. One evening, he made the following comments:

> Policemen who are ambitious do a lot of questioning of citizens. For example, when patrolling the streets, it is fairly easy to do. If someone has a light out on his bicycle, he can be stopped and rather easily persuaded (if he is initially evasive) to give basic information about himself—what his name is, where he is from, where he is going. He will cooperate, although reluctantly at times. I might do this six of seven times a night.

This is a prime example, along with the routine family visits, of how Japanese police penetrate, as David Bayley (1991) stated, deeper into the community than do their American counterparts. The reasons are obvious. In the United States a citizen would no doubt loudly voice his "rights" if confronted by the kind of police behavior just described.

Occasionally, one hears of complaints from foreigners who are offended by what they consider the audaciousness of the Japanese police. A professional woman employee of a U.S. government office in Tokyo offered the following episode as an example. This Japanese American spoke fluent Japanese and had lived in Tokyo for a number of years. She stated that she and an acquaintance, a male American scholar, were stopped by two men in business suits while heading for lunch in the Akasaka area of Tokyo. The officers inquired where the couple were going, to which she responded by asking who they were. The men immediately furnished their police identification cards. She then asked why they had been stopped, but they did not reply. The officers repeated their questions and the woman reluctantly replied that they were headed for lunch. One officer smirked and again repeated his question, to which she angrily retorted, "To lunch!" The police then asked about the nature of their relationship and in the process discovered that her companion was not carrying his alien registration card, which all foreigners are legally required to have with them at all times. The officers then asked the couple to accompany them to the nearest police box, despite the woman's protest that the man's alien registration card was easily accessible—a three-minute walk to his office. At the police box, the man was asked the purpose of his being in Japan, and he informed the officers that he was seeking employment. They responded that there was no way that they could be assured of the veracity of his statement. The American visitor was then asked to provide further identification and to sign a form letter of apology. In addition, he had to promise to report back with the alien registration card. This incident illustrated the ease with which Japanese police can make inquiries at their own discretion (a privilege that would be the envy of American police) and the indignant and angry feelings of foreigners subjected to such tactics.

Courts in the United States have continued to be sensitive to possible rights violations by police. A variety of court rulings, including one by the U.S. Supreme Court involving a California law that allowed police to arrest vagrants, has been ruled unconstitutional. A vagrant in California law had been defined as one "who loiters or wanders from place to place without apparent reason or business, and who refuses to identify himself when asked by a police officer." The key issue becomes to what degree police may detain, question, or otherwise impede a private citizen when they lack "probable cause" to make an arrest.

The Akabane Police Station

The Akabane station area covered approximately twenty-five square kilometers (about ten square miles) and was located at the northern end of the Tokyo Metropolitan Police Department's jurisdiction, bordering Saitama Prefecture. The low-income housing projects found here have historically had somewhat higher crime rates than the surrounding areas, but it has been crime against property and not violent—bicycle theft, petty larceny, and similar offenses.

Concerning changes in the nature of police work over recent years, the problem of dealing with citizens intent on expressing their "right" was once again voiced. This issue, in various forms, was raised by more officers during the field study than any other. One officer put it this way: "Before, people were obedient to their seniors, but now you have to explain before asking a person to do something."

A discussion with one officer concerning domestic disputes was revealing. Asked about their frequency and how they are handled, he commented:

> We receive such a call about once a week, but usually it's quieted down by the time we arrive. We are ready to protect ourselves when we walk in, but usually there is little violence between the husband and wife—rather, it may be directed at an object, like breaking a window. Only once or twice a year do we have to break up a fight and often it's because they are drunk. If it is necessary to intervene, our training in judo or kendo is sufficient.

Concerning wife beating, the officer suspected that there was some but that unless the wife wanted a divorce, there was not much use in reporting it. Furthermore, he noted that there was a tradition that prevented the enforcing of laws related to crimes within the family.

In the Akabane and Motofuji *kōban*, and in fact all over Japan, I saw posters with slogans. A cynical American policeman might view these with disdain, but they seemed to have real meaning to Japanese police. Sometimes officers submit their own slogans to M.P.D. headquarters, and these may appear later in a published circular. Some *kōban* police even repeat these slogans before starting a shift. One "permanent" poster spotted on several occasions said, "To have good contact with people and show understanding, to get the confidence of people." Another poster declared, "Don't take it out of the holster, don't put your finger on the trigger, don't point it at people." Occasionally, a "goal for the month" poster was observed. One said, "Try hard to stay in good condition mentally and physically," while another exhorted, "Try your best to be responsible and maintain a sense of duty." A more elaborate poster spotted on the backroom wall of the *kōban* was entitled "Five goals."

1. Try to meet each person honestly and try to gain the respect and understanding of the local community.
2. Try to melt into or fit into the community by taking the initiative and grasping the area of your jurisdiction.
3. Try actively and constructively to question people on the street in order to prevent crime and make arrests.
4. Be alert and be nimble in terms of organizing your activities in order to solve each case as quickly as possible.
5. Work properly, correctly, and with dignity. Be fully alert in preventing any crime or accident.

The Motofuji Police Station

This station's jurisdiction included the main campus of Tokyo University, but officers were quick to point out that it would take a serious emergency for an officer to dare to enter the campus. Tokyo University had been the scene of some pitched battles between police and students during the late 1960s; it was now required that the chief of the Motofuji station be a Tokyo University graduate. At the time of my visit the chief, a man in his mid-thirties, was a law-department graduate, who had been a student when the police entered the campus. An agreement was reached that the president of the university would be consulted before any police officers were allowed on campus. The young chief was particularly receptive to my questions and was extremely helpful in explaining the problems of policing this area. A member of the elite police, he, like his colleagues, had been rotated through various assignments and had recently left a post on the northernmost island of Hokkaido. His rank was superintendent. Officers under his command noted that he placed great emphasis on family visits.

One interesting piece of information that emerged from visits to *kōban* in the Motofuji area came from an officer about to be transferred to a prison. He commented that he would still be a police officer and that he was doing this to further his career aspirations as a detective. He explained that this prison exposure to "see how criminals are handled" would expand his understanding of the justice process.

During a brief visit to the Hongo Crossing police box, just a few blocks from the Tokyo University campus, it became clear that giving directions was the main activity; typically over two hundred inquiries were answered daily. University students occasionally teased an officer, but the violent clashes between police and students common in the late 1960s no longer occurred.

Among the four different shifts of the patrol division stationed at the Motofuji station, there was competition concerning the number of traffic violations recorded, robberies solved, and so on, although investigations of the latter crime are pretty much in the hands of the detective division. Traffic enforcement is a controversial subject since administrators are concerned that too rigorous an enforcement of traffic laws leads to the alienation of citizens, but it was the judgment of one senior policeman that the competition between the four shifts had more advantages than disadvantages: "It increases the individual's incentive to do a good job and it betters the team spirit—it peps up the whole morale."

At the average *kōban* there were approximately four hundred and fifty households assigned to each officer for the purpose of the routine family visits. Sometimes officers were selected to do the residential survey exclusively. Officers at one *kōban* admitted that the transient population presented serious problems in terms of knowledge of the neighborhood.

Policing Sanya

Sanya, a lower-class section of Tokyo, had many transients, and police officials pointed it out as one of the most crime-ridden areas of the me-

tropolis. It is a small, skid row district of Tokyo in which criminal offenders often attempt to elude authorities by disappearing among the
many jobless transients. Residents lived in run-down, single-men's rooming houses and hotels.

One television report focused on the plight of one Sanya resident. A
former businessman, then in his sixties, he had been fired by Mitsui
Trust for diverting funds into a loan, which he had been unable to repay.
Relatives ridiculed him and his wife divorced him. Ashamed, he sought
shelter in Sanya, where people do not inquire about one's background,
and had lived there alone for half his life.

Accompanied by my interpreter, I paid a visit to this area on a late
afternoon during early autumn. Groups of disheveled men loitered around
the kōban area. This police box, like most others, was a very small,
inconspicuous, two-story building with a drab façade. A young inspector of the National Police Agency had joined us that day, and we decided
at the last moment to make this stop after having visited the nearby
Asakusa Juvenile Counseling Center. An inspector in his late forties received us in the rather crowded space on the second floor of the kōban, a
small, open room with several other officers seated at desks. (It is
common practice for section chiefs and supervisors, in business and government as well as police work, to sit in an open area with their subordinates.) The chief was friendly and explained that men in the area contracted
for daily work and that this lack of stability and the emotional difficulties that often accompanied their circumstances contributed to the excessive drinking and fighting that were common in the section.

Later, wandering through the side streets of the neighborhood, one
older man reached out to touch my female interpreter. On the whole
though, aside from this one feeble gesture, for a neighborhood considered to be among the most dangerous in Japan, it paled in comparison
with crime-infested neighborhoods in cities that I have seen and worked
in, in the United States. Most urban areas of Japan are relatively clean
and pleasant to live in, by American standards. Police, even in this area,
were not deeply concerned about the safety of a foreigner walking through
the narrow streets. While a mugging or purse snatching might occur, a
serious assault or a homicide would be extremely unlikely.

Bayley (1991) noted that because many of the residents of Sanya
were too poor to own watches, the local kōban erected a large, illumi-
nated clock to assist men in reporting to work on time. A message board
on which were posted weather reports and notices to individuals from

friends or family members was also constructed. This, however, is hardly a new service of the Japanese police, since Westney (1982) observed that as early as 1884 the police were posting daily weather reports near the station houses and *kōban* as a means of inducing the public to read police bulletins.

The next chapter explores the role of police in the northern prefecture of Hokkaido and the western prefecture of Okayama. Attention is focused on the *chūzaisho* or residential police box in the countryside.

5

Attitudes of the Police toward Their Work

During my visits to *kōban* and *chūzaisho*, there was ample time to talk with police officers about their attitudes toward their work, including how they became interested in their occupation and their perceptions of the future of police–community relations. Occasionally I made inquiries about discipline problems, weaknesses within the organization, and how family members felt about their employment as police officers. For instance, the changing shift pattern of American police officers has been such an irritant for spouses that it is often cited as one of the causes of divorce. I was interested to know whether the Japanese police experience similar difficulties.

These conversations were held at police boxes with street-level officers, usually those holding the rank of policeman, senior policeman, sergeant, or assistant inspector. However, I also discussed these topics with higher-ranking personnel, including members of the elite police— those who had entered as assistant inspectors. Usually they were administrators working out of the headquarters of the National Police Agency, the Tokyo Metropolitan Police Department, the Hokkaido Prefectural Police Office, and the Okayama Prefectural Police Office. Some were superintendents, others senior superintendents and occasionally even higher-ranking personnel at the apex of the administrative hierarchy. Meetings with these top-level officials were somewhat different in tone and often proved to be events in their own right. I particularly remember a luncheon with a chief police superintendent who was second in command at a prefectural police agency. I was given the red-carpet treatment, complete with a chauffeur-driven trip to an expensive restaurant nearby. Information gathered from high-ranking as well as low-ranking personnel was supplemented by contacts with other justice personnel and private citizens who helped to deepen my understanding of the attitudes of the police toward their work.

Street Police

I attempted to create an informal atmosphere in my conversations at police boxes, and the flow of conversation was far more important to me than adhering rigidly to a prearranged set of questions. Responses, of course, varied tremendously, and occasionally avenues of discussion opened up that were totally unanticipated. Frequently I had the luxury of time on my side—I usually spent a full day at a police box. Unless the police were unusually busy, there was ample time for conversation. This portion of my research was decidedly dependent on the candor of the officers interviewed and on my ability to establish a rapport.

Given this background, I have selected the following excerpts from interviews, which I believe help to capture the flavor of the encounters and the attitudes of these men toward their work. The information lends itself to this narrative style as opposed to a survey approach in which data are categorized and presented in tabular form. While the latter approach has the advantage of presenting a large amount of material in a concise manner, it fails to convey the subtleties and nuances of individual answers to specific questions.

How They Become Interested

As is the case in the United States, it appears that aspiring young officers in Japan began with notions of becoming detectives and investigating crime. Television programs and films, imported and domestic, glamorize the role of the detective. An officer who was approaching retirement and who worked out of the Tsukiji *kōban* in Tokyo mentioned this as the reason for his original interest in joining. He noted that while he felt disappointment over never having become a detective, he nevertheless enjoyed the contacts with citizens in his day-to-day work at the *kōban*.

A sergeant at a *kōban* in the Akabane area of Tokyo had been a police office for thirty years. He noted that he became interested in police work at the close of World War II, when "life was a mess" and few jobs were available. He said that, "Despite the hierarchical paramilitary structure of the police force and the strict discipline, younger people who enter now speak more frankly and occasionally with humor to their superiors." I countered with, "Don't you lose discipline in a more relaxed system?" To which he responded, "Yes, but working in a police box is more like working in a family setting. It's not that I command them." When I asked if he could generalize about these attitudes, he remarked, "Well, of course it is difficult, but practically speaking (and perhaps inevitably) living overnight here at the *kōban* creates an environment that encourages close working relationships." At another point, he was nostalgic for an earlier period: "Obedience still characterizes the attitudes of older citizens toward police, even if they tasted the fear of the earlier prewar period, while young people are not particularly obedient. Routine visits used to be made, and the families known thoroughly. We used to have much more knowledge—very complete—but now there is just a brief visit. For example, if a woman lost her husband during the war, she would talk to police about it and feel gratitude for the assistance she received. Also, during that period they had a relationship more like that of friends and today that has been lessened, but there is still a carryover."

A problem concerning the future of policing that was raised on a number of occasions by different officers was also voiced. "There is a group of us [in the Tokyo M.P.D.], around six thousand in number, who have worked for many years and who are rapidly approaching retirement. There is concern about the void in police skills that will exist when we leave."

Finally, concerning the demands of the job, he said that it is both physically and psychologically less taxing than it used to be. The shift patterns that were adopted after World War II, which imitated the American system, were quickly abandoned in favor of the present four-day pattern described earlier. Furthermore, in recent years there has been less emotional tension compared with the previous decade, when political dissidents were active.

It was not uncommon to hear officers talk about the "stability" of police work as a factor in their choice of an occupation. One thirty-year senior policeman mentioned this as his main reason for joining. In addition to being attracted by stability, he had been encouraged to join by his *sensei* (teacher or mentor), and he had ruled out a desk job.

Table 5.1

Reasons Given for Joining the Police in Okayama Prefecture

	College graduates (total: 140)	High school graduates (total: 102)	Total (242)
To serve society	20.0	15.7	18.2
Because it is a stable life	14.3	23.5	18.2
Because of an advancement examination system based on ability	25.7	8.8	18.6
Because it is a good job for a man	28.6	38.3	32.6
Was attracted by the uniform	0.7	0.0	0.4
No other suitable job available	2.1	4.9	3.3
Wanted to ride a patrol car or motorcycle	0.0	2.9	1.2
Other	8.6	5.9	7.4

Source: Walter L. Ames, *Police and Community in Japan* (Berkeley, CA: University of California Press, 1981), p. 166.

While the economic conditions of different periods of Japanese history have affected the recruitment process, stability was still an important factor for younger officers even in the prosperous 1970s, as Ames's data show. In 1974, 18.2 percent of recruits offered this as a reason for joining. The responses offered by recruits from Ames's research in Okayama are shown in Table 5.1.

A large majority of Tokyo's police are recruited from outside the prefecture, where 98 percent of Okayama's officers had lived in the prefecture. Despite this difference in recruitment, however, it is probable that the responses of the Okayama police can be considered representative of the force as a whole. In Okayama in 1974, 312 applicants who took the police entrance examination gave the following answers to the question of who had urged them to join the police: family, 24 percent; relative or friend, 8.7 percent; teacher, 3.8 percent; and police officer, 48.1 percent.

Data gathered by police on Japan's northernmost island of Hokkaido concerning the reasons for joining the police agency resemble that recorded by Okayama authorities. The vice chief of the patrol division of the Hokkaido Prefectural Police mentioned the following reasons (presented in order of frequency): (1) Being a policeman is a manly job; (2) Police stand on the side of justice and punish criminals; (3) The income is steady.

Another sergeant, fifty-seven years old, who was working out of a *kōban* in the Seijo station area of Tokyo, also entered police work im-

mediately after World War II. He made similar comments on the disorder that existed in Japan at that time, limiting his choice of occupation.
Raised in Fukushima Prefecture, he attended school in Tokyo. For him,
retirement was just six months away, and although his retirement plans
were vague, he wanted to do something active to keep him healthy. The
job was physically demanding, and kendo had helped him maintain his
physical condition.

A younger officer, aged thirty-four, shared the assignment at the same
police box in this outlying area of Tokyo. Raised in Hokkaido, he was
attracted to police work because he liked judo. Proud of his physical
prowess, he said, "I never lost a fight when I was growing up." He worked
on his parent's dairy farm until he reached the age of eighteen. His wife,
like those of most officers, accepted her husband's choice of occupation, but it is unclear to what extent this represented mere acquiescence
or a more positive acceptance. A Japanese wife would be expected to
support her husband's choice of occupation to a greater extent than her
more outspoken counterpart in the United States. Notwithstanding his
self-confessed combativeness at an earlier age, he said he had never
drawn his firearm. He recounted one incident, eight years earlier, when
he was called to a family quarrel where the father was drunk and wildly
swinging a sword, frightening family members. He had been required to
disarm the man, but even on that occasion he had done this without
resorting to the use of his gun. His greatest job satisfaction, he indicated, was "being of assistance to others," while having to "sit around"
was clearly the most boring feature of his work. Like many officers, he
took pride in his work and observed that while there have been occasional lapses, police work tended to have few instances of corruption
because officers were "obedient and faithful" to their job. This last comment reflects the esprit de corps and the high performance standards of
Japanese police.

One rugged, thirty-seven-year-old sergeant, assigned to a *kōban* just
three years previously, had spent six years with the riot police (see
photo 5.1). Earlier, he had been assigned to the Traffic Information
Center at the headquarters of the Tokyo Metropolitan Police Department. His responses to my questions were short and clipped, as if he
were determined to meet only the minimal professional requirements
of the situation. Nonetheless some information emerged. "Police work
is clean work; it's good for a man. It's also a special type of service
work that, unlike other public service jobs, demands more activity—it's

Police in Riot Gear

Source: National Police Agency 1998.

not desk work." ("It's good for a man" reflects the popular image of what police work is like, and this was by far the most frequently given reason for wanting to join the police force in Okayama Prefecture— 32.6 percent of applicants mentioned it.)

Work with the riot police was difficult during the 1960s when students were on the rampage, and he admitted having been frightened on one occasion when the windshield of his car was smashed. Like most riot police, he was unmarried at the time, but out-of-town assignments and the constant readiness had still been a chore. The high level of physical training was one of the more enjoyable features. Most riot police officers are rotated out of that duty every three years, but he had spent six years in the assignment as a mechanic working on the various types of vehicles required by this paramilitary unit. As one learns about and observes units of the riot police during street demonstrations, a comparison with U.S. Army National Guard becomes inevitable. The National Guard unit also operates independently, and its methods, including training, are militaristic, but the comparison goes only so far; Army National Guard units are not nearly as well-trained or disciplined as the riot police. Ames spent time with one of the riot police units in Tokyo and his comments are illuminating. He goes so far as to say that the organization is "modeled directly after the abolished Imperial Japanese Army" and that the "Way of the Warrior" (the *samurai* ethic) is exemplified in the riot police.

Another sergeant I interviewed had been a member of the Japanese Self-Defense Force before joining the police. The term "Self-Defense Force" is a euphemism for the armed forces as Japan's post–World War II constitution does not permit the development of an offensive military machine. He decided to join the police force because prior military service allowed him to start with a high salary. He confessed that prior to joining he had worked as a "public officer"—a person who investigates communists.

An older veteran of the Tokyo M.P.D. revealed an incident that had drawn him to policing as an occupation. He had been brought up on a farm in Okayama Prefecture before joining the army during World War II. After a bombing raid near Osaka, he and an uncle were assisting two children who were in "bad shape." Apparently disoriented, the children were crying and hungry. They met a police officer, who arranged shelter for the children and gave them food. This act of kindness, which was in sharp contrast to his image of police as authoritarian, was primarily responsible for his decision to become a police officer.

Family ties to police work were not infrequently mentioned as being responsible for interest in the occupation. This reason was cited by two officers, one young and one middle-aged, assigned to a *kōban* in Sapporo. In one case, a grandfather had been in police work; while in the other, a friend's father, who was a police officer, had encouraged him to take the examination. Another Hokkaido officer, from the Asahikawa area, had become interested in police work because his father worked for the Hokkaido Prefecture Police. One sergeant in Tokyo said, "When I was small, my grandfather and uncle were policemen, mainly that was it."

One young officer at a *chūzaisho* on the outskirts of Tokyo noted that "a sense of justice" had contributed to his choice of police work. This thirty-one-year-old senior policeman had witnessed the student uprisings of the sixties in which barricades had been erected on his college campus. Unlike some of his friends who sympathized with the demonstrators, he felt angry when many classes were canceled: "It didn't seem fair." This contributed to his desire to become a policeman.

One young, recently promoted sergeant in his thirties, whom I met at a police box in Tokyo, became a good friend. He was the first officer I spoke with after my arrival in Japan, before I had officially commenced my research. It was a chance meeting: I had asked for directions at a police box where the officer could not speak English, and this man, stationed at a neighboring police box a mile or two away, was phoned. This downtown area of Tokyo is frequented by foreigners, and most inquiries from English-speaking visitors were referred to this man when he was on duty.

After a few minutes of conversation, I was amazed to discover that he had read David Bayley's (1976) original book, *Forces of Order: Police Behavior in Japan and the United States*, and so I eagerly sought his impressions. The book was accurate in his opinion; he indicated that many Tokyo police had read the Japanese translation. Not only had he read Bayley, but he was eager to learn of other American criminological works. On a piece of paper he had scrawled the title of a sociological text by Walter Reckless, a well-known American scholar. His lively intellect and interest in American police practices contributed to a friendship that has grown over the ensuing years.

His English was excellent, which is rare among Japanese street police. Some members of the higher-ranking police of both the National Police Agency and the Tokyo Metropolitan Police Department speak English fairly well, but it is unusual to find such a fluent street-level officer. He graduated from college with a degree in engineering and then worked in the sales department of a Japanese firm that specialized in international business. This permitted him to travel to other Asian countries. Several years later, he left the firm and joined the M.P.D. Like other Japanese, he had received some exposure to English during junior high school, but this did not explain his fluency. He credited this ability to having listened to the U.S. Armed forces radio station, which broadcasts programs in Tokyo.

While he thoroughly enjoyed his work, his wife found it a bit taxing to adjust to his hours. His police box, like many others, was pleasantly decorated with flowers. Like most police, he took a gentle, low-keyed approach with drunks—there were many wandering the streets in his section of Tokyo after 11:00 P.M.

He noted that womanizing and drinking and driving occasionally presented a discipline problem among police, but he added that if an officer loses his police identification card, disciplinary action can follow. Serious disciplinary problems, however, are unusual. In one instance he knows of, an officer had an affair with a married woman in the neighborhood of his *kōban*. The ensuing gossip and complaints registered with his superiors resulted in his transfer to a different *kōban* and a reprimand. Noting that while businessmen engage in a fair amount of extramarital activity, he hazarded a guess that few policemen do. Officers are frequently reminded about their conduct by superiors. One weekend when he was among a group of thirty policemen headed out of town for a vacation trip, they were, he said, "preached at not to get into trouble." Some in the group complained, "They treat us like children." By the mid-1990s this officer had left police work and joined his in-laws' construction business. With the advent of the new millennium, it has been more common for businessmen in Japan to shift jobs, as the vaunted lifetime employment scheme is under assault. Still, it is a bit unusual for a police officer to leave in mid-career.

In one police box I interviewed three officers together, and asked them how they had become interested in the police. One was from Kyushu, in the south of Japan. His family was poor, and he came to Tokyo for a college education. He dropped out of college, and police work became one of the few available jobs he could find in a tight job market. The second officer grew up on a farm as the oldest son but found farming dull. He left the farm for police work, which seemed exciting. The third officer said he had consulted a Buddhist priest. He had a vague notion that people relied on policemen. The priest supported his interest in this aspect of police work and he subsequently joined the force. When asked what jobs they would seek now if required to choose alternative careers, they mentioned Buddhist priest, teacher, and farmer, respectively.

Officers are not immune to verbal abuse although they generally receive much less than their American counterparts. One policeman, who seemed a bit unhappy with his choice of career, said, "There is a kind of obligation around your neck. When local teenagers hurl bad names or insults, you can't talk back." He said, "I've been called '*bakayaro*' [you dumb jerk] and '*wakazo*' [the equivalent of 'punk' or 'kid,' implying a lack of maturity]. Often when people are drunk, they say, 'Why do I have to get bossed around by a punk kid?'"

The fact that "service to the public" links occupational interests as diverse as law enforcement and teaching is revealed in one officer's comments. "I got interested in police work because 'service' runs in my family. My parents were teachers, and other relatives worked for various government agencies, and therefore it seemed natural to go into police work."

Police Crimes

More serious acts by police, including criminal offenses, while less frequent in Japan than in the United States, are occasionally reported in the
press. A number of examples follow.

Arrested for stealing goods from a supermarket, a forty-two-year-old
police inspector, who was chief of the crime prevention section of a
police station in Chiba, was discharged in disgrace. He had attempted to
blame the shoplifting on his eleven-year-old daughter until eyewitnesses
forced him to admit to the crime. He had picked up three cassette music
tapes worth 12,000 yen ($50) (Sims 2000).

A former police inspector was arrested for robbing a credit union of
500,000 yen ($2,200) in Yokohama. Police reported that a masked man,
brandishing a kitchen knife, broke into a branch of the Yokohama Dai-
Ichi Credit Union and threatened a teller with a knife. The credit union
immediately telephoned the police, while three employees armed with
wooden swords chased after the thief (Sims 2000).

In 1982, there was a rare case of alleged corruption at higher levels of the
police force. The man who had been the head of the Osaka Prefectural
Police at the time of the incident killed himself, a typically Japanese suicide
in which he assumed responsibility for the wrongdoing. While he had been
reassigned as the director of the Police Academy before the corruption case
unfolded and while there was no indication that he was directly involved,
he nonetheless took responsibility for not having prevented it.

In a different vein, a thirty-three-year-old detective of the Fukuoka
Prefectural Police was accused of having "intimate relations" with the
wife of a local gang leader and receiving 4 million yen ($18,000) from
her. He had become acquainted with her at a snack bar and borrowed
money from her to repay the loan he had obtained to buy a 12-million-
yen ($60,000) condominium. The officer was suspended pending fur-
ther investigation. Fukuoka Prefecture had been one of the most active
areas for gangsters in the 1980s, and police claim that 3,200 gangsters
were associated with 144 underground organizations in the prefecture.
The officer involved had investigated 600 gangsters in forty gangs.

Problems and Future Prospects

I sometimes asked lower-ranking police about problem areas within
police work, including organizational weaknesses. Naturally, they were

not always eager to specify things they were dissatisfied with or identify problems within the police agency. Occasionally, I managed to "tease
out" criticisms. Sometimes I linked this discussion with inquiries concerning future problems and prospects facing the police. A number of
officers provided perceptive and thoughtful answers.

One *chūzai-san* from Hokkaido linked the frequently mentioned issue of citizens citing their "rights" with a growing sense of individuality
and social distance among the people in his village.

> People feel freer to argue with police. But in town associations, too, there
> is an increasing reluctance to serve others. Compared to earlier years,
> people seem to lack a spirit of cooperation, not only toward the police but
> among themselves. This tendency will increase in the years ahead, which
> will make it difficult for police to do their work. In order to inspire coop-
> eration, we will have to make a greater effort. For example, we were
> trying to catch a man who was making explosives in his apartment, but
> his next door neighbors "didn't know about it." We had been working
> with the local TV station on it, yet the growing distance among Japanese
> prevented us from getting help from this criminal's neighbors.

One assistant inspector in his early forties who had worked undercover was concerned about the problem of ferreting our radical students.
During the early 1980s there were fewer dissidents, and the main difficulty emerged from violent infighting between extremist groups such as
the *Chukakuha* and *Kakumaruha*. The police had been unable to penetrate their ranks and break them up.

An officer at a Motofuji area police box in Tokyo mentioned two
problem areas for police. The first, traffic enforcement, was of concern
to administrators. Officers on traffic detail are sometimes accused by
kōban police of overzealous enforcement of the law. He acknowledged
that a balance is required and commented:

> As you know, it is important to maintain good communications between
> officers and the surrounding community. Traffic is regulated by the traf-
> fic section and sometimes by the patrol department. The possibilities of
> hostile reactions by the public mostly arises because the traffic section
> too strictly enforces the code. One example is illegal parking. But in most
> cases when citizens are warned, they go home with the realization that
> they have done something wrong. Therefore, it isn't just a matter of re-
> sentment directed toward the police.

A concern for police, he believed, was the continuing rise in juvenile delinquency, which had been observed over the previous thirty years. "The fact is that the age is dropping—it used to be high school students, but now it is junior high school students or even younger ones. Some are prospective very dangerous criminals."

Some responses to questions about future prospects and improvements needed in police work yielded statements reminiscent of those of American police. A detective in the Shitaya station area responded, "We need to expand the size of the police force to deal with growing criminality." While police in the United States might agree, scholars and students of policing have become increasingly skeptical of this stock response, and with good reason. A study conducted by the Police Foundation found that saturating an area in Kansas City with police patrols was not effective in reducing crime and that a comparable region of the city with a minimal police presence had similar crime rates.

This M.P.D. detective went on to note that officers like himself were sometimes unhappy with the limitations imposed upon them when they interrogated suspects. He added another complaint: "Some officers with ability feel too much emphasis is placed on the paper exam, which restricts their opportunities for promotion."

Occasionally officers expressed concern about the planning for and the management of earthquake-related problems. One superintendent stated that this issue was currently being studied by high-ranking officials. The citizens of Tokyo, at least, are understandably concerned about a possible repeat of the 1923 quake that devastated the city. A major quake has been forecast for this region of Japan, and the number of minor earthquakes that occur are an ever-present reminder of potential devastation.

Police Administrators

Not surprisingly, a different pattern of vocational and professional interests characterizes many of the higher-ranking officers. There are two groups: those who have risen through the ranks to inspector, superintendent, or higher, and those who are identified from the outset as elite, having entered as assistant inspectors. The latter, as previously mentioned, are frequently graduates of Tokyo University's law department. Many of the superintendents and inspector-level middle managers I met were part of the elite group of those who had passed the National Public

Service Examination. Some of this elite had considered other public service careers (the ministries compete for the most able graduates from the most prestigious universities) before joining the National Police Agency. Unlike the street-level police, few had family members in police work.

All who do manage to enter as assistant inspectors are marked for top careers with the National Police Agency. Many will rise to become chiefs of the forty-seven prefectural police agencies. Some will graduate into high-level positions within the headquarters of the National Police Agency in Tokyo, while others will be posted to Japanese embassies overseas. It is very difficult to enter this level of police work, but once one has done so one can feel secure. It is rare for a person to be fired, mediocre job performance notwithstanding. If a person is not performing well, he will be shifted to a different position.

Promotions in the police, except at the top levels, occur very regularly, and an officer keeps pace for the most part with his "classmates." While in the late 1990s the business world of Japan has seen a very gradual shift toward the concept of merit as opposed to seniority in promotions and advancement, this concept barely touches the police field. Only at the very highest levels of management (above prefectural police chief) would consideration be given to merit and then in only a handful of cases. Entering bureaucrats generally are very conscious of colleagues who enter at the same time, and a sense of camaraderie often develops among them. Salary increases and regular bonuses that are given out twice annually, as in industry, are generally similar, and neither salary increases nor bonuses are linked to meritorious performance, contrary to the practice in the United States.

In 1999 I had the pleasure of joining a group of eight National Police Agency officials for a night on the town in the Ginza section of Tokyo. They came together at least once a year informally because they had all belonged to the same martial arts club at Tokyo University—not all during the same four-year period. Sophisticated and cosmopolitan, they had taken assignments, not only all over Japan, but some had been assigned to Japanese Embassies in Indonesia, the United States, and England. Some had earned graduate degrees at the University of Michigan, State University of New York at Albany, and at the University of British Columbia in Canada. Some National Police Agency officials become "security officers" at embassies throughout the world, and like most foreign service personnel, they take intensive language training before assuming their assignments. I was impressed by their strong educational backgrounds, broad-mindedness, and general intelligence. Several admitted that they would have liked to have careers in law, but they had been unable to pass the entrance examination for the Judicial and Legal Training Institute. As mentioned earlier, thousands of applicants annually seek admission to this training institute, which accepts just a small number. Moreover, just ten to twenty individuals are selected annually to become assistant inspectors in the National Police Agency's program to train and develop top managers. As in industry, the large majority of entering recruits will continue with the police agency throughout their careers. In Japan, management-level positions in the national ministries and agencies carry more prestige than do similar positions in private industry, the converse of the situation in the United States.

One inspector impressed me especially. His intellectual approach and willingness to confront problem areas with a visiting researcher struck me the first day we met. He discussed police work candidly and commented on Bayley's book, which was, at the time, the only Western publication on Japanese policing. With a good command of English, he had a knack for effectively conveying his analysis of an issue. Still in his twenties, he had been a police officer for approximately two years. Asked about career goals, he indicated that he hoped to become the first officer at an embassy abroad.

At the outset of his career, after completing the mandatory three months of training at the National Police Academy, he was given an additional six-month field training assignment. Typical of other elite officers, he was given supervisory responsibility over a group of street police—in this instance at a station in Aichi Prefecture—an opportunity for a newcomer to get a feeling for grass-roots policing.

He noted that attitudes of young patrol police have changed, as evidenced by the fact that today officers desiring promotion spend time studying materials published monthly by the National Police Agency. During an earlier era, one avenue for promotion consisted of impressing one's superior through effective off-duty work. This took the form of intelligence gathering—for example, trying to get in with the head of a neighborhood dissident group. Older officers sometimes viewed with disdain younger officers who failed to devote off-duty hours to police work.

From his perspective in the Safety Bureau of the National Police Agency, gangsters present the most serious problem facing police in the immediate future. The Safety Bureau is charged with drug enforcement and the investigation of white-collar crime, and it coordinates policy in these fields for the entire country. At the time we were discussing these issues, he had been asked to generate a plan for a public media campaign to deal with increased stimulant use among young people. I asked if he could rely on other National Police Agency officials for assistance, which led to a discussion of factionalism and its impact on decision making. Workers are prohibited from seeking assistance from offices outside their bureaus.

A police superintendent working at the National Police Academy told me he was also a Tokyo University graduate, but, unable to gain admission to the Judicial and Legal Training Institute to become a lawyer, he had chosen police work because of its uniform status. Noting that if he had chosen to enter the Self-Defense Force, he would have worked among the nonuniformed ranks, and he confessed to finding the uniform attractive. After completing the Training Academy program, he was assigned to supervise ten experienced men in the field, a difficult task for an inexperienced assistant inspector. Later, he worked in the Traffic Division for several years and then in "public security" (a euphemism for intelligence work), which involved gathering information on student radicals. Like his middle-management colleagues, he seemed intelligent and highly professional.

Discussing disciplinary problems, he mentioned that sometimes officers are required to appear before a committee of supervisory personnel. In the case of drinking or "woman" problems, an officer's supervisor might suggest that he resign. If the person balks at this, he could be assigned to trifling jobs with no opportunity for promotion—in effect, disgraced. More serious cases, such as shooting a suspect, might involve review by a public prosecutor.

Discussing the future, he repeated the observation that many older officers were due to retire at the same time, leaving a vacuum. Adding to the problem was the difference in attitude between older and younger police. Older police perceive "work as life itself." Younger officers take a "salaried man" point of view, that police work is a nine-to-five type of job and only the required hours are logged. He also emphasized that officers do not work during their off-duty hours "cultivating the field," as they did in earlier times.

A day I spent with a chief superintendent, the second in command at a prefectural police agency north of Tokyo, was particularly gratifying because of the candid give-and-take conversation. Fluent in English, this maverick had studied political science at Johns Hopkins University on a Fulbright scholarship in the 1960s. I was startled to hear him challenge the efficiency of the *kōban* and *chūzaisho* system. This was practically heresy! It was not working in its present form, he claimed, because rapid urbanization created different kinds of demands on the system. Traffic control, criminal investigation, and delinquency in schools required manpower allocation based on a centralized administration. At that time, teams of officers were sent out to handle investigations and delinquency problems in schools. In his view, a single officer out of a police box could not handle these tasks. Efficiency was a key word for him, but he acknowledged that change was difficult because local neighborhood residents were wedded to the *kōban* system. "Changing the *kōban* system quickly would bring an outcry from the public and politicians."

In a major city in his prefecture there was approximately one policeman for every nineteen hundred residents. "How is it possible," he asked rhetorically, "for the officer to know everyone?" Though he was not completely without sympathizers, few other top administrators agreed with his philosophy. This prefecture, slightly to the north of Tokyo, was undergoing more rapid industrial and population growth than most, and this might have influenced his different perspective on the system. He favored phasing out at least some police boxes so that the limited manpower could be reallocated to deal with the previously mentioned problems. Needless to say, although his opinion apparently represented a minority view, that in itself did not invalidate it. Indeed, conventional thinking in any field follows those creative enough to work at the cutting edge of social change.

Since 1989, approximately fourteen or fifteen women have been brought into the elite program, where an officer starts as an assistant inspector. A woman police superintendent, the highest ranking woman in the National Police Agency in 1999 (and assigned to the Tokyo M.P.D.), was asked about changes that she had observed in police work during her career. Earlier, she had studied law at the University of Michigan. As of April 1998, there were 8,100 females assigned to prefectural police agencies throughout Japan.

She mentioned that police training had more recently focused on exposure to social and nonprofit agencies—including brief assignments working as a volunteer with the elderly, and so forth. She mentioned an administrative change—the department that had been called "crime prevention" had been elevated organizationally to "community safety"—

and it embraced the patrol division. The functions had not shifted in any significant way but allowed the integration of community policing services with the mobilization of private citizens under the umbrella of crime prevention. In 1995, with the increase in international crime, the international department had been created.

The working hours for these high-ranking officers were not a standard nine-to-five routine but rather frequently included evening work and a half-day on Saturday.

A superintendent in the Crime Prevention Division of the National Police Agency was particularly helpful to me. Flexible and possessing a good sense of humor, he applied himself conscientiously to his work at the agency. We had many conversations and contacts as he coordinated some of my research activities. Family background was a factor in his selection of police work; his father had worked in crime prevention at the prefectural police agency in Osaka. A graduate of Tokyo University's law department, he was a strong supporter of the kōban system, remarking that, "It is the only thing that makes Japanese police unique." Juvenile delinquency along with "internationalization of crime" were two problem areas facing police at the beginning of the new millennium.

On average he and his fellow elite officers were transferred every one to three years and occasionally more frequently. There is a serious question as to whether these officers can attain a high level of productivity in their positions, given their short-term assignments. Comments from several lower-ranking police officers and legal scholars support such skepticism. On the other hand, one could hardly quarrel with the breadth of their training for eventual top prefectural police assignments. Furthermore, the officers themselves told me that they felt they could master a new assignment in three or four months and that two years in one post was just about the right amount of time.

William Ouchi's analysis in *Theory Z* of Japanese and American business practices attempted to make the case for "nonspecialized career paths." A number of examples were cited, but one of the advantages of this approach was offered in this description:

> In the Japanese case virtually every department will have in it someone who knows the people, the problems, and the procedure of any other area within the organization. When coordination is necessary, both sides will be able to understand and cooperate with the other. Perhaps more important is the fact that every employee knows that he will continue through

his career to move between functions, offices, and geographical locations. The person from another department who is asking for assistance today may be the person who will be his coworker or even superior tomorrow. Thus there is not only the ability but also the incentive for taking a broad, organization-wide point of view and for cooperating with everyone. (1981, p. 27)

Examples of the breadth of training of upper-echelon personnel are offered in the following chronology of assignments of two elite superintendents. After graduating from the three months of training at the Police Academy, one officer was assigned to supervise *kōban* officers in a prefectural policy agency south of Tokyo for six months. He was next assigned to a police agency in the western part of Japan for approximately eighteen months, and he followed that with a three-year commitment to the Self-Defense Force. (It is not uncommon for officers to be assigned temporarily to the military agency or even to the Japanese National Railways.) This assignment was followed by an appointment to the Crime Prevention Division of the headquarters of the National Police Agency in Tokyo for several years. Later, he was shifted to the Juvenile Delinquency Section of the Hokkaido Prefectural Police in Sapporo. This was followed by an assignment in Mia Prefecture and then a three-year assignment with the Japanese Embassy in Jakarta, Indonesia. Later he was made chief of Okayama Prefectural Police for two years and then returned to Tokyo (on loan) as Director of Public Investigation in the Ministry of Justice.

The professional career of the other superintendent, in brief outline form, was as follows:

- National Police Agency (pre-service executive training course for successful applicants from the national Public Service Examination) as assistant inspector: three months.
- Kyoto Prefectural Police, supervising patrol police: eight months.
- National Police Agency in Tokyo; Security Division. Assignment included investigating problems associated with left-wing infiltration of labor unions, strike activities, and the Japan Teachers Union: one year.
- National Police Agency in Tokyo; transferred to International Criminal Affairs Division (Criminal Investigation) (required two months of training in Criminal Procedural Law, National Police Academy): one and a half years.

- Kagoshima Prefectural Police; chief of criminal investigation with a focus on fraud, embezzlement, and organized crime cases: one year.
- Prime Minister's Office (technically on loan); counselor, coordinating functions with other ministries and agencies: two years.
- National Police Agency in Tokyo; assistant director, Juvenile Delinquency Section, in charge of "guidance" (relationship of adults, including gangsters, to youth): three years

One final problem should be noted. It is not easy on the personal lives of police managers to have to move every two to three years, and it can be a wretched and painful experience for wives and children. As children become older, their schooling becomes extremely important, and sometimes families will decide that it is best for them to stay in a particular location while the father moves on to his new assignment. He will then return home on weekends or, if he is in a distant prefecture, he may even be forced to fly home once a month. However, one administrator noted that when his children entered high school in Tokyo and he was made chief of prefectural police in Okayama, he was allowed to leave the prefecture only twice a year. While his wife and two children could visit on the "bullet train" in five hours from Tokyo, the cost was prohibitive. One round-trip ticket in 1999 was around U.S.$350. Therefore they visited rarely.

In Kobe, a personable superintendent assigned to the Foreign Affairs Section of the Hyogo Prefectural Police was very conscious of social changes taking place within Japan and pointed to the changing structure of families as contributing to weaker social controls. "We used to think of the family as grandparents as well as mother, father, and children. Now there is only mother, father, and sometimes a single child. Families are having less influence as children are exposed to many other influences." By way of example, the superintendent described the case of a college-aged man who had murdered his parents: after two unsuccessful attempts to get into the college of his choice, he became a *ronin* (the term literally means "masterless *samurai*"), that is, a student who spends extra years preparing on his own in the hope of passing the entrance examination to a university. In the course of studying for his third attempt at the Waseda University examination, he was reprimanded by his father for drinking and stealing money. The twenty-year-old student retaliated by bludgeoning his parents to death with a metal baseball bat. In an editorial on the incident, the *Japan Times* (1980) noted the excessive pressures experienced by the *ronin*, and another "characteristically Japanese element," namely, "that the parents were victims of credentialism, obsessed with the notion that their son must go to a well-known university."

Another aspect of juvenile delinquency reported by this officer was that, "Historically, delinquents came from poor families, but increasingly they are drawn from the middle class, as in the case of shoplifters."

Talking with the young chief of the Motofuji police station in Tokyo concerning the controversy surrounding the *kōban* system and whether it should be dismantled, he said that it was dangerous to generalize because situations varied throughout the country—for example, there were residential areas, urban districts, entertainment sections. "Size alone shouldn't be the exclusive determining factor—regions change and evolve. Decisions on increasing or decreasing [the number of] *kōban* should be dealt with on a case-by-case basis."

Concerning the possible need to centralize manpower to handle problems on traffic control, criminal investigation, and delinquency in schools, he responded, "there's a need to take into consideration not just police perceptions, but the proven fact that the *kōban* system acts as an effective pipeline of communication that has strong implications for crime control and juvenile delinquency." The chief cited as an example of cooperation between police and citizens in his jurisdiction the use of "walking patrols"—citizens, both with and without police, patrolling the neighborhood. The December holiday season typically involved a rash of house break-ins, and crime-prevention block-watch groups had apparently reduced the number of such incidents during that time.

Concluding the discussion of the *kōban*, he offered an illustration of a different approach. Kanagawa Prefecture had experienced rapid population increases, but due to financial constraints combined with the need to occasionally mobilize significant numbers of men, it had decided to use a mobile *kōban*, a police box operation that worked out of a large van.

Among problems facing the police, he mentioned disaster and crisis relief associated with earthquakes. He felt that the need to coordinate all municipal services, including fire, was a challenging one. One wrap-up session with a police inspector at the Seijo station yielded this analysis: "It's primarily based on population, and there are plans to switch personnel more often instead of keeping them in one post for such long periods. Also, we're considering increasing the number of patrol cars throughout the district—to that extent it's a move toward centralization." The inspector reported that Shinjuku (a large shopping and entertainment section of Tokyo) had solved the problem of increasing manpower in one of its own areas by establishing a "mammoth" *kōban*. As suggested by the name, this type of *kōban* has more manpower assigned to it than the average police box.

Despite the problems mentioned above, in general the Japanese police seem to find fulfillment in their work. Relatively good police–community relations have been maintained over the twenty-year span of this research. This along with a highly organized system of benefits and promotion and the lack of violence in Japanese society continue to make police work a desirable profession.

Figure 5.1 Organizational Chart of National Police Agency

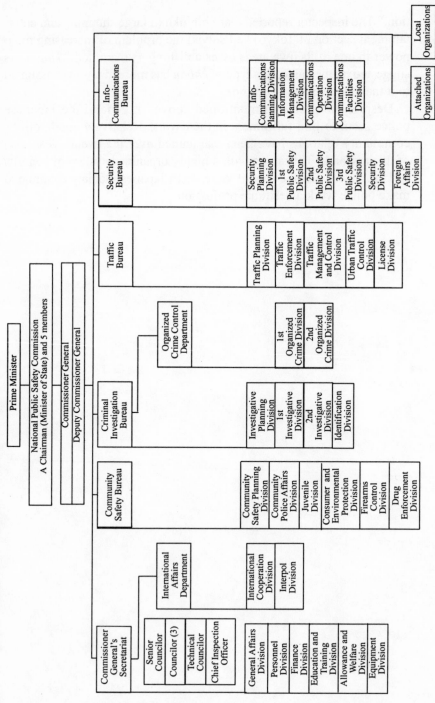

6

The Hokkaido and Okayama Prefectural Police Forces

The Hokkaido Setting

Hokkaido ranks second to Honshu in size among Japan's five major islands, accounting for 85,513 square kilometers out of Japan's total 377,643 square kilometers. While primarily rural in character, with the major activities being dairy farming, fishing, and forestry, industrial growth has taken place in cities like Sapporo, Hakodate, and Asahikawa. Hokkaido is one of the few regions of Japan that is not densely populated—it has fewer than ninety-nine persons per square mile, and a stroll through Sapporo's streets might remind one of a northern United States city like Minneapolis or a Canadian city like Edmonton. Boulevards are wide and laid out in a grid pattern, and there are many high-rise office buildings and hotels. There was a spurt of growth, including the creation of a huge underground mall, at the time of the 1972 Winter Olympics. Sapporo's population was listed as 1,241,000 in 1975, but it has grown since then to 1,804,000, and is Japan's fifth largest city as of 1999.

Hokkaido is cold during the winter, with temperatures averaging minus five degrees centigrade during January and February. The heavy annual snowfall, along with the mountainous terrain, make it very attractive for skiing, and one resort, Furano, has been a regular stop on the international World Cup Ski Tour.

While the police in Tokyo have been described by Western scholars, Hokkaido's police force has never been studied in any depth. Furthermore, given the preeminent position of the Tokyo Metropolitan Police Department, I decided that a study of regional police forces such as those of Hokkaido and Okayama would lend some balance to my research. The Tokyo Metropolitan Police Department is at the cutting edge of new developments in policing and has been since the Meiji era, but I also wanted to see outlying police agencies.

Policing Hokkaido

As of 1997, the Hokkaido Prefectural Police employed 9,224 officers (National Police Agency 1998). While the Hokkaido Prefectural Police is referred to formally as a "Communications Division," in fact, along with the Tokyo Metropolitan Police Department, it functions like the seven other regional police forces.

The organizational chart of prefectural police agencies provides an outline of the major departments and lists some of their functions (see Figure 6.1). Figure 6.2 sketches the organization of police at the station and police box level.

The principle concern of the Hokkaido police became apparent in one of my early discussions with the vice chief of the Patrol Division, who remarked that, "Patrolmen are the face of the police—they're always interacting with citizens." Because of the rural nature of the territory, there are 506 *chūzaisho*, as opposed to only 291 *kōban*, in Hokkaido. The problems of police–community relations and defining the proper role of the police officer are particularly crucial to the functioning of these residential *chūzaisho*, and the administration is conscious of the fact that it is the behavior of the men who staff these *chūzaisho* that is viewed as the real nature of the police by citizens.

While there might be some debate on this point, I believe the same is true of American police. True enough, many United States programs advertised as police–community relations have been superficial public relations approaches. However, the true relationship of police and community in the United States has been very much a function of the day-to-day relationships of patrol police and citizens. In fairness to American police, it must be noted that from the late 1980s major strides in police–citizen relationships have been achieved through the adoption of "community policing" programs that have put hundreds of thousands of officers back on the streets in walking and bicycling patrols.

An ideal relationship between a patrol officer and the citizens he serves

Figure 6.1 **Prefectural Police Organizational Structure**

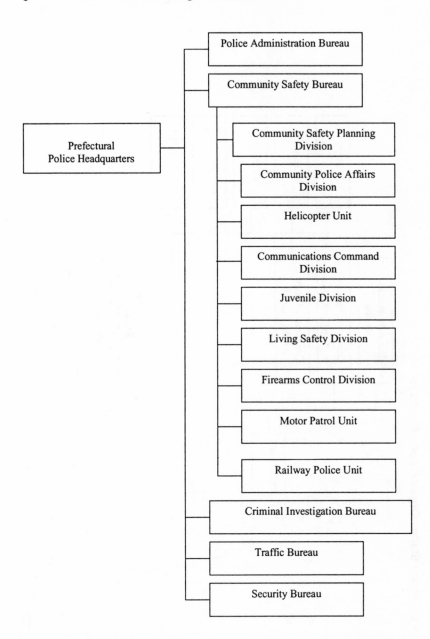

Source: National Police Academy 1998.

Figure 6.2 **Police Station Organizational Structure**

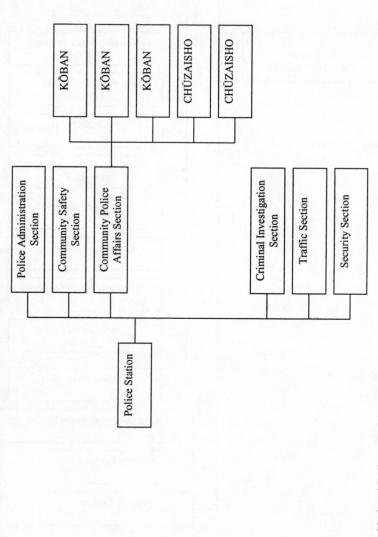

Source: National Police Academy 1998.

is not easily achieved. One Hokkaido police administrator observed that in any country there are problems both in becoming too friendly and in remaining too distant. In the view of this veteran officer, "One must stand at the neutral point." He explained that a *kōban* or *chūzaisho* officer cannot mingle freely in the neighborhood. If an officer is friendly with one person, others may suspect him of favoritism. Moreover, administrators are concerned that close friendships between police and citizens render the officers vulnerable to corruption. Hence, officers are rotated every few years to prevent such ties from developing.

Since the system was first introduced, the *chūzaisho* officer (or *chūzai-san*, as he is called) has traditionally been able to develop closer relationships with the people in his district than his urban counterpart in the *kōban*. While administrators may hope that the *chūzai-san* will concentrate on being vigilant, the actual circumstances of the social setting—usually a small village community—encourage a friendly, helpful attitude on the part of the officer, rather than an official, formal one. Usually, he has the luxury of being able to spend more time in visits to households than does the *kōban* officer. The isolation of some rural outposts means that the *chūzai-san* does not have the company of fellow officers on a regular basis and thus must turn to family and neighbors for companionship. People in rural areas are generally more interdependent in their relationships.

In contrast, the dormitory-style living of a considerable number of police in the cities, particularly young, single officers, contributes to a sense of community and cohesiveness among officers. Critics charge that it also creates a certain insularity among police and a bit of the "we" and "they" feeling so prevalent between American police and citizens. For example, a probation officer noted that the complex for police in Ebetsu (a city in Hokkaido), which houses around one hundred twenty police officers and their families, is referred to as being the *kidotai* by nearby residents. *Kidotai* is the word for the sometimes fearsome riot control police, and applying it to this housing area reflected the subtle hostility and apprehension felt by citizens. Another person informed me that children of police officers are sometimes treated differently by their classmates in school; other youngsters feel they cannot "fight" with sons and daughters of policemen. In cities, these disadvantages seem to be outweighed by the advantage of having the police together in their own housing complex, ready for mobilization in case of emergency. In much of Hokkaido, where the force is represented by one man in a residential *chūzaisho*, police–community relations, for better or worse, are much more personal.

When a new officer arrives at a police box, whether it is residential or nonresidential, he must try to get to know the people in his area. Ideally he would get to know all of the people in his jurisdiction, but he is most concerned about the persons he must interview as part of the residential survey. The task is made more difficult if he is officious. New recruits among both American and Japanese police tend to accentuate the "professional" role; but in Japan, the general attitude is as important as the actual performance. For instance, if an officer rigorously enforces traffic regulations, he will not be approached by citizens as frequently with tips on criminal offenses.

The head of the Miyuki *kōban* in Sapporo estimated that through the routine family visits and confidential files kept at police boxes, the officers know approximately 90 percent of the residents in terms of basic information but are able to match the names and faces only of neighboring residents.

According to the National Police Agency's document on "Community Police in Japan" (National Police Academy 1998), a model *chūzaisho* consists of forty-one square meters of floor space for official office use such as computer room, toilet for visitors, reception room, office, investigation room, and storage area. An additional seventy-seven square meters are for private use by the police officer and his family such as living room, bedroom, children's room, bathroom, toilet, and kitchen. Although women have become much more integrated into the mainstream of police work by 2000, men staff the *chūzaisho* and are almost always married with children. These *chūzaisho* often have motorbikes as well as bicycles and a car. Some *kōban* and *chūzaisho* have fax machines as well as computers. It is acknowledged that due to the frequent overlap between personal life and police work a certain strain is imposed on officers and their families. In recent years, due to the fact that wives often have to cover for their husbands when they are out in the community, they are now financially compensated for their work. This amounts to approximately 1 million yen (U.S.$9,615) annually. Due to the very nature of the *chūzaisho* assignments (often in rural settings) not all officers can adjust to this type of living arrangement and therefore the additional compensation for the wife's assistance is probably necessary to attract candidates. As already noted, the residential nature of this police assignment encourages closer relationships with the citizens within these jurisdictions.

Police Van Outfitted for Public Relations

Source: Tokyo Metropolitan Police Department 1998.

Occasionally mobile *kōbans*, or especially equipped vans with desks and chairs, are now used by police agencies to provide a temporary base of operation to augment police stations and other police boxes. One type of van is equipped for public relations work (see Photo 6.1). Often these are used in areas of rapid urban population growth where there are large-scale apartment complexes. (National Police Academy 1998).

The *Chuzai-san*

From the early days of policing, the *chūzai-san* has occupied an honored place in the community and, along with the village headman and school principal, has been considered one of the top-ranking town officials (e.g., Dore 1978). While administrators may set a policy that urges a "neutral" stance, the nature of rural life encourages close ties between an officer and his community.

To help to cement ties, an officer may leave behind his name card (*meishi*) when he visits a home that he finds unlocked and with no one at home. The *meishi* has the officer's name on one side, and frequently he writes a note on the other. Ever alert to his crime-prevention role, he might comment on something that indicated the house was empty: "The many milk bottles that have accumulated during your absence are an invitation to criminals. Therefore you should suspend the milk delivery when you are away." Since police behavior in Japan reflects a moral norm as much as a legal one, this type of note with its paternalistic tone is acceptable. Most Americans would regard such a note as overly intrusive.

Police in Japan appear to use print media to a much greater extent than American police. Three-quarters of *chūzaisho* and *kōban* publish their own short articles and notices in local newspapers; they also distribute circulars. Contents vary from reports on crimes and accidents to specific crime prevention measures, explanations of laws, citizens' opinions, and children's activities. Events of interest to the community and profiles of citizens who perform outstanding services are often included. Police–community relations are also enhanced by telephone lines called "*Jumin* Corner" (*jumin* means "resident"), which have been established in a number of prefectures to allow people to call in with various problems. This service will be described in more detail later.

By the mid-1990s, both *kōban* and *chūzaisho* were using "facsimile networks" and local television to get information to the public quickly in case of emergencies and alerts on criminal offenders, and so forth. (National Police Agency 1999).

Regarding lost items, police officers handled about 2.89 million reports of lost articles in 1997. Reports of found items the same year totaled about 4.12 million. Perhaps startling to an American, a significant number of lost items that were turned in included purses and wallets. The police reported that the total cash turned in amounted to 14.4 million yen in 1997.

On a crime-prevention level, over 13,152 sites for *kōban* and *chūzaisho* liaison councils existed by the end of 1997, according to the National Police Agency (1999). These efforts were directed at improving dialogue between police and citizens at locations throughout Japan. Police agencies and citizens throughout the world pay attention to response times—or the time an emergency 110 call is received and time it takes for an officer to respond. For 1997, the average response time throughout Japan was five minutes and forty-five seconds.

Attitudes of rural citizens toward the police are different from those of their urban counterparts. One officer assigned to Konbu *chūzaisho* noted that when he had worked at the busiest police station in Sapporo, engaged in traffic investigation, people gave only necessary, minimum information. In his new rural outpost, hundreds of miles from Sapporo, people volunteered information and at times sought him out for conversation. One elderly man came regularly to the *chūzaisho* to talk. One day he came at around 7:00 A.M. and the officer invited him in for breakfast. Due to the heavy annual snowfall in this mountainous area, the officer also occasionally helped motorists shovel out. While he actively encouraged residents to bring their problems to him, because of his brief tenure of just ten months, people still preferred to seek out the town assemblyman. The Konbu *chūzaisho* is responsible for more than 114.3 square kilometers (forty-three square miles), but there are just 450 houses and commercial enterprises in that large area. As with many one-man rural *chūzaisho*, a mini–patrol car is provided. Most of this officer's time was spent in routine family visits and an occasional traffic investigation. He informed me that no husband–wife domestic fights were brought to his attention during his ten months at this location.

A visit to the two-man Niseko *chūzaisho* offered only slight variations of the *chūzai-san*'s role. This police box is located in the center of a village of 4,595 people. Because the nearby hot springs and mountain trails attract tourists in the summer and skiers in the winter, the principal duty of Niseko police is giving directions. The police estimate that 45 percent of their time is spent with directions, 20 percent with traffic accidents, and just 10 percent with crimes, with the other 25 spent on administrative matters or other duties. The most common crime is petty theft. There was one report a few months prior to my visit of an altercation between six drunken construction workers and two highway patrol officers. The problem occurred when the car the workers were riding in was stopped at midnight because it was weaving all over the road. The occupants became incensed and started punching the police. Another incident had occurred the previous July: Several workers became involved in a street fight during a Niseko festival, probably as a result of drinking. These were among the few incidents of violence that police could recall during the previous year.

The Kuchan region encompasses five towns and two villages and has a population of around thirty-eight thousand. Fifty police officers and six civilians are assigned to this station area, which includes one *kōban* and twelve *chūzaisho*. For the entire region covered by the Kuchan station there had been just two homicides in the previous ten-year period. In one case, a young man murdered a high school classmate who had rebuffed his sexual advances. In the other case, a bar hostess had been murdered by a *yakuza* (gangster). There were an estimated twelve or thirteen such gangsters engaging in gambling and narcotics-trafficking in Kuchan. The head of this local group was reputed to be a "lieutenant" to the chief of a larger group in Otaru.

By 1997, there were approximately eight-three hundred residential police boxes in Japan, a reduction from the 10,239 that existed in 1974. As Japan has become more urbanized, officials have moved to replace *chūzaisho* with *kōban*. The geographical area covered by a *chūzaisho* jurisdiction is usually almost four times greater than that of a *kōban*. For example, the largest jurisdiction in Hokkaido covered almost half the area of Osaka Prefecture.

Profile of a *Chūzai-san*

One example of a man who thoroughly enjoyed his work is offered here in this sketch. This man was one of the most delightful police officers I met during my stays in Japan. He was a *chūzaisho* officer working in an outlying area covered by the Tokyo Metropolitan Police Department. I spent several days at his police box observing his daily routine and his interactions with citizens. I was surprised to find that there are residential police boxes under the M.P.D.'s jurisdiction until I learned how large and diversified Tokyo metropolitan area is. This man—Officer Saito let us call him—was thirty-seven years old, married, and had three daughters. He was a sergeant. He had always sought a residential police box assignment. Born and raised in an agricultural community far to the south of Tokyo, he had considered taking over his parents' farm but had decided against it. "These days," he said, "the oldest son is not automatically expected to take over the farm. Rather, the son who likes the work will take it over." He traced his early interest in police work to the "little kindnesses" he had observed the local officer offering to neighbors in his community. He had hoped to avoid working in a large city, but it proved to be his only access to police work. After completing high school, he had been assigned to Nakano for police training. Later, he took evening courses at his own expense at Nippon University, a Tokyo-based institution with over a hundred thousand students. Eventually, he received his degree. He had been a policeman for seventeen years and had worked in a variety of other police assignments, including traffic control, and his last assignment before receiving this posting had been in a jail working with presentence detainees. As mentioned earlier, police administrators agree that married, slightly older officers like Saito are the best choice for *chūzaisho* assignments, but, according to one official in Chiba Prefecture, they are increasingly difficult to find.

Saito was friendly and outgoing and appeared to enjoy thoroughly the most trivial, mundane encounters with citizens. He went out of his way to make such meetings agreeable. His police box was gaily decorated with flowers, and a colorful bird chattered in a cage near the window. This *chūzaisho* is located in a park across the street from a cemetery, and there are some cherry trees nearby. It was the first *chūzaisho* I visited, and the setting was so idyllic that I found myself wondering at the time whether or not it had been "spruced up" for my benefit. Later, after visiting other flower-bedecked *chūzaisho*, my skepticism vanished.

Saito said he found his job very enjoyable because it allowed him to get to know people and that, in his opinion, was the most important part of a *chūzai-san*'s job. This seemed evident when he conducted the residential survey, visiting neighborhood homes, shopkeepers, and the residence of a Buddhist priest. His wife was cooperative and helped by answering the phone and occasionally assisting with a drunk. He noted, "When drunks are talking to women, they are less aggressive."

In discussing police work, he remarked that most officers are very committed, that morale is high, and that while some people, like his brother, feel that the police take their duties too seriously, he disagreed. He added that the discipline of police work creates a sense of pride in many officers.

A number of officers I interviewed provided thoughtful answers to my questions. For example, in response to the question, "How much does society or one's life circumstances versus one's own sense of responsibility contribute to criminal activity?" Saito answered, "They both do, although it is difficult to separate the individual's control over his own behavior from society's impact upon him. In the case of a young person who gets involved with a particular group, he may be under pressure to commit a delinquent act. However, I believe the person must try to resist the pressure of the group and act with responsibility." Then, somewhat as an afterthought, he said, "It's my job to improve the environment."

He demonstrated compassion toward offenders when I asked, "Once arrested for a serious crime like rape, murder, or robbery, how should criminals be treated by authorities (i.e., courts and prisons)?" He answered, "They may be disturbed and they may need to be handled with care—otherwise they will feel isolated if put into prison. Everybody has the potential of committing a crime, and the authorities should make sure that a person who comes out of prison is able to live independently." It is uncommon to hear American police express concern for the conditions in prison and often they express contempt for offenders. Saito's compassion was tempered with realism, however, when I asked specifically about the rehabilitation potential of adult offenders. He viewed youthful offenders as having a good potential for living a crime-free life if they are provided with education and/or job training, but he acknowledged that with serious offenders, many returned to crime. "When one commits a crime, it reflects on the rest," he observed, referring to the interdependence and mutual responsibility felt by Japanese family members, coworkers, and friends.

While enjoying the social interaction of his job, Saito was also required to make more official observations at times. For example, he was participating in an investigation of radical students, who, though fewer in number and generally less active than during the late 1960s, are still considered dangerous, as well as difficult to locate and arrest. Though he claimed he did not enjoy doing it, he said that for this kind of work it was necessary to learn what one could, even during the friendly routine family visits.

Saito's jurisdiction included 467 households and businesses in which 1,300 persons lived and worked. His muscular frame reminded one of a football fullback, and, combined with his husky voice, it belied his friendly attitude toward local residents. He hailed almost everyone who walked past his police box. Like a number of officers I met, he enjoyed giving judo lessons to neighborhood children, in this case a class of seventeen youngsters. Saito viewed judo as an activity that discouraged juvenile delinquency and "built character." He could not resist a slight parenthetical admonishment to parents who were "too careful about their children." He maintained that children should learn "fighting spirit." Like many sports enthusiasts, he felt that the benefits of physical conditioning flowed into other areas. Some mothers had voiced concern that the judo training would affect the study habits of their children, a subject that obsesses Japanese parents, but he had allayed their fears. In his eyes, judo served as a vehicle for developing better relationships not only with the children he taught but with their parents as well.

Earlier in his career with the M.P.D., he had been frustrated with his traffic assignment, and in contrast the *chūzaisho* allowed him a much greater variety of tasks that he enjoyed. Other *chūzai-san* who enjoyed the work voiced similar sentiments. He felt this sense of job fulfillment so deeply that if a possible promotion meant reassignment he would have preferred to stay at his rank of sergeant and remain at this location.

It would be misleading to fail to point out that there are police officers in the United States who function much like the *chūzai-san*. As in Japan, these officers are often found in small towns and rural areas where they are less pressured and have more time to develop relationships with citizens.

One such American was described by Rout (1981) in an article for the *Wall Street Journal*. His name was "Virgil," and he was the sheriff of Grant County, South Dakota. During his thirty years as sheriff, he fired his gun just once—straight up into the sky. He patrolled a sprawling jurisdiction of over 750 square miles, and, like his rural counterpart in Japan, he spent most of his time counseling and visiting people. The service aspect of his job predominated in his territory of 9,000 inhabitants. While he served summonses, took care of prisoners, and collected taxes, his personal relationships were such that one county resident remarked, "Virgil is God around here; you have a problem about anything, you call Virgil."

Visits to Other *Chūzaisho* in Hokkaido

Unlike the situation with the Tokyo Metropolitan Police Department, in which officers are frequently drawn from outside the M.P.D.'s jurisdiction, the Hokkaido Prefectural Police selected most of their men from the island of Hokkaido. It was not uncommon to hear that an officer's father or another relative was a policeman.

It took one hour to reach the Ishikari *chūzaisho* by driving north from Sapporo in a blinding snowstorm. The police box was just 200 meters from the Sea of Japan. It was staffed by one officer and served the village of Ishikari, which had 3,000 inhabitants. Like his counterpart in Konbu, this officer was required to spend time during the winter clearing snow away from the police box. The daily routine usually consisted of processing paperwork—perhaps including a report on a traffic accident—for an hour or so in the morning. This *chūzai-san* estimated that he would have approximately forty-five accidents to report on during any given year, fifteen of which might involve personal injury. After completing any snow clearing or report writing that was required, he went out on patrol, usually on foot, but occasionally in his mini-patrol car. After lunch, for approximately two hours, he made routine visits to residences and to the handful of commercial establishments in this small town. Late in the afternoon, he worked on traffic control, then wound up his day with some paperwork. Officially, he stopped work at 6:00 P.M. Like other *chūzai-san*, he was not infrequently called after he had closed the front office area of the building. He estimated that every two or three days he received a call concerning a traffic accident or perhaps one about a drunk who was sleeping in the street. Occasionally, he was called upon after hours to give directions.

Generally, there was little criminal activity for the sergeant to be concerned with in Ishikari. For example, in the previous year, sixteen thefts were reported, including four house burglaries and two automobile thefts. There were three reported instances of theft from unlocked motor vehicles. One homicide had occurred, but this was considered extremely unusual: An emotionally disturbed man who had just come to town killed his younger brother with a knife. An additional dozen or so incidents, including fights and a person who refused to pay a bill in a restaurant, were all there was to report for the previous year.

This *chūzai-san* seemed to strive for the middle ground in relationships with citizens. Choosing not to work hard at fostering close relations with local citizens, he nevertheless occasionally went drinking with some of them. However, he commented that he was always mindful of the fact that he might have to turn around and "lecture" one of them for speeding.

Like other officers, he had observed over the years that people had become more concerned about expressing their individuality and less interested in "serving others." He was concerned that decreasing cooperation among community residents did not augur well for the future of crime control.

Juvenile delinquency in this rural community took the form of group theft, running away from home, and sexual promiscuity. He cited a recent case of a high school girl who had frequently arranged nighttime visits by her boyfriend to her room in her parents' home. According to the sergeant this situation would not have arisen when he was growing up, but in the present era it could be attributed to the increased tendency for parents to give their children their own rooms. In an attempt to keep abreast of the juvenile situation, he often met with schoolteachers and administrators to discuss problem students. While this officer was willing to counsel juveniles or adults with problems at the police box, he acknowledged that some felt a reluctance to come to him for assistance.

Along with the fear of becoming the subject of rumors, he said that most people wished to "solve their own problems."

Contacts with *chūzai-san* and observations at other residential police boxes provided information that generally conformed with the examples sketched above. A veteran of eight years at one *chūzaisho* in the Tokyo area complained at length about the system of evaluation. It is inherently unfair, he claimed, because it is based on brief, intermittent visits by supervisors. In addition, there is no feedback for the officer from these evaluations. The officer maintained that these feelings are shared by other *chūzai-san*.

In Sapporo, observations of police boxes such as the Susukino and Miyuki *kōban* yielded information similar to that which I had gathered earlier in Tokyo. The Susukino police box was located in the heart of a brightly lighted entertainment district. As a consequence, police were concerned about controlling the activity of overly aggressive pimps. Susukino is quite famous in Japan as a prostitution quarter, and there are more than thirty-five hundred pubs, cabarets, and restaurants compressed into this small district, as well as some eighty-five Turkish baths that also offer sex to their customers. As in other districts of this kind in Japan, *boryokudan* (gangsters) have made inroads into the nightclub and cabaret businesses. A "turf" battle had erupted between a gang from Honshu and a local Hokkaido group, with the outsiders being rebuffed. Once again, despite this huge amount of nighttime activity and the element of organized crime, there were just two incidents involving firearms. In one case, a *yakuza* had accidentally fired a weapon, while in another a member of the same group had been charged with the illegal possession of a firearm.

The Okayama Prefectural Police

Okayama Prefecture, in the western part of Japan, is around five hundred miles below Tokyo and was chosen for research in part because of the author's friendship with a former chief of the Okayama Prefecture Police. The friend, an NPA senior superintendent, had been chief in Okayama for two years in the late 1990s, but had been reassigned on a normal rotating basis to a new assignment as the director of public security in Tokyo. This was one of several assignments he had taken during his career when he was "on loan" to another agency—in this case the Ministry of Justice. The position involved gathering intelligence on radical groups in Japan. The long-term relationship with the former head of Okayama's police was critical, and the author was assured of full access to the agency and an excellent research opportunity. Personal relationships are even more critical in Japan than in America in getting things done. The research centered around Okayama City, the capitol of the prefecture and a picturesque and appealing tourist destination. The Chugoku Mountains provided a beautiful backdrop for visitors, along with Japan's Inland Sea. The total population of the prefecture was 1,950,000 in 1998, and it ranked sixteenth in size among the nation's forty-seven prefectures. One guidebook warned that a visit to Okayama City should be enjoyed before it merges into the east-west megalopolis spreading from Tokyo to Fukuoka. The city itself was just over five hundred thousand in population. Like many Japanese cities it has its share of shrines, castles, and gardens, including the popular *Korakuen* (translated as "Garden for Taking Pleasure Later"). This peaceful sprawling park area along the banks of the Asahigama River, was built by Lord Ikeda in 1686 (Bisignani 1993).

The Okayama Prefectural police structure, like most others in Japan, is organized into districts, each with its own police station operating directly under the control of prefectural police headquarters. Of course, under the police stations are the omnipresent police boxes (both *kōban* and *chūzaisho*). As of 1998 the Okayama police force had 3,028 officers and 530 civilian employees. It had 23 police stations and 105 *kōban*, along with 200 *chūzaisho*.

The structure of Okayama's police force is depicted in Figure 6.3. The following emerged from an interview with the second in command, a newly assigned chief superintendent, at Okayama Prefectural Police headquarters. In response to the question about the public's receptivity to the annual household visits by patrol officers, this administrator stated that 90 percent of individuals were cooperative, but 10 percent did not respond. However, he added that a majority of the latter group were often not available because both spouses were employed. Therefore, he added, police are now visiting these households during early evening hours as well as on weekends in an effort to make contact. This chief superintendent had taken this assignment just several months earlier. Again, this was a standard practice among the upper echelon of 600 National Police Agency administrators—the large majority were rotated every two or three years. In response to a question concerning any recent changes that had taken place in Okayama, he mentioned that (simi-

Figure 6.3 **Organization of Okayama Police**

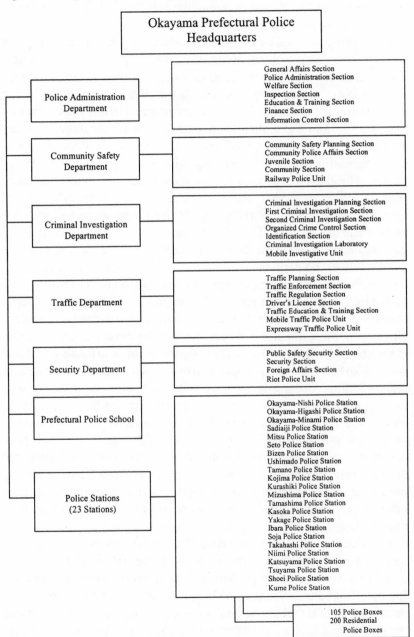

Source: Okayama Prefectural Police 1999.

lar to what had been noted in Hokkaido) there had been an introduction of *kōban* and *chūzaisho* liason councils, vehicles to help create better citizen–police relationships.

Concerning my inquiry as to how women were performing in police work, this chief superintendent remarked that only in the use of physical force did he see a difference. And this was confined to circumstances when officers in the worst neighborhoods were required to subdue drunken brawlers. Guns were such a rare problem in this prefecture that this administrator stated there were perhaps just two or three instances over the past year in which officers were required to draw their pistols—"occasionally [when dealing] with a foreigner who might be armed." He added that perhaps fifty to sixty arrests of Chinese had taken place in the previous year. They had been arrested primarily for illegal entry, overstaying their tourist visas, and larcenies—none had committed a homicide in 1998. The other major group of foreigners in Japan were Koreans. They are to be distinguished from the more than seven hundred thousand permanent Korean residents, who in some cases are now second- and third-generation residents. Most are not citizens, and this points to another example of the prejudice and insularity of Japanese society that makes it extremely difficult for non-Japanese to achieve citizenship. Most important, this is also true for those who have resided in the county their entire lives. Still, Japanese police officials noted that some Koreans, coming legally from South Korea, engaged in pickpocketing, slashing of bags, and other petty crimes. Okayama has a small population of foreigners, but other prefectures have some larger numbers, particularly of Chinese and Koreans, as they are the two largest groups of foreigners. The overall issue of foreigners and their relationship to crime is addressed more fully in a later chapter. Suffice it to say their role in criminal activity is a complex one in which a confusing portrait emerges because of the way the media have played up their offenses. Often foreigners appear to have been scapegoated or their crimes exaggerated by both print and electronic media.

High-tech and white-collar crime has not yet become a major problem in Okayama, although officials acknowledge that it would probably increase given the rapid growth of information technology and the Internet. Robberies were rare in Okayama. One assistant inspector said that he recalled a robbery several years earlier of a post office and that the culprit held up the post office with a knife. The chief superintendent reported that there were just 104 felony offenses in 1998 including homicides, rapes, robberies, arsons, and abductions (kidnapping). Interestingly, and consistent with the general picture nationwide concerning the underreporting of domestic disputes, this chief superintendent remarked that, "We have no stats on this subject. We are starting to look into this carefully—we can deal only with someone who has committed a physical assault. This is one of the hardest offenses for us to prosecute successfully, so we often suppress it. In rural areas people are starting to band together to try to combat this problem to reduce it. There are few shelters for battered women in this country."

On the subject of suicides in Okayama, the headquarters office furnished the following statistics—for 1997, 401, and for 1998, 484. They acknowledged that the deep recession of the 1990s had not spared Okayama Prefecture from the loss of jobs and the bankruptcies that have plagued all other geographical areas in Japan.

The Okayama-Higashi Police Station

The first police station the author visited in Okayama City was the Okayama-Higashi police station near the center of the city, but in the eastern sector (*higashi* means east). Most of the police boxes under its jurisdiction were *kōban* (nineteen) as opposed to *chūzaisho* (one). The author inquired of the station chief as to what the most common crime was in his jurisdiction. "Larceny," was the response, with the station chief noting that the category included bicycle theft, residential burglaries, motor vehicle theft, and stolen motorbikes. In 1998, he stated, there were 3,191 criminal cases in his jurisdiction with 1,304 arrests. For larcenies there were 2,913 cases, but just a 38.5 percent clearance rate for 1998. Other crimes for 1998 in Okayama-Higashi district were fraud cases 161, assaults 67, "moral" offenses 4, homicides 5, and "other" cases 41. Overall, the station chief reported that crime rates had remained stable in recent years with no marked increase in any category. Among juvenile offenders he reported a slight increase in shoplifting during 1997 and 1998, but (consistent with nationwide statistics and anecdotal evidence) there were additional incidents involving violence among teenagers but also occasionally directed at teachers. Finally, while rare, there had been instances of extortion among juveniles.

Asked about organized crime activity, the chief reflected for a moment and said that there had been some crimes by *boryokudan* members, typically involving extortion sale of stimulants (mostly amphetamines), prostitution, sale of pornographic materials, and loan-sharking. He noted that there were ten organized crime groups (totaling 130 individuals) operating in Okayama Prefecture. Asked if they were typically armed with guns, he replied that for the most part they possessed knives and clubs. Nationwide, however, and notwithstanding the low incidence of firearms violations in Japan, a significant portion of handguns seized by police forces throughout the nation are owned by *boryokudan* members. For the following years these statistics apply (National Police Agency 1999).

	Number of guns seized from *boryokudan* members	From nonmembers
1994	1,242	505
1995	1,396	484
1996	1,035	514
1997	761	464

In 1995 the amendment to the Firearms and Swords Control Law made it a more serious offense to possess guns. Along with law enforcement's intensified effort to crack down on the illegal possession of guns, *boryokudan* members have systematically devised ways of concealing firearms according to the *White Paper on Police 1998*. (National Police Agency 1999). In 1997 in Japan generally, there were 148 shooting incidents, or 15.6 percent more than during the previous year, with much of the increase linked to an incident in which a leader of the *Yamaguchi-gumi* gang was shot dead by rival gang members. This set off internecine warfare that resulted in twenty-six shooting incidents among gang members.

Given the strength and efficiency of the overall justice apparatus in Japan it has always puzzled me that the justice system has not effectively routed and dismantled the various *yakuza* groups in Japan. The Okayama-Higashi chief's response to my question on this subject was, "The biggest reason is they have invested in legitimate businesses and that its been difficult to follow the money trail; money laundering laws don't have the same teeth in them as they do in the United States." One of the chief's colleagues, a superintendent from prefectural headquarters who accompanied the author on the visit (and who had worked with U.S. authorities on organized crime matters) added, "In the United States the burden is often on the organized crime figure to prove that he got his money legitimately, but here the burden is on the prosecutor. However, in some cases we have been effective in using the tax law to tax their illegal funds or make an arrest." As a footnote to this discussion the chief added that there had been eighty arrests of organized crime figures in Okayama over the previous two years. No homicides among gang members or involving Japanese citizens had been reported in the previous two years. Several years earlier there had been a grenade incident. This episode involved a turf conflict between a group that moved into an area in which another group had set up its illegal business. The event was triggered when the new group muscled in on a protection racket that the first group operated.

In this station, eyewitness issues were handled by the police through published sketches in newspapers, *kōban* bulletin board postings of artists' sketches, and television presentations of photos and sketches. Photos are sometimes presented to witnesses in arrays, but Japanese often allow for one-on-one encounters of suspects through the one-way windows of interrogation rooms. These "show-ups," as they are called in the United States, are illegal according to a ruling by the U.S. Supreme Court because of the heavy prejudicial impact of asking a witness, "Is this the guy?"

Throughout the author's visit to Okayama Prefecture he was accompanied by two officers from prefectural headquarters. One assistant inspector in his late thirties had joined the agency just a few years earlier, after leaving his first career with a subsidiary of Honda Motor Company. That position had taken him to Ohio and California, and this had helped his English fluency. He had been hired as an assistant inspector and his fluency in English was an obvious asset to the Okayama Prefectural Police. Interpreting was one of his major duties. The other official had superintendent rank and was in mid-career, having worked for the National Police Agency in various assignments all over Japan. He was a classical music buff and he performed in a major chorale group in Okayama. He was an avid gardener as well. He lamented the fact that he had missed an opportunity, because of a police assignment, to perform with his chorale at Carnegie Hall in New York City. This group had appeared with several American University chorales at a festival at the famous venue. His career had required him to visit the United States on a number of occasions to coordinate with the FBI and various American police forces on international criminal investigations. He too conversed easily in English. As we traveled together in an unmarked police car over a number of days we talked about a variety of matters, both police and nonpolice. Socializing, along with eating and drinking together, was not only enjoyable but aided in establishing rapport.

I asked if police officers became cynical in Japan. (It has often been reported that many American police officers become cynical or "burned out" as they accumulate time on the job, and some research has documented this phenomenon.) My interpreter stated that yes he thought that in his brief career of six years he had seen some of it. A different response was offered by his colleague. Superintendent Fujioka's area of responsibility was personnel and human resources, and he noted that because most citizens respect the police in Japan they probably had an easier time of it with citizens compared to their counterparts in the United States. Furthermore, he noted that the recession had contributed to an even larger applicant pool of police recruits in Okayama. For 1998 there had been 1,400 applicants for just forty openings, and the applicant pool had further been culled after background checks along with both physical and psychological screening. Incidentally, lie detector tests were not included in the screening process, although they are often employed during screening in the United States.

The Okayama-Nishi Police Station

The visit to this station started with an interview with the chief of the station, Mr. Matsumoto. This friendly and extroverted man offered a variety of information during the one-hour interview. Approximately two hundred seven thousand citizens (or 35 percent of the Okayama City population) lived in the jurisdiction of this station.

Matsumoto-san had been a police officer for thirty-seven years and at fifty-seven years of age was close to retirement. Officially he was scheduled to retire at age sixty, but he acknowledged that he might be nudged out a little earlier "to make room for a colleague." Upon retirement many police officers go to work in allied areas, such as private security. Partly because of the early age of forced retirements for police in Japan, and also because of the meager pensions, I asked about his post-retirement plans. Preparing this answer by noting that many people are still healthy at age sixty, he said he might choose a consulting role—some retired officers do part-time consulting back with the police agency. He mentioned that his pension would be around 3 million yen (U.S. $27,000) upon retirement.

Asked about recent developments in police work in Okayama, he stated:

> Crime correlates with the economy and organized crime prospered during the "bubble economy" because of a lot of loose money. Similarly, *boryokudan* have taken a hit during these recession years—they are dormant now. Also, concerning loan sharking, you should know that ordinary citizens don't borrow from *yakuza*—they loan to shady business groups.

On this matter of citizens citing their rights, he offered that "ten to twenty years earlier police had a stronger position of authority, but citizens increasingly insist on their rights today. For example, if you are doing a criminal investigation and talk to people who might have some information concerning a crime, they are no longer as eager to cooperate as earlier."

Another issue mentioned by this open and friendly chief was the emergence of victims' rights. I had heard no discussion on this issue when doing the research in the 1980s, but had recently became aware of a major thrust into this arena by various justice agencies, including the police. Matsumoto noted that a systematic nationwide approach had been generated around four years earlier. Perhaps not by coincidence, the U.S.' efforts in the field of victims' rights had become a major force only a few years earlier. He went on to say that a great variety of support systems had been put into place for all kinds of victims and families of victims. These included those who had been raped, mugged, or assaulted, and the families of those who died from homicides and accidents. Furthermore, the support took various forms—financial, psychological, and legal. A network of lawyers, schoolteachers, psychiatrists, and counselors were available to offer services. The police actively publicized services through bulletins, leaflets, and television public service announcements. Examples of crime prevention leaflets distributed by the Okayama police are presented in Figures 6.4, 6.5, 6.6, and 6.7.

The National Police Agency (1999) reported that international pressure from the Seventh United Nations Congress on the Prevention of Crime and Treatment of Offenders had helped spur Japan to take action in this field. Specific attention was drawn to the clause "Declaration of Basic Principles of Justice for Victims of Crime." The statement also proposed that victims should be treated with compassion and respect for their dignity.

In February 1996 Japan's National Police Agency adopted a policy entitled "Guidelines of Relief Measures for Crime Victims." A full-blown system of assistance was implemented that included a policy of maintaining contact with crime victims including informing them of the name of the suspect, the name of the prosecutor's office handling the case, and the police progress in investigating the case. NPA requires police officers at stations and police boxes to contact and visit victims. In 1997, 3,560 such contacts were reported (National Police Agency 1999).

A counseling service for crime victims is still developing, and by 1997, fifteen prefectural police agencies had hired psychological counselors and another twenty-one agencies had hired private practice psychiatrists and counselors to aid victims. Included in the array of services offered are policies to provide financial benefits to victims.

Another dimension of the approach to crime victims has been a major effort by the police to respond more effectively to the victims of sex crimes including rape. Each prefectural police agency now has a director and guidance officers assigned to investigate and coordinate handling of sexual crimes. More policewomen have been appointed to these positions in an attempt to be more sensitive and effective in dealing with rape victims. The National Police Agency (1999) reported that by April 1998 there were 1,759 women assigned as sexual crime investigators.

The matter of the existence of street crime units was raised with Chief Matsumoto, and he noted that only in special investigations such as a kidnapping did the Okayama-Nishi station resort to the use of large numbers of undercover or plain clothes detectives. In such a case, he commented, "this station might have one hundred detectives out of three hundred in civilian attire." Generally the widespread use of aggressive undercover police work, as in the case of New York City in the late 1990s, is viewed as unnecessary in Japan.

A controversial topic in police circles in the United States in the late 1990s has been "hot pursuit," with various municipalities and states adopting different policies. In Okayama City, Chief Matsumoto reported

Figures 6.4 through 6.7 **Crime Prevention Cartoons** (*Source:* Okayama Prefectural Police)

Figure 6.4

Stop Molesters!
It takes courage to get rid of molesters

[Thought balloon:] Show COURAGE
[Heart:] B-Boom

To report a molester or related matter, call the
Railroad Police Molestation Victims Bureau
Tel 086-222-7405
   *Completely confidential for victims.

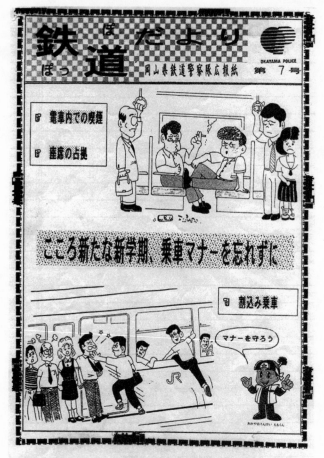

Figure 6.5

Railroad News...ch ch ch ch

Okayama Railroad Police Bulletin No. 7

⇨ Smoking in the train
⇨ Occupying seats

In the new school term, don't forget your train manners
⇦ Pushing on board

[Momo-kun:] Use good manners

Figure 6.6

Railroad News...ch ch ch ch

Okayama Railroad Police Bulletin No. 5

The Bon* Rush Home

[Momo-kun:] Take care!

Pickpockets
Purse-snatching
Luggage Theft

---

*A major summer Japanese holiday honoring the dead.

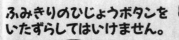

Don't play with the railroad crossing emergency button.

Don't play dangerous games.

"3 Promises" to Keep

1.   I will not play near train tracks or crossings.
2.   I will not put stones or other things on the train tracks.
3.   I will not play with the emergency button.

Don't play near train tracks.

Don't play like this.

Railroad Police Corps

that there was no official policy but that generally there would be a hot pursuit on waterways, with the marine police, but that in the city in the case of "hot rodders" and the like, they were rarely pursued because it was easy to use other methods to identify them. This problem of a felon fleeing in a motorized vehicle has been a more frequent problem for American police forces.

Visit to an Okayama *Chūzaisho*

A personable *chūzaisan*, Mr. Hideaki had received an honor as the best *chūzaisan* in Okayama for 1998. My police interpreter, showing off his English, used some American sports jargon referring to him as a "most valuable player." This residential police box was in a somewhat rural area, but just a fifteen-minute ride from Okayama City. He was married with three children ages sixteen, fourteen, and ten. On this summer weekday afternoon the entire family was there to meet me, and green tea and cookies were served. I inquired about the breakdown of his job activities, and he proceeded to tell me that he usually started work at 8:00 A.M. and worked at his desk for a while to organize his day. This might mean writing up a report or perhaps making a phone call or two. Then he might go out to an elementary school to give a talk. Typically, he spent around three hours a day doing the routine family visits that he covered twice a year.

In his sixteen years of police service he had worked two and one half years at this particular box, but five years overall as a *chūzaisan*. Historically, he noted, the police agency used to give ten-year assignments at one *chūzaisho*, but now moved officers every four to five years but gave some consideration to officers' feelings. The rationale seemed to be that while the policymakers wanted officers to have good working relationships with citizens, they didn't want "overly cozy" relationships to develop. Still, it was not easy on family life with children being forced to change schools—his youngest had changed three times.

The balance of his day usually involved being on patrol in the car or motorcycle and covering his 16.15-square-kilometer area. Foot patrol averaged around one hour per day. The population of his jurisdiction was 7,629 individuals and included 2,158 households.

Traffic cases, including accidents, amounted to 122 for 1998. His wife typically assisted in these matters, taking calls, making reports, and giving directions. As noted earlier, wives are now paid for their work. Typical of most *chūzaisho*, this one had the desk and workrooms in front, and the family resided in a connecting rear section. Officer Hideaki stated that he typically handled the initial phases of criminal investigations and traffic accidents but called the station for backup when necessary.

Generally he worked forty hours per week and had two days off. However, he always responded to an emergency when he was at home. When he was away with his family, he would post a sign on the door, and there was a telephone with a direct line to the station. The starting salary was approximately 200,000 yen per month (U.S.$2,000). As mentioned earlier, a *chūzai-san*'s wife receives around U.S.$800 per month to pay for her part-time work. Housing, of course, was free, but the family covered other expenses such as food.

A final question to Hideaki-san was what was the most unusual thing that had happened in the past year? He paused and said, "We had a robbery committed by three guys from another prefecture who stopped in a rest area on the main road. They approached a couple and physically threatened them (although no weapon was produced) and stole their money. Their vehicle had been identified and the parties were arrested two days later."

During the visit to the Okayama region an incident occurred to the author that reflects one of the memorable features of Japanese people that gets replayed thousands of times annually for the benefit of *gaijin* or visitors. Having stopped for a brief lunch on a twenty-mile bike tour of the surrounding countryside, I pulled out a map at my table to try to locate my position. I asked for the assistance of a young Japanese man in his twenties at the adjacent table. He introduced himself as a junior high school geography teacher. He not only offered assistance, but dashed to his car to get a more detailed map of his own so he could draw a clear map of my route. I thanked him, and we both headed out onto the road. After I had been biking for a mile or so he drove up beside me and stopped. He apologized for having made a mistake on one of the turns he had drawn on the map and wanted to set me straight. This Japanese penchant for being helpful to foreigners is very widespread, and while I used to think it was a wonderful, friendly gesture (that I experienced many times over the years), I came to understand that it also springs from the sense of obligation that Japanese feel for visitors. This sense of obligation translates, of course, not only to a willingness to assist a foreigner but to various interpersonal relations among Japanese. It also contributes to the greater cohesiveness of Japanese society compared to American society.

The Railway Police

I paid my last visit in Okayama to the railway police office. Generally the railway police serve both a deterrent and an investigative function. In the case of the former activity, they patrol trains and railway station property. They focus on low-level crime such as pickpocketing and petty theft. They also assist at accidents and provide a vehicle to help locate lost children. Occasionally they provide protective custody, mostly to young people. Sometimes, like police at *kōban*, they provide counseling and consultation on a variety of matters. Each prefecture has a railway police section.

In Okayama, the main train station is a huge complex with shops and offices connected to an underground passageway that leads to the end of the main street of the city. The station serves not only local commuters but long distance travelers en route on the national rail line operating from east to west. High-speed *Shinkansen* (or bullet trains) also stop at the Okayama train station. The Okayama railway police are organized into three teams headed by an inspector. Two teams consist of investigators, while the third group engages in patrol. Crime prevention is a key element in the latter's work as evidenced by many posters and announcements. Some offered advice on protecting valuables and others offered cautions to young people. Often a "hot-line" number was included. Police, interviewed at their offices, stated that they rarely encountered serious crime. One officer recalled a kidnapping, but that was two years earlier in 1997. One of their tasks was to search for "wanted offenders" as part of a nationwide network, and mug shots were displayed on bulletin boards. Several fugitives had been apprehended in the previous two years in Okayama. The police inspector I interviewed said he had been assigned to the railway police just one year earlier, having previously been assigned to a team investigating *boryokudan*.

7

The Investigation of Crime

The amount of crime in Japan, as in the United States, is only partly a function of the efficiency and quality of the justice system. The basic nature of the society yields a more powerful influence. The role of the justice system, however, is perhaps larger in Japan. In many ways, although it is a cliché, "crime does not pay" for the Japanese. The chances of a criminal being caught are greater than in the United States, due partly to the simple fact that Japan is an island country, only slightly larger than California. A very important additional factor in Japan is that there is no plea bargaining, the negotiating between lawyers and judges that frequently reduces the seriousness of the charge. Occasionally a criminal offense in Japan is seized upon by the media because it touches a sensitive chord in the society or because it reveals a unique aspect. Two examples follow. First, unlike the United States where subjects like poverty, racism, drugs, and family breakdown are often identified in discussions of crime causation, in Japan the focus is often on the "pressure cooker" educational system with its stressful effects. The widespread intensity of the experience, in which families and the educational system both play a role, can be so damaging that various problems erupt in its wake, including early school dropouts, assaults by children, the scapegoating of classmates, psychological depression, and even suicide. The last is sometimes the product of "examination hell" or the stressful period at the end of high school in which achievement or a university entrance exam is critical to making or breaking a future. Joining a motorcycle gang (referred to as *bōsozōku* in Japan) or running with low-ranking *yakuza* (the earlier romanticized term for organized crime) are examples of how adolescents may respond to the pain of failure within the school system.

Perhaps astonishing to an American, the problem can arise for the family of a two-year-old when parental ambitions for a youngster's educational future can get out of hand. The case of a two-year-old competing for a slot at a "top" kindergarten was reported by French (December 7, 1999). A two-year-old girl, who had just passed an entrance exam, was killed by the mother of a child who failed the exam. The enraged and jealous mother admitted that she had strangled Haruna and stuffed her body into a bag. She then boarded a train to dispose of it near her own parents' home on the outskirts of Tokyo. Of course, numerous editorials decried the homicide and railed against the system that places intense academic pressures on children at this absurdly young age of two. Still, discussions of this type, which have been common in Japan for decades, have not yet contributed to any significant reforms. The shocking nature of the case plunged the Japanese into a related discussion of family life in general and the pivotal aspect of a mother's role (they are often called "education mamas" because of their central role in supervising the education of their offspring) in all of this. Some of the discussion explored the emptiness of some mothers' lives that appeared to have propelled them into "desperately projecting so many of their aspirations upon their young children" (ibid.). Some academics have observed that materialism, academic success, and extreme competitiveness have pushed a more sincere traditional humanitarian approach to relationships and to life in general to the sidelines. A virtual educational industry exists in Japan in which cram schools (*juku*), prekindergarten prep schools, and extra study are accepted as necessary vehicles for getting a youngster into a top school. It is widely accepted in Japan that mere acceptance into a top university will guarantee a good job upon graduation. Furthermore, unlike the United States, where there are second and third opportunities for those who do not excel in the early years or even at the college level, the Japanese system (like that in many European countries) shuts out those who do not show early academic promise. Some trace the Japanese approach to the Meiji era of the 1860s in which the county attempted to catch up rapidly with the West. Despite the overall egalitarianism and broad distribution of economic resources that Japan has enjoyed, this ferocious academic competition has taken a heavy toll on the lives of parents as well as their offspring (ibid.).

A second case reveals a different side of Japanese society—the way in which foreigners sometimes run afoul of the justice system. In this instance, the account comes from a twenty-seven-year-old British illustrator, Stephen O'Toole. O'Toole was arrested while arguing about a taxi with a Japanese man and two women. He admitted to hurling the handbag of one of the women to the ground after it was shoved into his face. Later, he acknowledged that his actions were stupid, but he welcomed the intervention of police. He claimed that the officers made no attempt to hear his side of the story and blamed him for the argument. During investigations in Japan suspects can be detained for twenty-three days and kept in police custody—often with limited access to their attorneys. The court must approve detention beyond seventy-two hours, and then again after thirteen days, but these extensions are almost pro forma. Court approval is granted in 99.9 percent of cases (Astill 1999).

O'Toole claimed that neither his friends nor their taxi drivers were allowed to give statements. After his friends' prompt release, he described his questioning as nothing more than an effort on the part of interrogators to corroborate the other side's version and to obtain a confession. Furthermore, he alleged that they persisted through the entire first night and kept trying to obtain his signature on a confession he could neither read nor understand. After seventy-two hours his detention was extended to ten days, and although the woman changed her story—admitting that he had not attacked her but had merely touched her handbag—the charge was still "violence without causing injury" (lowered from "assault"). O'Toole complained that he had difficulty walking and breathing due to rib damage and a knee injury that were inflicted at the time of his arrest. Furthermore, he stated that a police doctor checked only his pulse and blood pressure. A visit from his girlfriend, allowed only after the mandatory three-day waiting period, was highly restricted—the parties were forbidden to speak English. Neither O'Toole nor his friend knew much Japanese.

While waiting for his lawyer in Tokyo District Court, he said, he was forced to sit handcuffed and in silence for several hours at a time. O'Toole's lawyer, Yasuto Tanisho, urged him to plead guilty to avoid an additional eighteen days in jail. He complied and signed a confession. The British citizen was then fined 100,000 yen (U.S.$96) and released two days later. Neither Katsuhiko Iguchi, a member of the Japanese Bar Association's legal review committee, or Hideki Morihara, of Amnesty International, found this episode exceptional. Morihara commented, "It's a real disgrace that people might confess to crimes only to avoid extended police detention" (Astill 1999).

Clearance rates, a favorite topic of officials in both Japan and the United States, are remarkably different for both countries. Generally, the U.S. Department of Justice (1998) defines an offense as cleared "when at least one person is arrested, charged with the commission of the offense, and turned over to the county for prosecution." The Japanese *White Paper on Crime* (Ministry of Justice 1998) defined an offense as cleared when it was "reported to the police, which resulted in the identification of a suspect."

In 1997, in the United States, a total of 10,928,483 penal code offenses were known to the police, of which 21.6 percent were identified as cleared. In Japan, for the same year, 2,518,074 penal code offenses were identified by the police, and 54.7 percent of them were categorized as cleared. Thus, Japan's clearance rate overall is much higher. More specifically, a comparison of violent offenses such as homicide and robbery offers a sharp contrast. In 1997, the United States rate for robbery was 26 percent cleared, and the rate for Japan was 79.5 percent of cases cleared. For the same year, in the United States 66 percent of homicide cases were cleared while in Japan 95.6 percent were cleared. Comparable numbers exist for the crime of larceny in the United States—the clearance rate was 20 percent, while in Japan the rate was 35.2 percent.

The Japanese *White Paper on Crime* (Ministry of Justice 1998) reported that the overall crime rate for 1997 was the second highest in the post–World War II period and that the clearance rate showed a slight drop of 0.6 percent from the year of 1996. In general, the Ministry of Justice reported that the clearance rate for homicide had always exceeded 95 percent for the period 1987 to 1997 and that the clearance rate for robbery had been around 80 percent since 1993. Larceny, of course, showed a much lower rate, but still a higher rate than in the United States, and it too has consistently been around 30 percent since 1990. Larceny generally covers pickpocketing, shoplifting, purse-snatching, bicycle stealing, and other nonviolent crimes. Because American offenders are arrested less frequently than their Japanese counterparts, it could be inferred that American offenders are rewarded more often for their illegal acts than their Japanese counterparts. In other words, social and cultural controls are weaker in the United States and therefore fewer restraints are imposed on both juvenile and adult offenders.

Complementing the police efficiency, reflected in the high clearance rates, are strong psychological pressures within the tightly woven, competitive Japanese society for citizens to conform and obey the law. Japanese who commit crimes and who come to the attention of justice officials generally feel a deep sense of shame. Family members and relatives feel an obligation to deter illegal acts. If an individual is arrested, his or her family feels responsible—and probably experiences the embarrassment and shame the individual may feel. Though families in the United States may have similar feelings, they are much more pronounced among the Japanese. Nor is this sense of shared shame confined to families of offenders. For example, in one instance, a police officer raped a woman and the chief of his police station felt obligated to resign. (It should be noted that it is extremely rare for a police officer to be convicted of assaulting a citizen.) This action was taken despite the fact that the police station chief was in no way directly responsible for the offender; he did not even directly supervise the officer. However, in Japan, it is expected that the person in charge will assume a significant share of the responsibility.

Another factor in the sharply higher U.S. crime rate is the weakened family structure, reflected in the higher frequency of broken families and divorce. American families do not provide young people with fixed standards of right and wrong behavior to the same degree that Japanese families do. In Japan, there has been a slight increase in the divorce rate from 1983, when the rate was just 1.51 per 1,000 persons, to 1.78 in 1997. However in the United States the rate was 5.2 in 1980 and it dropped only slightly to 4.4 by 1995 (Foreign Press Center 1999).

Rates are much lower in Japan, in part because there is still some stigma attached to divorce, while there seems little social disapproval attached to ending a marriage in the United States. Also, the marriage rate, which has declined markedly in the United States, along with the increase in the numbers of couples cohabitating, has shown a modest decline in Japan. With a slight increase in the number of Japanese women entering the workforce and those pursuing higher education, there has been a subsequent decline in the marriage rate. Also, the average age of a first marriage has now climbed to 26.6 for women in 1997 from 24.2 in 1971. Historically, the pattern has always been that employed young women who have reached their late twenties have been expected to get married and leave employment for purposes of child rearing. This powerful expectation on the part of Japanese employers, in the context of general conformity pressures, has made it extraordinarily difficult for

Japanese women to get solid, long-term career positions and to advance within their chosen fields. Rounding out this picture is the change in household structure in Japan (Foreign Press Center 1999). For example, single-person households have increased to 25 percent in 1997 from just 18.1 percent in 1980 (Foreign Press Center 1999). Also, there has been a gradual increase in the number of single-parent households in Japan, with 552,000 existing in 1990. Of these, 74.5 percent resulted from divorce and 22.5 from death of spouse (Foreign Press Center 1996).

Another dimension of family instability, which has been widely reported on in the United States, is that of unwed mothers. Here, the United States has seen improvement in some categories but not in others. The National Center for Health Statistics reported that the proportion of unmarried teenagers giving birth continued to increase in 1998 to 78.8 percent of teenagers (Lacey 1999). However, among girls fifteen to seventeen years of age, the lowest birthrate in forty years was recorded. Also, African American teenagers recorded the lowest birthrate since 1960, and the rate among Hispanic women dropped sharply. But in the context of worldwide trends among developed nations, the United States lags behind; teenage birthrates are much lower in countries like Japan, France, Germany, and Great Britain (Lacey 1999).

Life in the United States seems cheap, at least by Japanese standards. In the United States in the late 1990s, there continued to be a spate of shootings in schools and workplaces where sometimes one or two gunmen were able to kill significant numbers of their fellow citizens. The Columbine High School deaths in Colorado provide only one of the more notorious examples. The widespread availability of guns clearly contributed to the ease with which one individual could unleash lethal violence on others. There are some estimates that there are as many as 200 million guns scattered across the American landscape and that many are unregistered or illegally purchased on the black market.

As previously alluded to, many criminal acts in the United States are committed because of circumstances of social and economic deprivation that do not exist in Japan, where middle-class affluence is widespread. Racism continues to flourish in the United States, and it is exceedingly difficult for many minorities raised in neighborhoods such as the South Bronx and Bedford-Stuyvesant to improve their standard of living. Thus, from their perspective, they have something to gain and little to lose by risking a criminal act.

The beginning of most criminal investigations is, of course, the citizen's report that a crime has occurred. The Japanese report crime at a rate that comes closer to the actual incidence than Americans do. Therefore, the huge discrepancy in reported crimes between Japan and America is probably even larger for the actual occurrence of crime, and this is supported by the fact that both countries have conducted direct household "victimization" surveys. One of Japan's victim surveys revealed that in a random survey of 15,000 households the number of unreported crimes was 1.005 times greater than the number of reported offenses. In the United States, the National Crime Survey of 60,000 households conducted in the mid-1970s revealed that the unreported rate of index crimes (homicide, rape, robbery, aggravated assault, burglary, larceny, and auto theft) was more than twice the rate reported in the FBI's *Uniform Crime Reports*.

Japanese police investigators, like their counterparts in the United States, employ mobile investigation units, DNA crime lab analysis, recorded voice analysis, document and handwriting analysis, and police dogs. Also, it has been necessary for police agencies to expand the number of interpreters as the pool of non-Japanese suspects has increased. More experts from the private sector have been added to assist police in investigations, and, of course, advances in computer technology have allowed for the development of an "automatic vehicle license plate number reading system" (National Police Agency 1998).

One more feature of criminal investigation by the police themselves is worthy of note. According to Walter Ames, investigations conducted by police detectives use informants, or *kyoryokusha*. Initial routine investigations are handled by *kōban* police, but more serious problems are dealt with by specialists. In the case of criminal investigations, detectives assigned to the nearest station become involved. Like investigators in most countries, their ability to "cultivate the field," or develop working relationships with local individuals, including ex-offenders, is closely related to their success. The people who act as informants and tipsters include bar hostesses, bar operators, managers of rooming houses, *pachinko* hall operators, and pawnshop proprietors. They are encouraged to spend time expanding their contacts and deepening their relationships with tipsters. Ames noted that "whenever there is a death in the family of a tipster, a marriage, or any other event the *keiji* (detective) always comes with an appropriate gift to symbolize the relationship." Often to maximize the benefit of the relationship between a detective and an informant, the detective must spend off-duty time socializing with the tipster by drinking and playing mah-jongg with him. This approach by Japanese detectives, along with the broad powers of the prosecutor, helps the Western observer begin to understand the reasons for the effectiveness of the Japanese justice system (Ames 1981).

Financial and Computer Related Crime

Over the decade of the 1990s financial and "high-tech" crimes have been on the rise in Japan as they have been in other developed countries. Following the burst of the economic bubble in Japan in the early 1990s, a number of financial institutions were stuck with huge amounts of nonperforming loans. Police cleared 172 cases of financial and loan-related crimes (see Table 7.1). These included companies involved in real estate and housing loans. Numbers in parenthesss in Table 7.1 refer to cases involving *boryokudan* or gangsters. The latter category also includes so-called *sokaiya*, or racketeers, posing as social-movement activists and occasionally infiltrating stockholder meetings. Overall, while the numbers of cases cleared are small they have continued to increase, and the numbers jumped by sixty-five from 1996 to 1997. Given the unwillingness of many Japanese companies—not just financial institutions—to clear away bad debt, restructure through employee layoffs, and declare bankruptcies, these numbers are probably the tip of the iceberg. Many experts believe that Japan's moribund economy, which continued into 2000, was directly linked to the heavy burden cast by the speculative bubble of the 1990s, and they predict little economic growth in the early years of the new millennium.

The National Police Agency in the late 1990s intensified training of computer-sophisticated personnel to cope with the growth of computer-related crime. High-tech crimes have been defined as "those perpetrated by abusing computer technology and telecommunications technology." As of 1997, the number of high-tech crimes known to the police was 263, and in 262 cases the offenders were charged. Table 7.2 provides a breakdown of high-tech crimes cleared in 1997. The numbers of crimes both identified and cleared jumped eightfold over the previous five-year period. The numbers are expected to increase dramatically in the years ahead. The police reported a large-scale increase in the use of the Internet to market pornographic images and related material to various groups including teenagers. The National Police Agency condemns the "pernicious" nature of this material, and states that youngsters who have access to a personal computer can access it.

Table 7.1

Financial and Bad Loan–Related Offenses Cleared, 1993–1997

Classification	1993	1994	1995	1996	1997
Total (cases)	34 (8)	43 (8)	38 (18)	107 (55)	172 (79)
Financial and bad loan–related offenses committed in the process of financing	5 (4)	7 (2)	6 (5)	15 (4)	21 (2)
Financial and bad loan–related offenses committed in the process of debt collection	4 (4)	6 (6)	13 (13)	56 (51)	87 (77)
Other financial and bad loan–related offenses involving financial institution officials	25 (0)	30 (0)	19 (0)	36 (0)	64 (0)

Source: National Police Agency 1999.
Note: Number in parentheses refers to *boryokudan*-linked crimes.

Table 7.2

Breakdown of High-Tech Crimes Known to the Police and Cleared in 1997

	No. of cases known to the police	No. of cases cleared
Computer fraud	163	162
Illegal production of private electromagnetic records	5	4
Illegal production of public electromagnetic records	8	7
Obstruction of business by destroying a computer	4	2
Destruction of public documents	1	1
Destruction of private documents	0	0
Crimes committed through computer networks	83	83
Other	1	1
Total	265	260

Source: National Police Agency 1999.

The agency vaguely warns "appropriate measures to shield" teenagers from this information has become more urgent (National Police Agency 1999).

Violence

While there is less violence in Japan than in the United States, recent instances of violent crime have shocked the Japanese people. Particularly disturbing is the increase in "senseless" crimes, those that are perpetrated on strangers without any apparent motive. During my stay in Japan, there was a noticeable rise in newspaper reports of such crimes, which often resulted in the victim's death. In one case, an apparently emotionally disturbed man tossed a firebomb into a Tokyo bus, killing several people. Another case involved a middle-aged man who stabbed two women and two children to death on a Tokyo street, then took another woman hostage and held her at a nearby restaurant. While this sort of random crime is, unfortunately, not uncommon in the United States, it has become a problem in Japan only since the early 1980s.

They are generally attributed to the mental instability of the accused, often brought on by the extraordinary pressures of the highly organized and competitive Japanese society. The outbursts can occasionally be traced to some particular failure or disgrace, such as being unable to pass the entrance examination to a university. But such explanations are little comfort to the police, who are beginning to experience the same bewilderment familiar to their American counterparts in the face of such meaningless, patternless, and thus unpreventable crime.

An example reported in late 1999 (*Japan Times* September 30, 1999) involved a thirty-five-year-old man who drove a car into a train station in Yamaguchi Prefecture and indiscriminately stabbed passersby, killing three people and injuring twelve. A hospital diagnosed him with a mental disorder. He had crashed into a ground floor concourse area at a Japan Railway station traveling at around seventy miles per hour and his car slammed into several people before coming to a stop. He exited and, brandishing a kitchen knife, he climbed the stairs to a train platform where he indiscriminately slashed a number of people returning from work.

In another example of an outraged attacker engaging in random violence, a knife-and-hammer-wielding man went on a rampage in a shopping area of Ikebukuro (*Japan Times* September 9, 1999). One person was killed in the attack, and the man was quickly subdued by citizens in the vicinity. The offender told police that he was angry because he could not find work. The culprit first positioned himself in front of the first floor of a hardware store and attacked people coming up from an underground passage. The incident caused panic and mass confusion.

The National Police Agency reported that there have been fifty murders or attempted murders in similar arbitrary attacks from 1989 to 1999, and forty-seven of the assailants have been apprehended (*Japan Times* September 9, 1999).

Occasionally, people have been robbed in the evening in marginal social areas. Most of those robbed were drunks older than fifty who were knocked down in alleys near entertainment centers or railway stations between 9 P.M. and midnight. The robbers operated in groups of two to four and appeared to be between twenty-five and thirty years old, according to reports given to the Tokyo Metropolitan Police Department. Though these muggings pale when compared to those in large American cities for a similar period, they represent an alarming increase in violence from the Japanese point of view.

However, notwithstanding the various crimes discussed in this chapter, the overall rate of felonious crime has remained at a stable, low level over the past two decades. Any attempt to understand why violent crime for the most part is so well controlled in Japan leads inevitably back to the discussion of Japanese society, with its emphasis on group values and conformity. Japanese values and customs are the key to this phenomenon.

On two different occasions, I asked a group of social scientists at the National Police Agency's National Research Institute of Police Science for their views on the role of violence and aggression in Japan. Haruo Nishimura, a psychologist, opened the discussion by noting that, "Aggressive people are not well received here." He added, "We do not like to express everything directly." Verbal communication is typically more indirect and polite in Japan with fewer direct confrontations. While some Japanese concede that the "frankness" of Westerners is appealing, they point out that it is achieved at the price of rudeness and hurt feelings. The Japanese emphasize getting along and promoting interpersonal harmony with as few conflicts as possible. While Americans, upon their arrival in Japan, are often frustrated initially by the lack of candor they perceive in their relationships with Japanese, many eventually come to appreciate the subtlety and nuances of Japanese social relations.

The following points were suggested by the above-mentioned social scientists at the National Research Institute of Police Science—a group that, in addition to Haruo Nishimura, included Yoshiaki Takahashi, Shingo Suzuki, and Kanehiro Hoshino. These statements might be described as widely shared views held by the Japanese about their society:

- The low level of violence is significantly related to the socialization process. At a very early age, parents teach their children that aggression will not be tolerated.

- Teachers exert strong controls on the expression of violence and/or aggression. Two- or three-day suspensions from classes are not unusual if a child acts up even in a minor way.
- The homogeneous nature of Japanese society, with less than 1 percent of the population being non-Japanese, contributes to a greater degree of empathy for one another.
- There are relatively few broken families in Japan and the divorce rate is low (as noted in the earlier discussion).
- The environment is less stressful in Japan according to these social scientists, several of whom had studied at the University of Chicago or at Harvard. While life is fast-paced, particularly in the major cities, there are environmental supports that help to cushion the consequences of modern urban life. Notwithstanding some weakening in the lifetime employment scheme, most Japanese employees still have more job security than their U.S. counterparts. The emphasis on group life, in which fellow workers, students, or neighbors offer emotional and social support to one another is important.
- Family life and child rearing are a high priority for Japanese couples, notwithstanding the increasing number of women working outside the home.
- Japanese society offers many forms of recreation and leisure activity. It is common for groups of workers to go off together to a resort for a few days of fun and recreation, enjoying the camaraderie that they prize. Workers frequently drink sake together or play popular games like mah-jongg or *pachinko* after work. (Another outlet is provided by the attention and caresses of Japanese hostesses in nightclubs and cabarets.)

This list was not, of course, intended as a comprehensive statement of the factors contributing to the lack of violence in Japan. Nonetheless, I think it provides a good framework for understanding this remarkable phenomenon.

There is, unfortunately, no way for an outsider (or for that matter, I suspect, an insider) to tell whether the police institutions are a cause or an effect of this social system. Do the powerful and respected police draw that power from this willingness to be obedient and cooperative, or does the obedience come from the constant pressure from powerful authorities, first in the family and then in society at large? The answer, of course, is obscured in the national history and psychology, but it is doubtful that either history or psychology will be of much help in un-covering it. Obedience and authority are almost a single phenomenon in Japan. I am not hoping here to solve that puzzle, but to describe an aspect of it. We have looked at the grassroots level of policing—the cop on the beat, or in this case in the *kōban* or *chūzaisho*. I would now like to look at the role of another authority figure who is at a different place in the hierarchy but has perhaps equally far-reaching power to promote law and order, namely, the public prosecutor.

The Role of the Public Prosecutor

The grass-roots investigation of crime, including violent crime, is for the most part conducted by police officers, but prosecutors play a major supervisory and policy-making role. They occupy a powerful position with broad-ranging authority to pursue as well as suspend prosecution of cases. In a Japan Society seminar held in New York in 1980, Public Pros-ecutor Shikita described prosecutors as having a quasi-judicial function:

> Each prosecutor is authorized to decide on the appropriate scope of in-vestigation, to decide whether to prosecute at all and, if so, on what charges and, finally, to request the imposition of sentence as he feels appropriate. Decisions are to be based only on the interplay of the individual prosecutor's conscience with the "substantive truth" as he discovers it. Thus, he is not merely an assistant to the agency head but is vested with independent powers. In this sense, a prosecutor's decision-making pro-cess is similar to that of a judge (Japan Society 1980, p.5).

Clifford (1976) expanded on this independence of judgment and the discretionary power of the prosecutor:

> However nobly impartial the courts in the West might be, the Japanese, like so many of the Chinese thinkers, preferred to take the blindfold off the symbol of justice and to take a closer look at the scales they were balancing. Discretion was necessary to them to take account of the spe-cial circumstances of each crime and to apply the law only when neces-sary. If a *penalty* could be mitigated by circumstances, so could a charge. Here again was the familiar particularism of Japanese thinking being opposed to the universalism of the West. For the West, justice is a matter of principle. The Japanese accept that, but only with the proviso that the principle needs to be adjusted to take account of special circumstances.

Thus a public prosecutor in Japan may suspend prosecution at his own discretion, even if the evidence is sufficient to ensure a conviction, if he believes it to be in the best interest of society and the offender (p. 67).

In discussions of the history of the role of the prosecutor in Japan, one frequently reads accounts of the European origins of the system, not unlike the case of the police discussed earlier. In this connection, during the early Meiji period *samurai* visited France, Germany, and other European countries to study their legal systems. The resulting institution, known as the "procurator" in Japan, had wide discretionary powers to prosecute or not to prosecute certain cases. Nagashima (Von Mehren 1963) explained, however, that the role of defense counsel was rather limited until the influence of Anglo-American law was felt in the post–World War II period. Tanaka (1976) has offered a critical perspective on the role of both the defense counsel and the public prosecutor during the early part of the twentieth century:

> In the field of criminal law as well, the Japanese notion of law seems to have been pretty different from that of the Westerners. Though at the level of theory, we imported, during the Meiji Era, the Western concept of emphasizing the role of criminal law in protecting an individual from the power of the state, much time was needed before this concept took root in our soil. This becomes obvious if we look at the actual working of criminal law. It is notorious how easily the human rights of suspects were neglected before 1945. The blame for this is not to be ascribed solely to the police, but also must be cast upon public procurators and judges for their failure to develop rules and practices to prevent or discourage such unlawful methods of law enforcement. Turning to practicing attorneys, I cannot help having the impression that only a minority of them fought hard for the protection of the rights of suspects, though I can also give a number of names of those who worked for this objective.

The above-mentioned quasi-judicial function of present-day prosecutors is a remnant from a period when they actually were part of the judiciary. Tanaka (1976) observed that up until 1974, the prosecutor's office was regarded as one of the components of the judiciary and that the intertwining of both judicial and prosecutorial functions resulted in a concentration of the powers of the state. This dual authority in the Ministry of Justice also allowed many prosecutors to have political influence far beyond their prescribed function. Many occupied top positions in this agency. Furthermore, it should be remembered throughout this discussion of the investigation of crimes and prosecution of criminals that jury trials, only briefly in existence, were abandoned by 1943, and all criminal trials were handled by judges.

The present-day prosecutor (or procurator) has a substantial amount of power, and in addition he has a broad range of situations and opportunities throughout the judicial process in which to exercise it. Though generally the prosecutor acts in a supervisory role for an investigation initiated by police, there are occasions in which the prosecutor will initiate the investigation himself. Horiuchi (1995) stated that prosecutors perform four main functions in Japan:

> They investigate criminal wrongdoing by interrogating suspects, interviewing witnesses, and examining written and physical evidence gathered by the police; they decide whether or not to formally charge suspects with a crime; they present the state's case at trial; and they supervise the execution of sentences imposed by the courts. (p. 70)

In Japan, crimes are not described as felonies or misdemeanors. Rather they are classified as "penal code offenses" and "special code offenses." The latter category includes minor road violations and many drug crimes.

A major function of the public prosecutors is to separate out those offenders who might be acquitted if prosecuted (along with those who might be convicted but whom, for other reasons, the state chooses not to punish) from those who will be prosecuted. This is in the context of a system that has neither a grand jury nor an examining magistrate and therefore relies on the police and public prosecutors for investigations (Horiuchi 1995). Warrants are required at the arrest stage and are issued by a judge. The Japanese system allows for two exceptions. First, a person may be arrested without warrant in an instance where an offender is committing or has just committed an offense. Second, a person may be arrested for an offense punishable by up to three years of imprisonment because of "great urgency" (i.e., a warrant cannot be obtained before the suspect flees).

After having a suspect in custody, the public prosecutor must inform the person immediately of the alleged offense and his right to defense counsel (UNAFEI 1998). Only a public prosecutor has the power to ask a judge for a detention order. The judge reviews the detention request and may order the suspect's detention for ten days. In most instances the judge grants the request. A prosecutor may make a request for an extension, and then the detention period can be extended by an additional ten days. The maximum period of custody before indictment is twenty-three days.

During detention no suspect is entitled to bail. After prosecution a judge may grant bail, but the Code of Criminal Procedure specifies conditions for denying bail. They include cases where the defendant has been charged with an offense punishable by one year or more and cases where there are reasonable grounds to believe the suspect may destroy evidence or flee (Horiuchi 1995). Before making the bail decision, the judge commonly hears opinions from both defense counsel and prosecutor, and the judge may also interview the parties who will guarantee the appearance of the accused at trial. The judge then fixes the condition of bail including the amount. Either counsel may appeal the bail decision.

Frequently used in the United States, undercover operations are rarely utilized in Japan, although they have been implemented in some drug and gun trafficking cases (UNAFEI 1998). Japan and the United States also differ in the use of written evidence. After questioning a suspect, the investigator will prepare a written statement of the interview and the accused will be asked to sign it after the last sentence, which declares that the statement is voluntary and accurate. This is admissible evidence in court when the witness does not appear to testify or when the witness testifies in a different or contradictory fashion.

Nonprosecution takes place, of course, when there is insufficient evidence, but also when there is a "suspension of prosecution." In the latter instance Japanese criminal law allows prosecutors to drop cases even when there is enough evidence to establish a conviction. The Japanese approach is described by justice officials as "a discretionary procedure in disposing of cases flexibly according to the seriousness of individual offenses and the criminal tendency of each suspect and in giving them the chance to rehabilitate themselves in society" (UNAFEI 1998). Also, critical consideration is given to compensation and the victim's feelings in any suspension of prosecution. Table 7.3 (Ministry of Justice 1998) provides data on cases disposed of in the Public Prosecutor's Office by type of offense and disposition for recent years.

In 1999 the Japanese Diet passed a wiretap law, which allowed justice officials to wiretap telephone conversations and fax and e-mail messages when investigating certain crimes (*Daily Yomiuri* 1999). However, outside experts pointed out problems in implementing the law, particularly the difficulty in intercepting cellular phone conversations. In 1999, there were over 50 million subscribers to cellular phones in Japan.

Concerning the disposition of cases by the Public Prosecutor's Office, relatively few are tried, as Table 7.3 reveals. Of those prosecuted,

Table 7.3

Cases Disposed of by Pubic Prosecutors by Offense and Disposition, 1988–1997

Year/Offense	Total	Prosecution		Nonprosecution		Referral to family court
		Trial proceeding	Summary proceeding	Suspended prosecution	Others	
1988	2,348,171	111,650	1,317,427	397,475	51,970	469,649
1989	2,221,317	102,283	1,204,014	418,900	50,709	445,411
1990	2,229,929	93,039	1,204,085	459,567	44,661	428,577
1991	2,195,771	90,112	1,152,950	512,241	40,569	399,899
1992	2,220,515	89,058	1,177,582	556,013	37,380	360,482
1993	2,205,478	92,312	1,150,217	603,244	37,387	322,318
1994	2,126,988	91,993	1,081,813	621,463	36,700	295,019
1995	2,028,491	94,833	989,289	637,254	36,223	270,892
1996	2,076,730	98,508	1,023,891	641,805	35,674	276,852
1997	2,100,006	101,478	1,053,112	615,908	34,357	295,151
Penal code offense	917,865	56,002	100,427	543,309	27,303	190,824
Homicide	1,288	769	—	40	439	40
Robbery	3,210	1,166	—	61	204	1,779
Bodily injury	26,852	3,758	8,304	3,751	711	10,328
Assault	5,148	271	1,971	1,702	78	1,126
Extortion	9,778	2,226	—	1,075	360	6,117
Larceny	143,204	26,326	—	17,940	3,166	95,772
Fraud	11,291	7,015	—	2,576	1,118	582
Embezzlement	36,947	949	36	4,579	426	30,957
Rape	1,702	880	—	125	284	413
Indecent assault	1,902	807	—	110	584	401
Public indecency	1,065	73	759	184	8	41
Distribution of obscene literature, etc.	715	326	232	132	15	10

Arson	906	522	1	81	191	111
Bribery	402	209	32	61	11	
Gambling and lottery	2,800	521	1,272	942	23	42
Violent acts	2,981	522	731	426	75	1,227
Traffic professional negligence	645,701	4,700	83,689	504,236	14,677	38,399
Others	21,973	4,873	3,400	5,288	4,933	3,479
Special Law Offense	1,182,141	45,476	952,685	72,599	7,054	104,327
Election	892	216	378	227	66	5
Firearms and swords	4,042	913	1,309	1,093	262	465
Stimulant drugs	27,067	22,500		1,302	1,327	1,938
Poisonous and powerful agents	6,625	758	1,555	126	19	4,167
Road traffic violations	1,093,276	9,982	927,414	55,685	4,041	96,154
Others	50,239	11,107	22,029	14,166	1,339	1,598

Source: Ministry of Justice 1998.

the majority are disposed of by a "summary proceeding," (when the offender can be assessed a fine not exceeding 500,000 yen and admits guilt). In "summary procedure" no public hearing is held, and instead a judge examines the evidence in his chambers and orders the offender to pay the fine.

Conviction rates in Japanese trials have been running at around 99.9 percent in recent years (Horiuchi 1995), but prosecutors and Ministry of Justice officials are quick to point out that there are sound reasons for this astonishingly high conviction rate and that it does not reflect weak legal defense. Tsuchiya (1980) has claimed that only when the evidence is strong are cases prosecuted. Furthermore he and other Ministry of Justice officials argue that many offenders are diverted from the criminal justice system at various stages.

Another factor influencing both the low crime rate and high conviction rate is that many crimes that are still "on the books" in Western nations, including the United States, are not treated as crimes in Japan. As examples, Tsuchiya offered vagrancy, homosexuality, and public drunkenness, which have never been considered crimes in Japan. Without the worries caused by these prevalent but victimless offenses, law enforcement authorities have been freer to pursue the solution of what most people would consider more serious crimes. As noted earlier, Japanese prosecutors actively consider the rehabilitation prospects of offenders in deciding whether to prosecute or not. This factor is also taken into account at the sentencing stage, should the defendant be convicted. Japanese officials frequently use the term "criminological" in discussing this aspect of their work. In describing the evolving role of the prosecutor in the 1960s, Nagashima (1963) noted:

> Before the second Code of Criminal Procedure, there was no provision giving procurators a discretionary power of nonprosecution. Nevertheless, it gradually became general usage for the procurator to decline prosecution of less serious crimes. Because the investigation and disposition of the matter were carried out by the procurator in closed chambers, the identity of the offender against whom prosecution was declined was rarely disclosed to the public; consequently, the offender could continue in the community as a good citizen rather than with the stigma of a criminal. This system contributed so much to the rehabilitation and reentry of the offender into society that it was explicitly approved and extended in the second code. Even an offender who had committed a rather serious crime

might be relieved from prosecution if he was a first offender, if the injuries caused by the offense were compensated for, and if there was reasonable ground to believe that he would not commit another offense. (p. 299)

What Nagashima did not mention in this statement, and what critics have been quick to point out, is that while it is true that in cases in which prosecutors decline to prosecute, though offenders are not socially stigmatized with a criminal record, they do remain marked men in the eyes of law enforcement authorities. Decisions to prosecute or suspend prosecution are strongly affected by the existence of a confession, sincere repentance by the suspect, and the forgiveness of the victim according to prosecutors.

In 1981, journalist Donald Kirk wrote critically about the high Japanese conviction rate, noting that 86 percent of all cases that were sent to trial included a confession, which, he sarcastically pointed out, was still "king of evidence" in Japan. Generally, Japanese officials have not quibbled with this assertion, but have viewed the process somewhat differently. Japanese officials note that there is a tradition of confessing among Japanese, and they are proud of their high conviction rate. Of course, to Americans, it smacks of heavy-handedness and coercion.

But from the defense side of the bench, one prominent Japanese private attorney who has defended many clients mentioned that as the suspect increasingly becomes the target of an investigation, authorities can get "harsh." "Unless you confess readily, questioning will be tough. Most guilty people do confess," he indicated. He noted that police methods had been the subject of three types of Supreme Court case: those involving the "voluntariness of citizens' cooperation in police questioning"; those involving "police abuse itself" (obviously he meant physical abuse); and, finally, those cases involving "civil damages." Along similar lines, one of my police officer colleagues who had worked as a sergeant in Tokyo, in response to my question about why suspects confessed so readily, commented that, "It is no use to protest against power." Kirk's journalistic piece (1981) also emphasized another element that has caused apprehension among Westerners, namely, the sheer power of a prosecutor who is allowed to hold a suspect for up to twenty-three days before bringing charges.

Prosecutors point out that the system has built in safeguards. Yoshio

Table 7.4

Courts of First Instance, Adjudicated by Offense, 1996

Offense	Total	Death	Life	Guilty sentences				Acquittal
				Sentenced	Suspended execution of sentence	Suspended with probation	Fine, penal detention, minor fine	
District/family courts								
Total	54,592	1	34	53,997	33,483	3,736	413	35
Penal code offense	25,453	1	34	25,274	14,236	1,832	54	31
Murder	588	13	13	563	127	30	1	3
Robbery	771	1	18	748	99	33	—	—
Bodily injury	3,007	—	—	2,982	1,615	288	16	6
Extortion	1,717	—	—	1,711	1,004	186	—	5
Larceny	5,524	—	—	5,516	2,181	413	—	2
Fraud	3,178	—	—	3,162	1,440	243	—	2
Rape	606	—	—	603	184	58	—	2
Arson	344	—	3	340	110	39	—	1
Gambling and lottery	390	—	—	390	341	9	—	—
Violent acts	387	—	—	387	155	23	—	—

Traffic professional negligence	4,758	—	4,724	4,006	246	15	5
Others	4,183	—	4,148	2,974	264	22	5
Special law offense	29,139	—	28,723	19,139	1,904	359	4
Election	230	—	206	204	1	2	1
Firearms and swords	556	—	551	143	12	4	—
Stimulant drugs	14,219	—	14,211	7,277	1,226	—	1
Narcotics drugs	111	—	111	63	2	—	—
Horse race	112	—	112	95	1	—	—
Alien registration	3,872	—	3,859	3,811	5	12	—
Road traffic violations	7,304	—	7,242	5,900	517	45	—
Others	2,735	—	—				
Summary Courts							
Total	1,031,747	—	8,288	5,432	1,150	1,023,315	19
Total Formal Trials	9,109	—	8,288	5,432	1,150	677	19
Total Summary Proceedings	1,022,638	—	—	—	—	1,022,638	—

Source: Ministry of Justice 1998.

Suzuki addressed this issue in the above-mentioned 1980 Japan Society seminar by discussing two other features of the Japanese system, the "inquest of prosecution" and the "analogical institution of prosecution." Briefly, the former involves a commission—which is attached to each district court—composed of eleven local voters chosen at random for six-month terms. A victim or complainant may raise the issue that "prosecution was improperly declined," and then the commission will conduct its own investigation based on case records and the examination of witnesses. If the commission decides that the criminal should have been prosecuted, the chief public prosecutor must reconsider the case, but he still retains the right to prosecute or not. The "analogical institution of prosecution" is an approach that is designed to counter any prejudice or bias of prosecutors. It attempts to prevent any appearance of impropriety when public officials are accused of abusing their power. It also has jurisdiction over charges of police brutality and abuses by other justice personnel. The approach is similar to that of the appointment of a special prosecutor in the United States. Action is initiated by a victim or complaintant as in the case of the "inquest of prosecution," and the court conducts an independent inquiry. If the court decides prosecution should be undertaken, then a private attorney is appointed in place of the prosecutor.

The *White Paper on Crime* (Ministry of Justice 1998) provides information concerning defendants adjudicated by district, family, and summary courts of the first instance. Table 7.4 presents data on the various types of offenses adjudicated and the outcomes. There were 54,592 defendants tried in 1996, or an increase of 5.2 percent over the previous year. Of those, one was sentenced to death, thirty-four were sentenced to life imprisonment, and thirty-five were acquitted. Again, as noted earlier, acquittal rates are extremely low in Japan.

As far as cases adjudicated at the district or family court level in which a sentence of imprisonment was administered, the rate for suspended execution of sentence varied between 50 to 59 percent for the period from 1960 to 1988. From 1989, it started to increase and has been above 60 percent since 1994. For example, in 1997 the rate was 62.3 percent (Ministry of Justice 1998).

Concerning sentencing in the Japanese courts during 1996, those sentenced to imprisonment for one year or more, but less than two years, accounted for 50.4 percent of the total. Those sentenced to two years or more, but less than three years, amounted to 16.8 percent. Those sentenced to six months or more, but less than one year, amounted to 14.4 percent of the total.

Finally, for those sentenced to more than ten years and up to life imprisonment there were a total of 157 individuals. Among that group, 91 were sentenced for homicide, 45 for robbery, 10 for arson, 3 for rape, 2 for violation of the firearms and swords law, and 2 for violation of the stimulant drugs control law. The roles of courtroom trials, the judiciary, corrections, and probation will be addressed in the next chapter.

8

Courts, Corrections, and Probation

Courts and the Trial Process

After World War II the Japanese legal system was reshaped by General Douglas MacArthur and the American Occupation Force, and an adversarial system of justice (as opposed to an inquisitorial type) emerged. The present constitution of Japan was put into effect on May 3, 1947 (Supreme Court of Japan 1998). The previous constitutional monarchy was superseded by this constitutional democracy and, as a result, the Japanese Diet (parliament) came into being. There is a separation of powers between the executive (prime minister), legislature (Diet), and courts (the Supreme Court at the top of the hierarchy) much like various Western democracies.

Under the Supreme Court are eight high courts, which act as courts of appeal from district courts or family courts. Appeals from summary courts go directly to the Supreme Court. There are 50 district courts, 50 family courts, and 438 summary courts scattered throughout Japan. At the trial level, cases handled by the district courts are often disposed of by a single judge, but some cases require a panel of three judges. In the latter instance, cases punishable by death, life imprisonment, or confinement for one year or more are heard by the panel of three. As previously observed, there are no jury trials in Japan, although they were briefly instituted during MacArthur's administration.

In Japanese trials, the suspect is presumed innocent until proven guilty, and the standard of proof in a criminal trial is "beyond a reasonable doubt" (Horiuchi 1995). Horiuchi (1995) described the typical steps in a criminal trial (see Figure 8.1). As in the United States, the accused has a right to cross-examine prosecution witnesses, and in principle hearsay evidence is inadmissible. In theory defendants have a right to a speedy trial, but once the trial commences, a few cases can take years to terminate as the players meet intermittently. For example the court may meet once or twice a month on a particular case. In an interview in his office in 1999, Yamakawa, a lawyer, claimed that the way lawyers are compensated makes it difficult financially for at least some defense lawyers to work continuously on one case at a time, even though over 90 percent of all cases brought to trial are resolved within six months. A report issued by the United Nations Asia Far East Institute (Horiuchi 1995) stated that for 1992 of 54,802 clients defended, 18,808 were given counsel by private lawyers while the balance of 36,720 were represented by legal aid.

Table 8.1 (pp. 150–151) provides a breakdown of the length of various criminal court proceedings during 1993. Japan has not adopted an arraignment system whereby it is sufficient for a defendant to plead guilty. The system requires additional evidence beyond a confession. Often, in complex cases, the defense counsel, judge(s), and a public prosecutor have a preparatory meeting in order for the trial to proceed smoothly (UNAFEI 1998). Actual evidence is not disclosed in these meetings until court proceedings are underway, as the judges (not a jury) are the fact finders. Once again, written evidence can be accepted by the court if witnesses or defendants are to appear or change earlier oral statements given to investigators. Furthermore, if the testimony of witnesses contradicts earlier statements, the written statement can be used by the prosecutor to impeach the in-court account. Unlike the Anglo-American criminal procedure, the trial process is not separated into the trial and sentencing stages. As in many European courts, at the time of the closing statement, public prosecutors often express their opinions as to the appropriate punishment.

Acquittal rates are low, as noted earlier, and complete judgments of "not guilty" occur in less than one-tenth of one percent of all decisions. For most offenses, the criminal statutes allow for a wide range of sentences. Table 8.2 (p. 152) provides data on the judgments rendered by criminal courts (Horiuchi 1995). In reviewing this information it be-

Figure 8.1 **Proceedings in a Criminal Trial**

OPENING PROCEEDINGS	1. Questioning the accused for identification 2. Indictment read aloud by the public prosecutor 3. Notifying the accused of the right to remain silent 4. Giving the accused and defense counsel the opportunity to make comment on the indictment (plea)
EXAMINATION OF EVIDENCE	1. Opening speech by the public prosecutor 2. Application by the public prosecutor for examination of evidence 3. Statement by the defense counsel responding to 2 above 4. Decision by the court about the course of examination of evidence 5. Examination of evidence adduced by the prosecution 6. Opening speech by the defense counsel 7. Application by the defense counsel for examination of evidence 8. Statement by the public prosecutor responding to 7 above 9. Decision by the court about the course of examination of evidence 10. Examination of evidence adduced by the defense 11. Questioning the accused
CLOSING PROCEEDINGS	1. Closing speech by the public prosecutor (including recommendation of sentence) 2. Closing speech by the defense counsel 3. Statement by the accused (if any)
PRONOUNCEMENT OF JUDGMENT	EITHER 1. Pronouncement of sentence, facts found by the court, evidence supporting the facts, applicable law, etc. 2. Notifying the accused of his right to appeal OR 1. Pronouncement of "Not guilty" or "Dismissal" and the reason for it

Source: Horiuchi, United Nations Asia Far East Institute for the Prevention of Crime and Treatment of Offenders 1995.

comes clear how few capital punishment cases exist and how few defendants receive "imprisonment with labor for life." Table 8.2 also highlights the large portion of judgments that result in fines.

Minor criminal cases are heard by a summary court and the proceedings may be less formal in that setting (Terrill 1999). In this setting, no public hearing is held and the prosecutor offers the evidence to the court. In a summary court, a punishment cannot exceed 200,000 yen, and finally, if the outcome is not agreeable to both sides, a formal trial will commence. Family court issues and proceedings, which often involve juveniles, will be discussed in a later chapter on juvenile delinquency.

Imprisonment

The Japanese correctional system, as in most countries, affects the crime rate, the courts, and policing. A brief sketch is offered. As noted in an earlier work by the author (Parker 1986) on parole and the community-based treatment of offenders in Japan, the modern prison system had its origin in the legislation of 1872. This was the time of the Meiji era in which Japan opened up to the West and concepts and ideas from abroad were sought out and implemented. Clifford (1976) noted that the legislation was patterned after Western-style institutions. Not only was the architecture Western—for example, penitentiaries housed individual cells—but the criminal codes were Western. Superficially, the Japanese correctional system looks somewhat like its U.S. counterpart, but initial impressions can be deceiving. The length of sentences, the rate of incarceration, and the culture of Japanese prisons is vastly different. In 1997, the total population of inmates in Japanese penal institutions was just 50,091 (Ministry of Justice 1998). Of that number, the population of convicted offenders numbered 40,977, while those detained awaiting trial numbered 8,859. In the United States, during a similar year there were over one and a half million individuals under lock and key, and the two million mark was reached in March 2000. The United States rate of incarceration escalated to 725 inmates for every 100,000 Americans (Shaw 1999). The Washington-based Justice Policy Institute claimed that the cost of incarceration was close to $40 billion per year. Former *New York Times* editorialist and Attica prison negotiator, Tom Wicker (2000), stated that America's draconian

Table 8.1

Average Length of Trials and Number of Trial Dates, 1988–1992

Year	District court					Summary court				
Classification	1988	1989	1990	1991	1992	1988	1989	1990	1991	1992
Number of defendants	(100.0) 57,883	(100.0) 52,755	(100.0) 49,821	(100.0) 47,539	(100.0) 46,983	(100.0) 12,558	(100.0) 11,428	(100.0) 10,374	(100.0) 9,383	(100.0) 9,621
Term from prosecution to disposal										
Within one month	(4.0) 2,309	(3.5) 1,828	(3.3) 1,658	(3.4) 1,604	(3.0) 1,389	(13.8) 1,736	(12.5) 1,432	(10.8) 1,125	(11.9) 1,112	(9.6) 925
Within two months	(39.0) 22,590	(38.9) 20,530	(38.0) 18,926	(39.0) 18,553	(38.0) 17,867	(52.7) 6,624	(52.4) 5,991	(53.6) 5,556	(53.4) 5,011	(54.2) 5217
Within three months	(27.4) 15,870	(29.0) 15,279	(28.5) 14,215	(28.5) 13,538	(29.6) 13,907	(18.9) 2,378	(20.3) 2,318	(20.8) 2,156	(20.7) 1,938	(22.0) 2,112
Within six months	(22.0) 12,725	(21.2) 11,182	(22.7) 11,306	(21.8) 10,345	(21.8) 10,249	(10.1) 1,267	(10.3) 1,180	(10.9) 1,126	(10.5) 986	(11.1) 1,072
Within one year	(5.2) 3,012	(5.0) 2,649	(5.2) 2,569	(5.0) 2,366	(5.4) 2,551	(2.3) 289	(2.4) 269	(2.3) 243	(2.0) 192	(2.0) 195
Within two years	(1.5) 867	(1.4) 740	(1.4) 686	(1.4) 652	(1.4) 681	(1.5) 194	(1.3) 148	(0.9) 94	(1.1) 105	(0.6) 59
Within three years	(0.4) 247	(0.4) 194	(0.3) 156	(0.3) 148	(0.3) 146	(0.4) 55	(0.3) 39	(0.4) 39	(0.2) 21	(0.2) 16

More than three years	(0.5) 263	(0.7) 353	(0.6) 305	(0.7) 333	(0.4) 193	(0.1) 15	(0.4) 51	(0.3) 35	(0.2) 18	(0.3) 25
Average term of trial (months)(A)	3.4	3.5	3.5	3.5	3.4	2.5	2.6	2.6	2.4	2.4
Average number of trial dates (B)	3.2	3.2	3.1	3.3	3.1	2.6	2.7	2.7	2.7	2.6
Average interval of trial dates (months)(A/B)	1.1	1.1	1.1	1.1	1.1	1.0	1.0	1.0	0.9	0.9

Source: Horiuchi, United Nations Asia Far East Institute for Crime and Treatment of Offenders 1995.

Table 8.2

Judgments by All Criminal Courts, 1989–1993

	1989	1990	1991	1992	1993
Found guilty and sentenced to: Capital punishment	5	6	5	5	7
Imprisonment with labor for life	49	32	24	29	27
Imprisonment with labor for a fixed term	25,389 (I) 31,962 (S)	23,372 (I) 30,745 (S)	21,598 (I) 29,221 (S)	21,440 (I) 29,941 (S)	21,727 (I) 31,753 (S)
Imprisonment without labor for a fixed term	273 (I) 4,118 (S)	265 (I) 4,121 (S)	228 (I) 3,441 (S)	175 (I) 2,956 (S)	197 (I) 2, 696 (S)
Fine	1,193,231	1,206,144	1,148,789	1,170,257	1,137,937
Penal detention	60	74	59	45	51
Minor fine	9,716	5,761	4,753	4,530	4,304
Found not guilty	131	107	197	91	124
Other	1,063	768	563	565	731
Total	1,265,997	1,271,395	1,208,878	1,230,034	1,199,554

Source: Horiuchi, United Nations Asia Far East Institute for Crime and Treatment of Offenders 1995.
(I) = immediate imprisonment.
(S) = suspended sentence of imprisonment with or without supervision by the Probation Service.

"three strikes and you're out" and mandatory drug sentencing laws have resulted in the inclusion of many nonviolent offenders in the costly overflow of incarcerated inmates.

As of 1997, 22,667 offenders were newly admitted to Japanese correctional institutions, a number that included a one percent increase from the previous year. Violations of the stimulant drugs control law (29.7%) topped the list followed by larcenies (27.5%), fraud (6.8%), road traffic violations (5.9%), and bodily injury (5.2%) (Ministry of Justice 1998).

Recidivism rates, as measured by those who were released from custody in 1992 but who were reincarcerated by 1997, amounted to approximately 50 percent. This number is not vastly different from the recidivism rates that have been reported in the United States, although various states have sometimes reported rates of over 60 percent.

A highly critical perspective on Japanese prison life has been offered by Amnesty International. The report claimed that "systematic cruel, inhuman or degrading treatment" was characteristic. They presented documented cases of prisoners severely beaten by guards for minor infractions of prison rules, detained in solitary confinement for long periods, and restrained in leather belts and handcuffs. The regulations and instructions to prisoners are presented in Figure 8.2 as handed down by Fuchu Prison authorities. A preface (not shown) to the excerpts offered in Table 8.2 makes clear that "good discipline" is maintained at all times, and "no prisoner is allowed to act as he feels" (Amnesty International 1998). Prison wardens are given wide latitude in implementing their own internal rules and regulations. Perusal of the information in Figure 8.2 makes clear that the Japanese prison environment is vastly more restrictive than that of the typical U.S. prison, and foreign prisoners have often claimed that they were abused. At a minimum they have found it enormously painful to adjust to the rigid demands of their keepers. Detainees who fail to obey the rules in the minutest detail risk severe punishment. Most offenders are held in communal cells with six to eight people per cell. Exceptions are granted to foreigners, the sick, and those under a death sentence. Those undergoing punishment for *keiheikin* (minor solitary confinement) undergo the following, according to Amnesty International (1998): they are required to remain motionless in a kneeling or cross-legged position for hours on end (sometimes from 7:00 A.M. to 5:00 P.M. for a period of

up to two months); all communication is cut off except when necessary between prisoners and guards; the cell is stripped bare of all personal items such as books, photographs, and paper; no physical
exercise, baths, or contacts with outsiders are permitted; offenders
are sometimes forced to fix their eyes continuously on a single place
on the cell wall where a poster has been hung exhorting the inmate
to "reflect."

"Protection cells," common in Japanese correctional institutions,
are designed for housing offenders who are viewed as demonstrating signs of vulnerability or instability. They contain no furniture
except for a bed made of vinyl chloride and a sink and toilet bowl
embedded in the floor. The walls are wooden and there is around-
the-clock video surveillance. Inmates are strip-searched on entry,
ostensibly to check for sharp objects, and are forced to put on trou-
sers with a slit cut in the seat for defecation. The slit cut is to allow
prisoners to go to the toilet without using their hands. This is because the prisoner is usually restrained with leather or metal handcuffs (Amnesty International 1998). Reportedly, these handcuffs are
not removed at any time, even during mealtimes or periods of sleep.
A number of summaries of individual cases were included in the
Amnesty International report and included numerous accounts of
abuse and beatings.

Probation, Parole, and Community-based Treatment

The Rehabilitation Bureau of the Ministry of Justice oversees the
probation, parole, and community-based programs for offenders in
Japan. As in the United States, these services are designed to provide a transition for offenders leaving prison, or in the case of probation, a vehicle designed to keep offenders out of prison.

Probation officers also engage in the parole function, but unlike
such services in the United States, the counseling and assistance
provided to released offenders are offered by a large corps of volunteers. Professional probation officer/parole officers number around
seven hundred fifty. They function as administrators, not counselors, and they supervise the volunteers. Toshiko Takaike (1999), a
probation officer and supervisor whom the author first met in 1983,
stated that there are approximately 48,000 volunteer probation of-

Figure 8.2 **Instructions and Regulations (Excerpts) Given to Prisoners of Fuchu Prison**

GENERAL INSTRUCTIONS

- Do not reveal names and addresses of your family to fellow inmates.
- While walking avoid folding your arms or hands, putting your hands in your pockets . . . waving your shoulders intentionally or dragging your shoes. . . .
- Always obey any instructions given by prison officers even if this booklet has not referred to the matter.

ROOM REGULATIONS

- Do not wash your head or body in your room at your own will. Do not wash clothes without permission.
- Do not lie down in your room whenever you please. Avoid leaning against the bedding or sitting on it.
- Your sitting position in the room should be as designated in the chart in your room.
- In a single room, sit facing the table while working, taking meals or during leisure hours. During bedtime, you can sit on the bed.
- Those under punishment should sit on the stool at the designated place in the correct position.

WORK REGULATIONS

- You are not allowed to leave your work area without permission. Idle talk is prohibited. Raise your hand to obtain permission from your factory guard beforehand when you have to leave your work area.
- When you go to the toilet you shall take a permission tag with you, and hang it in a fixed place. Conversation in the toilet is prohibited.

USING NOTEBOOKS

- Do not soil or tear off the permit attached to each notebook.
- Use each notebook for its authorized purpose only. Avoid lending it or asking others to write for you on it.
- Handle your notebook with care and avoid soiling and tearing.
- Use an eraser or draw lines to correct errors. Do not tear off any page.
- Use the notebook in the order of pages and do not leave blank pages.
- You may divide a notebook into two parts and use it from both ends. A notebook for study or vocational training may be divided into three or more parts when deemed necessary. Get permission from the officer in charge beforehand. . . . Indexes should be put in each section.
- Submit your notebook to officers for censorship when required.

Source: Amnesty International 1998.

ficers in Japan, and the ratio of volunteers to offenders was an excellent 1 to 1.6. In the United States, the probation/parole system has suffered from underfunding. While some states have experimented with "intensive" supervision—that is, staff to client ratios are small, and parole officers have at least weekly meetings with offenders—most states and municipalities have huge ratios of probation/parole officers to clients that can be in the range of 1 to 300 (Parker 1986). Practically speaking, it has meant that because there are few volunteers in the United States to supplement the work of professionals, there is minimal monitoring and little counseling of offenders. A recently released report on offenders in Massachusetts reflects the situation in the United States (Larivee 1999). As the author noted, because of the enormous increase in incarceration rates in the United States over the past twenty years, many of those inmates are now being released. Due to the minimal resources available to the released convict, few will be helped or assisted by society.

Once more, Massachusetts offers an example. For Massachusetts, 33,000 inmates were released between 1989 and 1999, but only 10 to 15 percent received any services. There was no supervision, mandatory drug treatment, employment counseling, or job training. Between 1989 and 1999, the percentage of clients under parole supervision dropped from 63 percent to just 27 percent (Larivee 1999). Halfway-house openings, which often provide not just a bed but a support system, fell from 693 in 1990 to 375 openings in 1999.

The Japanese government's financial investment in probation, parole, and community-based treatment or halfway-house facilities is modest in comparison with the resources dumped into police, courts, and institutional corrections. But the "after care" system is far more viable than that in the United States, and the bottom line is that volunteers have regular contact with their offender clients. The personal investment and contact is critical, as I discovered in my 1986 field research on this subject in Japan. As a former staff counselor at a prerelease center in Brooklyn, New York, I have always maintained a keen interest in this subject. In Japan, the halfway houses (called rehabilitation aid hostels) are often staffed by lay people, but some professionals trained in social work or counseling manage these operations.

In 1997, the number of Japanese offenders who applied for parole was 13,745, up 4.6 percent from the previous year (Ministry of Justice 1998). Of that number, 58.3 percent were paroled. In total, 76,078 offenders were under probation or on parole in 1997. In 1984, there were 18,718 parolees in Japan, but that number has leveled off to around 12,000 from the mid-1990s through 2000.

These various justice institutions—courts, prisons, and probation—all interact with police forces in Japan.

9

Crime by Foreigners

Overview and Role of the Media

Japanese justice officials and the public have become aroused by foreign criminality. The issue of the extent of the increase in crime by foreigners (sometimes called *gaijin*) is relatively clear, but how it is perceived and characterized by the media is a different matter. First, it should be noted, that the term *gaijin* means outsider as well as foreigner, and this says something about public attitudes toward foreigners. Surveys done by the prime minister's office in recent years have revealed that most Japanese do not wish to form "closer" relationships with foreigners. Also, the word *gaijin* has a pejorative meaning in some quarters, and one Japanese scholar friend once joked to the author that non-Japanese are viewed as less human by Japanese.

Within the insular bubble of Japan's historic homogeneous society, a strident rhetoric concerning foreign criminality has been trumpeted by justice officials, including the police and immigration authorities. Suspicion of foreigners can be traced back to the arrival of Commodore Matthew Perry and his "black" ships in the seventeenth century. The German scholar Herbert (1996), who conducted an extensive study of foreign workers and the role of law enforcement in Japan, has accused Japanese journalists of uncritically accepting press releases from government agencies and thereby contributing to the fearful atmosphere surrounding immigrant workers and crimes committed. His book on the subject examines the language of police reports and media releases (both electronic and print), and he concluded that prejudice toward foreigners was very much in evidence.

This chapter explores the issue of illegal activities and crimes on the part of foreigners. It attempts to separate the distorted perceptions and stereotypes of foreign criminal behavior from the reality of actual crimes committed. Why are there distorted and sometimes sensationalized media reports of crimes committed by foreigners? To what extent are these reports fueled by data and information provided by Japanese police agencies?

It was the thesis of Herbert's (1996) doctoral dissertation that prejudice played a major role in the way foreign criminality has been portrayed by the media—in both print and electronic versions. In his thorough and extensive analysis, which included data on the subject of foreign workers and the role of law enforcement, he reported that the overall number of foreigners in Japan was very small in 1992—0.8 percent of the 122 million population of that year. Koreans represented 69.3 percent of all registered foreigners. However, many Koreans who were born in Japan are still not citizens and carry an alien registration document much like the one I carried during the year I was a Fulbright scholar in Japan. Among Koreans, there are some second- and third-generation descendants who, after the annexation of Korea as a de facto colony in 1910, immigrated or were deported to Japan as child labor (Herbert 1996). In general, citizenship is difficult to obtain for non-Japanese, but it is remarkable that many Koreans and other long-term residents born in the country have been unable to gain citizenship.

A picture of foreign residents in Japan as of December 31, 1998, is captured by Table 9.1. Perhaps surprisingly, many Brazilians, along with Koreans and Chinese, reside in Japan. They numbered 222,217 at the end of 1998 and represented 14.7 percent of the total population of foreign residents. Much earlier, significant numbers of Japanese had emigrated to Brazil, and with changing economic conditions some, along with family members, chose to return to Japan.

The role of Chinese is very different. Their situation includes "illegals," or those who have overstayed their visas, and criminals who have arrived surreptitiously on fishing vessels and container ships and through other means. In addition, there has been a significant increase in the legal Chinese population since the mid-1990s, and that number reached 272,230 by 1998. There has been a parallel increase in the illegal and criminal element. They have been the focus of attention by Japanese justice officials, and the head of China's Public Security (Ministry

Table 9.1

Foreign Residents in Japan

Nationality	Number	% of total
Korean	638,828	42.2
Chinese	272,230	18.0
Brazilian	222,217	14.7
Filipino	105,308	7.0
American (U.S.A.)	42,774	2.8
Peruvian	41,317	2.7
Thai	23,562	1.6
Indonesian	14,962	1.0
British (U.K.)	14,762	1.0
Vietnamese	13,505	0.9
Total	1,512,116	100.0

Source: Ministry of Justice 1999.

of Justice) visited Japan in late 1999 to confer on the crime problem in an urgently arranged meeting. Herbert (1996) pointed out that authorities began tightening the screws on all immigrants through the passage of the Amendment of the Immigration Control Act of June 1990. It included new provisions for punishment of up to three years' incarceration (or a fine of 2 million yen) for employers who employed illegals (Herbert 1996). Herbert claimed that the Japanese Ministry of Justice used code phrases such as "potential for social disruption" (*shakai no bunretsu*) and the "necessity for the preservation of social order" (*shakai chitsujo no iji*) in a major publicity campaign directed at spotting illegal workers. The German scholar believed that the language in advertisements, in newspapers, and on billboards inflated and overemphasized the seriousness of the problems, reflecting prejudice against foreigners. In May 1988 a "special month for the exposure of illegal foreign workers" was proclaimed by the Immigration Control Office, and 1,371 persons were identified (Herbert 1996). Among the 1,371, were 698 Bangladeshi, 466 Pakistani, and 148 Filipinos.

One area of concern for governmental authorities was irregular migrant labor and the manner in which "illegals" came into conflict with authorities. Herbert (1996) reported that by far the largest category comprised individuals who entered Japan on tourist visas and engaged in paid employment without the appropriate occupational-legal qualifications. If their tourist visas expired, they kept working and they were described as "overstaying." Other illegals entered on an "entertainer or performance" visa (*kogyo biza*) which allowed six months of employment as a singer or dancer. However, these individuals were typically women employed in snack bars or nightclubs as "hostesses"—a designation that was not legally permitted—and they were often forced into prostitution. Often, feeling pressured to send money back to relatives or family in their native countries, they also overstayed their visas.

Another group of illegal workers were those "on-the-job trainees," or probationary employees, who took jobs outside their designated occupational specialties. Sometimes they were exploited as cheap labor. Finally, as in many countries, there were sham marriages or those in which a foreigner married a Japanese national for convenience, and in those cases all restrictions on gainful employment were lifted. The number of illegals in Japan has been variously estimated as between 200,000 and 300,000 (Herbert 1996).

Various scholars and writers have pointed out that *boryokudan* or *yakuza* elements have been involved in illegal arrangements for helping immigrants get into Japan and stay (Kaplan and Dubro 1986). These authors presented information to support their view that various groups of Asian women were exploited as "sexual slaves by organized crime." Often an illegal will gain entry to Japan by paying a huge commission (e.g., 400,000 yen) and then be forced into paying it off in an illegal job such as prostitution. The "agent" pockets the commission and then charges the migrant for a falsified passport and an airline ticket. The person may be in debt for years on the meager wages earned. Construction work is also a setting that has employed illegal immigrants. The migrant is lured to Japan, notwithstanding the outrageous commissions, because even at a menial job, one month's wages in Japan may be worth a year's income in the home country. Thus, pressure is exerted on the immigrant to grind out an existence in Japan in an effort to improve the lot of relatives in the home country.

As in many countries, illegals often end up in crowded and impoverished conditions after their arrival. According to Herbert's research, it was not uncommon for five to seven immigrants to live in a single room. Herbert noted that they often prepared meals together and avoided going out unnecessarily to avoid possible problems and complaints. Furthermore, they lived under the constant fear and stress of being discovered. Japanese citizens and the press have viewed them with anxiety as a potential "slum formation." Not infrequently they have been stereotyped as "dirty and noisy." The language of the media has some-times extended to words such as "filth" and "criminality." Herbert stated that because of this continuous xenophobic discourse, landlords often shunned foreigners. In Yokohama, for example, because only a few ten-ement houses accepted Filipinos, they became ghettoized, with up to a hundred Filipine nationals per tenement building. Finally, due to the high cost of living in Japan, low-paid illegals have been compelled to seek less desirable housing.

In the early 1990s there was some discussion in Japan about whether the country should change its immigration policy to allow increases in certain selected pools of immigrants to take mostly lower-level jobs that Japanese nationals seemed unwilling to assume. One well-known journalist, Nishio Kanji (1989) came out strongly against opening the door to more foreigners. He argued for a closed society, claiming for-eigners would pose serious "social problems" for Japan. At one point he argued that if the country of origin were given a say in who immigrated they might send "psychopaths and criminals." Wolfgang Herbert (1996) quoted Nishio:

> [T]hey would cluster by ethnic groups in neighbourhoods run by local bosses—miniature countries within a country, where the rule of Japanese authorities would not extend. The incidents of killings and other violence that have already occurred among foreigners living in Japan are an omen of worse to come if the gates are opened wider . . . they would engage in bitter feuds beyond the ken of the Japanese, causing social order to deterio-rate. . . . Many people in Japan worry that a rise in the number of foreigners living in this country would lead to an increase in crime, making it impos-sible for women to walk alone at night. (p. 215)

Admittedly, Nishio appeared to represent an extreme point of view, and not the mainstream point of view in Japan, but he undoubtedly repre-sented a xenophobic segment of Japanese society.

In late 1999, H. French, a *New York Times* correspondent based in Ja-pan, reported on fear-arousing advertisements offered up by the Japanese lock maker Miwa (French September 30, 1999). Miwa announced that "insecurity in society" is due to Chinese "theft gangs" that operate out of "secret bases." One ad stated, "the damage by foreign theft gangs is in-creasing swiftly now," and in bold face, "It is time to invest in safety like those in America and Europe." The advertising campaign was successful and prompted major interest in Miwa locks. French added that ever since a failed Mongol invasion of Japan in the fifteenth century there has been a " tendency to point a finger at Chinese," which reflects a mixture of fear and contempt (ibid.). Hiroyoshi Ishikawa, acknowledged the problem by identifying two sides of the same coin, "The Japanese government made a very conscious effort to copy the customs of Europeans first, and then Americans" (ibid.). He added, "In the depths of their hearts, the Japanese people have had some kind of contempt for the Chinese and Koreans. Since the end of the nineteenth century, the attitude has been whites are superior, other Asians are inferior." Another perspective on the scapegoating of foreigners was offered by Chiu Xiong Yin, president of the Tokyo Association of Chinese Residents (ibid.), "Many illegal aliens are causing crimes, but the media reports often say it is suspected that the culprits are Chinese, even when the facts aren't known."

As noted earlier in the chapter on criminal investigation, Japanese authorities can hold suspects for an extended period of time without having to bring formal charges. Unquestionably, the process of being held in a jail cell for the full twenty-three-day period would be coercive and take its toll on most accused Japanese, but in the case of foreigners the ante is upped considerably. Isolated and unfamiliar with Japanese culture and the legal system, foreign suspects find the pressure to confess is compelling. Two cases are offered by Herbert (1996):

> By virtue of international law, foreign prisoners on remand have the right to inform relatives of their whereabouts and to inform the embassy or consulate of their home country. Police in Osaka claim that they distribute information fliers in Japanese and English to suspects and inform the official representatives of the prisoner's home country if the prisoner wishes it. But given prisoners' diverse nationalities, lawyers criticize the provision of information in only two languages as grossly inadequate. In one case that came to the attention of a lawyer, a Pakistani was forced by the police to sign a declaration that he would not inform his embassy. His legal right to an attorney was also obstructed by police, who cited the high costs of legal representation. In the case of an American citizen who was arrested for a drug offence, a member of the U.S. embassy staff was prevented from seeing the prisoner by police who (falsely) said that the suspect did not want to talk to him. The provision of legal counsel was also delayed for a considerable time. The U.S. Embassy later filed an official complaint with the Japanese Ministry of Justice. (p. 235)

A much later case (*Japan Times* September 5, 1991) also highlighted the issue of duress during confinement. In this case a twenty-seven-year-old

Filipino woman was sentenced to eight years in prison for stabbing her lover to death. Her counsel planned to appeal the ruling, arguing that his client, Manalili Rosal, was confined for ten days in a "police dormitory" before she was charged and that this contributed to a false confession. She claimed an alibi and had retracted her confession before she was indicted. Furthermore, and in sharp contrast with American jurisprudence, the trial judge, Yasuro Tanaka, acknowledged that the police had detained her for that period of time, apparently because of the way they had processed her case, and the detention had been illegal (*Japan Times* September 5, 1999). Often the Japanese perception of the truth or substance of a case is allowed to prevail over procedural violations. Historically, until the late 1990s, the assignment of a lawyer for a foreigner posed a series of problems. As in the case of Japanese defendants, defense counsel was not usually made available until after charges were brought, but the practice has begun to change after pressure has been applied by members of the Japanese Bar Association (interview with Y. Yamakawa in 1999). Herbert (1996) reported that only after the arraignment were public defenders appointed. According to a survey of members of the Osaka Bar Association, who had worked on eighty-eight cases involving foreign nationals, there were just ten cases in which public defenders were appointed prior to indictments.

In reviewing many cases of foreigners, the data showed that English was the predominant language employed during the interrogation phase and that in many cases police interpreters were assigned, as opposed to neutral outside professional interpreters. Herbert's (1996) research noted, "analysis according to languages reveals that there is a clear preference for English over the mother tongue of the suspect." He added that Japanese judges meted out harsher punishment to Asian foreigners than to their Japanese counterparts and pointed to the discrepancy between the greater number of unconditional sentences handed down to the former group.

The *White Paper on Police, 1998* (National Police Agency 1999) presented data on the number of foreign visitors who legally come to Japan. From 1988 until 1997 the number increased from 2.4 million to 4.67 million, and, not surprisingly, an increase in foreign criminality occurred. While foreign visitors in 1997 represented 1 percent of the total population, they accounted for 1.7 percent of the total arrests for penal code offenses. This report on crime was followed by the NPA's (National Police Agency 1999) statement, "[T]he high rate of arrests involving foreign visitors as compared with the component ratio of the population of foreign residents is worth noting as a possible security threat." Whether this strong statement is consistent with the data provided is open to question. The data in Table 9.2 suggest that serious or "felonious" offenses for 1997 were actually down compared to 1993 and 1994. So-called intellectual offenses peaked during 1996, when 1,513 cases were reported, and in 1997 there were just 680 cases. A slight increase in violent offenses is revealed in Table 9.2, but the number has remained relatively stable over the past five years.

Table 9.3 (pp. 168–169), which identifies foreign offenders by country, shows that the majority are Chinese. Americans are a small portion of the total and numbered just 107 for 1997 (National Police Agency 1999). Since 1997 there has been an increase in Chinese criminality in Japan, and interviews with top National Police Agency and Tokyo Metropolitan Police Department officials in late 1999 provided a more detailed picture of the escalating problem.

Tables 9.4 (pp. 170–171) and 9.5 (p. 172) present additional data on offenses by foreigners. The information was provided during the course of an interview with Police Superintendent Y. Maki (Tokyo, August 29, 1999) of the International Criminal Investigation Division of the Tokyo Metropolitan Police Department (M.P.D.). Surrounded by staff members and an M.P.D. interpreter, Maki communicated a heightened sense of urgency regarding offenses committed by foreigners, particularly Chinese (Peoples Republic of China) offenders. Robberies by Chinese worried him most. He, along with a number of other high-ranking Japanese police officials, voiced great frustration over their inability to gain support in recent years from Chinese Public Security Bureau officials in their attempt to reduce crimes by Chinese. Chief Superintendent H. Munehiro was one of the officials who expressed frustration with his Chinese counterparts. He believed that Chinese authorities have been capable of doing far more to stem the tide of Chinese criminals embarking from mainland China, particularly on the seas. The crimes of Chinese included not only human trafficking but the stealing of clothes, medicines, cosmetics, and motorbikes.

At the time of my interviews with these officials the top Chinese public security official (Jia Chun Wang) visited Tokyo with colleagues from his ministry (*Japan Times* August 20, 1999, p. 2). This was the first time a top Chinese justice official had visited Japan. He had discussions with the chairman of Japan's National Public Safety Commission and top NPA and M.P.D. officials. Japanese officials were demanding that

Table 9.2

Number of Foreigners Arrested in Japan, 1988–1997

Classification	1988	1989	1990	1991	1992	1993	1994	1995	1996	1997
Total number of cases	3,906	3,572	4,064	6,990	7,457	12,771	13,321	17,213	19,513	21,670
Total number of persons	3,020	2,989	2,978	4,813	5,961	7,276	6,989	6,527	6,026	5,435
Felonious offense										
Cases	48	98	77	126	161	218	221	176	162	187
Persons	78	94	111	126	185	246	230	201	212	213
Violent offense										
Cases	92	107	140	128	196	244	220	247	272	265
Persons	135	138	157	174	213	277	246	255	279	313
Larceny										
Cases	2,689	2,353	2,719	4,506	4,277	9,134	10,120	14,145	15,952	19,128
Persons	1,816	1,776	1,656	2,493	2,944	3,995	3,937	3,900	3,399	3,155
Intellectual offense										
Cases	243	190	239	377	723	777	394	770	1,513	680
Persons	86	104	139	94	443	260	218	302	497	305
Others										
Cases	834	824	889	1,853	2,100	2,398	2,366	1,875	1,614	1,410
Persons	905	877	915	1,926	2,176	2,498	2,358	1,869	1,639	1,449

Source: National Police Agency, *White Paper on Police, 1998*, Tokyo: National Police Agency of Japan.

Stolen Cargo Prepared to Leave for Russia (Russian Organized Crime Operation)

Source: National Police Agency 1998

their Chinese counterparts cooperate in the efforts to reduce drug smuggling and people smuggling on the part of Chinese syndicates—particularly those from Fujian Province. A year earlier top Japanese officials had visited Beijing. Sometimes individuals smuggled in arrived in legally registered ships, and in our 1999 interview, Maki suggested they might be under Korean or Chinese registry and that sometimes crew members are bribed.

Police Superintendent Maki also claimed that container ships and even smaller fishing boats (see photo) had been used by Chinese crime groups in smuggling drugs, people, and other contraband.

Data on foreign criminality in the Tokyo Metropolitan region are presented in Table 9.4. A review of the numbers of foreigners arrested by M.P.D. personnel between 1994 and 1998 shows a decline in the number of persons arrested—3,328 in 1994 to just 1,462 in 1998, although the total number of cases rose from 4,527 to 4,756 for the same period. Similarly, the number of cases of theft rose, but the number of persons arrested declined between 1994 and 1998.

In Table 9.5 (p. 172), the data provided by the Tokyo Metropolitan

Table 9.3

Foreigners Arrested by Country and Region, 1992–1997

Year	1992		1993		1994		1995		1996		1997	
Country/regions	Case	Person	Case	Person	Case	Person	Case	Person	Case	Person	Case	Person
Total	7,447	5,961	2,771	7,276	3,687	7,183	17,213	6,527	19,513	6,026	21,670	5,435
Asia												
Subtotal	6,089	4,759	9,829	5,761	0,239	5,621	13,181	5,081	15,960	4,763	17,903	4,241
China	2,417	1,933	3,685	2,668	4,845	2,942	7,828	2,919	6,186	2,661	5,536	2,320
S/N Korea	1,254	876	1,858	987	1,793	775	1,574	752	1,965	732	2,001	522
Iran	862	771	846	544	686	294	380	167	458	150	294	103
Philippines	381	259	1,254	366	713	396	633	301	629	326	541	315
Vietnam	303	176	495	200	223	198	693	252	5,557	274	7,755	329
Malaysia	296	224	558	309	671	256	634	169	280	135	561	115
Thailand	197	158	387	260	328	223	607	213	276	145	186	119
Pakistan	121	111	131	86	204	87	227	59	97	46	247	34
Bangladesh	46	45	48	48	35	28	57	30	32	31	52	32
Others	212	206	567	293	741	422	548	219	480	263	730	352
Europe												
Subtotal	292	285	403	344	353	322	321	321	307	257	317	247
Russia	134	146	222	188	147	149	155	158	123	121	132	112
U.K.	72	62	53	54	71	61	51	55	50	34	68	63
France	22	23	26	25	28	27	25	25	36	17	19	20
Others	64	54	102	77	107	85	90	83	98	85	98	52

America												
Subtotal	907	801	2,187	1,016	2,965	1,131	3,551	1,027	3,138	906	3,308	859
Peru	331	310	1,449	470	1,618	470	1,170	386	1,098	310	990	264
Brazil	222	174	344	223	587	301	1,503	318	979	304	1,202	347
U.S.A.	195	162	187	153	280	161	351	135	496	131	365	107
Others	159	155	207	170	480	199	527	188	565	161	751	141
Africa												
Subtotal	62	44	256	68	65	49	100	36	56	43	58	46
Nigeria	32	15	216	33	41	21	8	5	25	15	25	20
Others	30	29	40	35	24	28	92	31	31	28	33	26
Oceania	95	70	92	86	65	59	57	58	51	57	82	41
Unknown nationality	2	2	4	1	—	1	3	4	1	—	2	1

Source: White Paper on Police 1998.

Table 9.4

(a) Number of Foreigners Legally Entering Japan, 1980–1998

1980	1990	1996	1997	1998
1,295,866	3,504,470	4,244,529	4,669,5114	4,556,845

(b) Number of Foreigners Illegally "Overstaying" in Japan, January 1, 1999

1	2	3	4	5	6	7
South Korean	Chinese	Filipino	Thai	Peruvian	Malaysian	Total number
52,123	47,020	42,608	37,046	11,606	10,141	276,810

(c) Number of Foreigners Arrested by Tokyo Metropolitan Police for Penal Code Offenses, 1994–1998

	Murder, robbery, arson, rape		Assaults		Theft		White-collar crimes		Other crimes		Total number	
	Cases	Persons	Cases	Persons	Cases	Persons	Cases	Persons	Cases	Persons	Cases	Persons
1994	60	76	74	88	2,781	1,511	83	83	1,529	1,570	4,527	3,328
1995	53	66	93	100	3,664	1,303	149	129	1,133	1,132	5,092	2,730
1996	44	67	77	87	3,532	988	203	148	945	971	4,801	2,261
1997	62	68	90	110	4,489	849	136	136	667	734	5,444	1,897
1998	73	82	84	94	3,881	602	104	104	536	580	4,756	1,462

(d) Number of All Foreign Offenders Compared to Number of Chinese Offenders, 1998

	Murder, robbery, arson, rape	Assaults	Theft	White-collar crimes	Other crimes	Total number
All foreign offenders	82	94	602	104	580	1,462
Chinese offenders	46 (56.1%)	29 (30.9%)	379 (63.0%)	76 (73.1%)	263 (45.3%)	793 (54.2%)

Source: Tokyo Metropolitan Police Department 1999.

Table 9.5

(a) Foreign Offenders Arrested by Continent, 1998—Tokyo M.P.D.

Origin	All penal-code offenses		Felony crime offenses	
	No. cases (%)	No. persons (%)	No. cases (%)	No. persons (%)
Total number	4,756 (100)	1,462 (100)	73 (100)	82 (100)
Asia	4,451 (93.6)	1,251 (85.6)	66 (90.4)	71 (86.6)
Europe	61 (1.3)	55 (3.8)	1 (1.4)	1 (1.2)
Americas	200 (4.2)	116 (7.9)	3 (4.1)	8 (9.8)
Africa	21 (0.4)	19 (1.3)	3 (4.1)	2 (2.4)
Oceania	23 (0.5)	21 (1.4)	0 (0)	0 (0)

(b) Foreign Offenses in Tokyo by Visa Status, 1998—Tokyo M.P.D.

	Illegal residents	Students	Short-term stayers	Long-term residents	Other statuses	Total number
All penal-code offenses	405	189	186	167	515	1,462
	27.7%	13.0%	12.7%	11.4%	35.2%	100%
Felony crime offenses	60	3	4	7	8	82
	73.2%	3.6%	4.9%	8.5%	9.8%	100%

(c) Felony Offenses (murder, robbery, rape, arson) with Weapons, Foreign Offenders and All Offenders, 1998

	All felony crimes	Felony crimes by foreign offenders
Number of arrests	689	73
Cases with weapon involved	229	37
	33.2%	50.7%

(d) Foreign Drug Offenses by Nationality, 1998

Iranian		Filipino		Korean		U.S.		Chinese		Others		Total number	
Cases	Persons	Cases	Persons	Cases	Persons	Cases	Persons	Cases	Persons	Cases	Persons	Cases	Persons
226	103	79	52	19	15	14	13	10	8	69	42	417	233
54.2%	44.2%	18.9%	22.3%	4.6%	6.4%	3.4%	5.6%	2.4%	3.4%	16.5%	18.0%	100%	100%

Source: Tokyo Metropolitan Police Department 1999.

Police Department reveals that for its region a higher percentage of arrests of foreigners included weapons offenses (50.7 percent) than all those arrested for serious offenses (33.2 percent) for the year 1998.

Concerning the subject of drug offenses committed by foreigners, Table 9.5 elucidates the picture for various nationalities. For example, in 1998 Iranian offenders headed the list and were responsible for 44.2 percent of drug crimes committed by foreigners in the Tokyo region. Filipinos were next, contributing to 22.3 percent of drug offenses. The problem of drugs in Japan is discussed in a later chapter.

In 1999 one of the National Police Agency's top officials, Chief Superintendent Munehiro offered this comment in an interview with the author regarding crimes by foreigners. "They become an elusive quarry, in part because of the sophisticated nature of the false passports they've created." Returning to the subject of foreigners who overstay their visas, the *Japan Times* (August 20, 1999, p. 5) reported that the number in that category on July 1, 1999, was 268,421. This represented a 10 percent drop from the peak of approximately 300,000 who had been identified as overstaying illegally as of May of 1993.

This chapter concludes with a summary of two cases of prominent foreigners that received major press attention in Japan in late 1999. They help to highlight the broader picture of the evolving perception of the role of foreigners in Japan as the year 2000 unfolded. The first case involved a Korean woman pianist, named Choi, a third-generation Korean residing in Japan (Kamiya 1999) who, like many of her fellow Koreans, had not received Japanese citizenship. She had "expressed delight" over merely having her permanent residency status restored. She had lived in Osaka, Japan, and traveled abroad. She had balked at being fingerprinted, a requirement for aliens and foreigners since 1955. In response to this case and others like it, the Japanese Diet passed a law that rescinded the requirement of fingerprinting on each occasion that an alien's registration came up for renewal.

The earlier bill, part of the Alien Registration Law, had been, not surprisingly, criticized as treating non-Japanese like criminals (Kamiya 1999). Six months earlier, Japan's Supreme Court had dismissed a 1986 lawsuit in which Choi had demanded that the government repeal its rejection of her reentry to Japan and reinstate her permanent resident status. She had travelled outside Japan, even to the United States, in pursuing her musical career. Choi's successful campaign was part of a broader attack on the law in which an increasing number of Korean residents had been refusing to be fingerprinted. In response, the Japanese immigration authorities had been denying reentry permits to those who had refused to be fingerprinted and who had left Japan for a variety of reasons. The political context of this matter was linked to the attempt at improving relations between Japan and South Korea. Recall that Korea had been a virtual colony of Japan until after World War II and that South Korea's President Kim Dae Jung was preparing to visit Japan. In this case the Japanese Diet caved in.

A second case that had drawn attention to the treatment of foreigners in Japan involved Ana Bortz, a Brazilian who had arrived six months earlier in Japan (French November 15, 1999). French stated that "she endured bureaucratic devices" like fingerprinting and reentry permits, even though she had a valid visa. Furthermore she had also suffered more blatant racism when Japanese avoided sitting next to her on subway trains. But Bortz was a reporter for a Brazilian satellite television network, and notwithstanding her being conditioned to earlier slights, she was unprepared for her ejection from a jewelry store in Hamamator City. The store adamantly claimed that they had a policy of refusing to wait on people of "her nationality." Bortz challenged this case of discrimination in court and, to the surprise of many, won. Japan's 1946 constitution states that "all of the people are equal under the law," but the Japanese version refers to Japanese people. The store owner in press interviews had argued that Bortz's behavior had been "unnatural" and that fears of crime by Brazilians had been justified and therefore it did not constitute discrimination.

In summary, Japan has stood out for years as "a stubbornly near monoethnic nation" (French November 15, 1999). Becoming a citizen is only a dream for many Koreans and others born in Japan.

10

Crisis with Youth

Overview

The term "crisis" is a strong one, but there has been a significant increase in problems with young people in Japan over the past twenty years, and the situation is perceived as a crisis by many Japanese. Some young people are riding motorcycles in groups—called in Japanese *bōsōzoku*—literally, "rough running tribe"—reminiscent of America's Hell's Angels, while others are on the rampage in the classroom, assaulting teachers and fellow students. The underlying causes of this rising delinquency appear impervious to a quick solution. Superficially, the lack of direction and sense of purpose of many young Japanese people resemble similar problems in the United States, but in Japan it is directly tied to the pressure-cooker atmosphere in schools, where the competition is almost unbearably intense. Success in Japan, as has been mentioned, is a matter of having attended the right schools. In the highly materialistic society of the new millennium, there is every indication that the level of competition and its unfortunate corollary, juvenile delinquency, will continue to be problematic for the Japanese.

Although statistics tell only part of the story, they are worth examining. As with adult crime, it is not easy to draw comparisons between the United States and Japan, especially since the two countries have different legal definitions of juvenile delinquency. In the United States, authorities define juvenile violators as those under eighteen years of age, while in Japan those under twenty are considered juveniles. I have used the Japanese definition and adjusted the United States data to include those under twenty to facilitate comparisons.

First, Figure 10.1 offers a picture of trends in four serious offense categories for Japanese juveniles from the period of 1988 through 1998. This bar graph portrays the jump in robbery, rape, murder, and arson for juveniles commencing in 1996. Second, in looking at the year 1998, for the same four offenses mentioned above, the Japanese total was 2,197. For the United States in 1998, when combining the same categories of murder, robbery, rape, and arson committed by those under twenty, the parallel figure was 60,081, according to the FBI's *Uniform Crime Reports* (United States Department of Justice 1999). In a comparison with four other countries, but one that still displays the large discrepancy in Japanese and American juvenile crimes, Figure 10.2 shows that for serious juvenile crimes cleared, the rate for Japan was just 1,100 (per 100,000), while the rate for the United States was 2,045 (per 100,000) for 1996. (*Note:* For these numbers the data are for those aged seventeen and under.)

A return to Figure 10.1 shows that in Japan the number of teenagers under age twenty arrested for felonies has risen by 57 percent for the period of 1988 through 1998 (French October 12, 1999).

An inspection of Japanese trends over a longer stretch of time shows that for all juvenile offenses since World War II there have been various peaks and valleys in the data. The Japanese Ministry of Justice refers to "three major waves" of juvenile crime. The first wave peaked in 1951 when records indicated that 166,433 juveniles were charged with crime violations of all types in the period of upheaval following World War II. The nation experienced many other disruptions in society as it sought to reestablish itself. A second wave of delinquency crested when 238,830 juveniles violated the criminal code around 1964. Scholars claim that during this period of rapid economic ascendancy, which included the shift to industrialization, there was also a marked increase in the number of teenagers in Japanese society. The sheer number of teenagers contributed to this second peak (Foreign Press Center 1998).

A third wave peaked in 1983 with 317,438 juvenile offenses recorded. This upswing took place during a period of economic prosperity, but also during an era when traditional Japanese values were brought into question. An apparent weakening in the traditional family roles of husband and wife, which included increases in divorce, also occurred. Data from the workplace showed that more women were entering the workforce and staying longer in the workplace, thus weakening the his-

Figure 10.1 **Teenagers Arrested for Murder, Robbery, Rape, and Arson, 1988–1998**

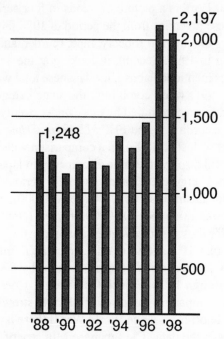

Source: French, October 12, 1999.

torically important role that full-time mothers had played in child rearing. These roles had been more clearly etched than in Western countries. For example, Japanese mothers are ofted called "education mamas" because of their reputation for intensely supervising their offspring in their educational pursuits. These trends continue into the new millennium (Foreign Press Center 1998).

Since World War II the number of women in the workplace grew from 13.76 million in 1950 to 27.01 million in 1995 (Bando 1996). In the post–World War II period, female employees were generally young unmarried women who worked until marriage or after marrying until they gave birth to a child. However, by 1995, 60 percent of all female workers were aged thirty-five and over, and married women were in a majority.

In the overall picture of juvenile delinquency in Japan and the United States there is no question that the problem of juvenile delinquency is much greater in the United States, but it is the rapid rise in juvenile offenses in Japan that has alarmed National Police Agency experts and scholars.

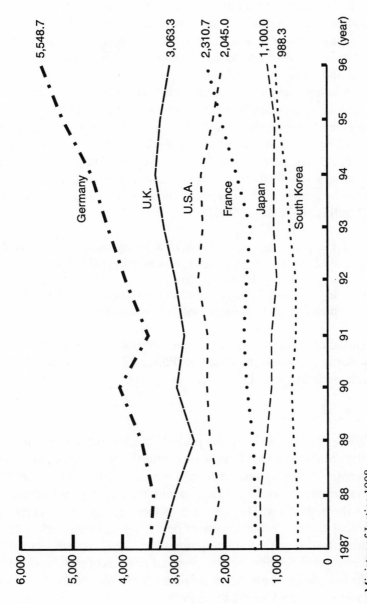

Figure 10.2 **Rate of Serious Juvenile Crimes Cleared (per 100,000) by Police for Germany, United Kingdom, United States, France, Japan, and South Korea, 1987–1996**

Source: Ministry of Justice 1998.

A frequently cited cause for the rise in juvenile delinquency in the United States, at least until recent years, has been a simple demographic one: the juvenile population was rising and there were thus more young people to get in trouble. This argument, however, does not help to explain the Japanese case. Japan's juvenile population has remained relatively stable in recent decades except for the increase mentioned as the "second wave" (mid-1960s).

Another phenomenon common to both countries, however, is one that many observers consider even more alarming than the overall increase in juvenile crime; that is, the growing number of very young offenders of junior high and even elementary school age.

The Japanese view the rise with concern. They fear that traditional values, especially those of cooperation and group action, are being threatened by growing individuality. A quote from the National State of Japan (1980) is applicable in 2000:

> The greater the degree to which a society respects individual freedom, the less the power of groups to control individual behavior. The root cause of present-day delinquency in Japan may well lie in the quickly weakening ability on the part of adults to exercise constructive influence on children through families, schools, and communities. (p. 23)

This alarm is echoed in newspaper editorials and by probation officers, juvenile counselors, and National Police Agency personnel charged with administering juvenile offender programs.

Bōsōzoku

While the source of various juvenile crimes may be similar—parental discord, weakening family ties, and the self-indulgence of young people—the symptoms vary. At least one manifestation, the *bōsōzoku* motorcycle gangs, has little to do with the creeping individuality feared by the authorities. The members of these groups are not seeking individual expression but a sense of belonging that their society has taught them to need, yet refused to grant them. The bikers are generally disaffected youth seeking the interpersonal rewards of membership in one of the few places where they can find it. As one biker put it, "When we ride together, we feel we are together."

Bōsōzoku members, as individuals, do not demonstrate a strong sense of self, but are far more assertive in groups, according to a number of psychologists and scholars. Keizo Hagihara, a psychologist who has worked extensively with juvenile offenders explained in an interview at a Juvenile Classification Home, that "Even in the case of motorcycle gang members, when you are observing them individually, they are quite obedient, passive, and polite. Surprisingly, they are occasionally university students. They don't have their own ego, but seek identity through gang behavior."

This analysis can be extended to most juvenile offenders. The typical juvenile offender, in Hagihara's opinion, has changed over the years and now reflects a dependent personality. Hagihara claimed that offenders have been indulged by their parents and are consequently immature for their age. Often, they have a sense of being "defeated," particularly by the educational system. The *bōsōzoku*, or "hot rodders," as one official called them, resemble American motorcycle gangs (*Newsweek* 1981):

> They dress in peg pants and black leather jackets; they are into German Army helmets and Nazi swastikas. They stomp all over traditional (Japanese) values of order, discipline, and decency. "Being bad is a badge of honor," says "Black Emperor" Masato Momose, sixteen. "It makes me feel strong, like I'm a man." (p. 58)

Incidents involving youthful violence are often featured in the Japanese press. The *Japan Times* (August 14, 1999) reported on increased acts of random violence inflicted on teachers in 1998. The article headlined, "Normal Kids Hitting Teachers," claimed that random acts of student violence in public schools soared to 29,685 incidents in 1998 and that represented a 25.7 percent increase from the previous year. Many of these were acknowledged as "relatively minor" and did not reach the criminal level. Nonetheless, educators were troubled by the trend, as many of the individuals were not among the ranks of those labeled "problem children." They seemed "normal" youngsters who engaged in impulsive acts. Most occurred in junior high school, where 23,005 cases erupted in 1998 (*Japan Times* August 14, 1999). So-called bullying cases fell somewhat in the late 1990s from 42,790 in 1997 to 36,396 in 1998. "Bullying" is defined by the National Police Agency (1999) as "the act of inflicting pain on a particular person or persons by repeating physical assaults or psychological pressure in the form of intimidation by words and acts, harrassment or snubbing." One Japanese educator, Haruhiko Tokuhisa (Shotaro 1998), stated that the decline was due to greater awareness on the part of both students and faculty. Still, bullying was more widespread than more serious violence, with 25.5 percent of all schools reporting cases of bullying (National Police Agency 1999).

The term for "bullying," *ijime*, first became a household word in Japan in 1985 (Foreign Press Center 1998). In February 1986 a Tokyo youngster took his life after suffering harassment at the hands of fellow junior high school students. The amount of bullying seemed to level off by the late 1980s, but the issue resurfaced in the public eye as a result of a string of suicides starting around 1994.

Another phenomenon of the 1990s, "dad hunting" (*oyaji-gari*), referred to a trend in which groups of young toughs beat up on adult males. One typical incident involved a man walking home at night from a commuter station when he was confronted by a group of five youths on a darkened street. In vulgar language they demanded money and when the man refused, they knocked him down and took his wallet. One criminologist, Fujimoto Tetsuya, claimed that there had been far fewer of these cases in the 1990s compared with the 1950s, but that the media labeling of these types of juvenile crime as *oyaji-gari* has helped to create a "trend" in the minds of citizens. Furthermore, criminologist Tetsuya has observed that while there had been just 2,500 of these cases a year in the 1990s and more than 10,000 similar assault cases in the 1950s, they had very different sources. In the mid-1950s approximately half of young offenders were from poor or dysfunctional families, whereas in the 1990s more than 70 percent of young offenders lived with both parents and in 90 percent of the cases the families could be called middle class (Shreiber 1997).

The Kobe Murders

Two of the more horrific incidents of juvenile crime that were widely reported took place in Kobe, Japan: A fourteen-year-old boy was convicted of killing eleven-year-old Jun Hase. The younger boy was beheaded and his head left at a school gate with a sinister note in his mouth. The youngster had also bludgeoned to death a ten-year-old girl. In 1999 the parents were forced to pay $952,000 in an out-of-court settlement involving the boy's death and a similar amount in 2000 involving the killing of the girl. The teenage killer was sent to a juvenile center for psychiatric treatment, but the case has caused an uproar in Japan and the Japanese Diet has been considering changes in the laws governing juveniles (personal communication from Ken Hattori, September 11, 1999). Presently, the juvenile law allows the government to turn cases of those over sixteen years of age who have committed serious offenses over to a prosecutor for processing like cases involving adults, but offenders who are younger than sixteen are shielded by the family court. Ken Hattori, the chief probation officer of Yokohama and a friend of the author's since 1980, sketched the government's position. First, the juvenile offender's name, address, family, and any other means of identification are currently protected under Japanese law, but the victim's privacy is not protected. The media often give wide exposure to the victim. The government wants to change the law to protect the victim's identity, but the process has been delayed because of some collateral issues that have intruded into the legislative process. Chief Probation Officer Hattori believes that it is important to pass the legislation for an additional reason—currently a public prosecutor does not participate in family court. Furthermore, the proposed changes in the juvenile law would allow the proceeding to be adjudicated by three judges instead of one as in the cases of serious offenses in adult court. As Hattori noted in an interview, "Currently the judge in juvenile court must play the role of prosecutor and judge." Hattori believes that requiring the judge to certify to the facts and also play the prosecutor's role is a serious inadequacy in the present system. He believes the Kobe murders have helped highlight these inadequacies in the juvenile system and that changes in the law are forthcoming.

A different perspective was offered by Junichi Seto in a Foreign Press Center report. The argument generated by Seto was that adult courts offer punitive sentences and that the large majority of juveniles need rehabilitation. Furthermore, according to Seto, they generally are able to receive effective treatment under the juvenile law. Finally, recidivism rates are low after young offenders are adjudicated by family courts, and grotesque crimes, such as those committed by the Kobe teenager, are rare. The Ministry of Justice policy is that three years or less is ordinarily required for rehabilitation of juveniles, but that in exceptional cases the term of custody may exceed this period (Foreign Press Center 1998).

These cases and similar ones of juveniles committing serious crimes have raised the same questions as those raised in the United States—when or under what circumstances should juveniles be treated as adults within the justice system? In the United States, many states have shifted gears and, under revised statutes, are presently more likely to try juveniles accused of serious crimes in adult courts than they were even a decade earlier. For example, the number of offenders under the age of eighteen serving time in adult correctional facilities has doubled between 1985 and 1997. In 1997, 7,400 juveniles aged seventeen or younger were committed to adult institutions in either juvenile or adult courts. Still juveniles represent just 5 percent of the 2 million inmates in adult facilities (Associated Press 2000). American critics have some of the same concerns as their Japanese counterparts. Because of high-profile school shootings, such as that at Columbine, the public has a distorted picture of the dangers posed by young people. This is the view of Eric Sterling, president of the Washington-based Criminal Justice Policy Foundation (Associated Press 2000). In the United States, there have been modest declines in juvenile offenses that have paralleled the overall decline in adult crime.

Violence against Teachers and Authority Figures

The report of the stabbing death of a junior high school English teacher in January 1998 by a thirteen-year-old was deeply shocking to Japanese. The youngster had not been considered a troublemaker, and the provocation had been merely a scolding for coming late to class. Apparently the student had built up resentment against his teacher and had been calling the teacher *mukatsuku* (someone who made him mad) to his classmates. Shortly after this incident, a fifteen-year-old boy in Tokyo attacked a police officer on patrol, stabbing the officer during a scuffle, and fled. Although wounded, the officer chased the assailant and caught him.

Some students in the past did hurl abuse at their teachers but did not go beyond that. They are now armed with bamboo swords and baseball bats. School violence involving teachers has become more widespread over the past twenty years. One school official declared, "It's increasingly vicious; they're using steel pipes and knives now." The fierce competition in schools and the pressure it creates have resulted in violence in the classroom (*kōnai bōryoku*) and at home (*kanai bōryoku*). Unable to deal with the oppressive atmosphere, young people lash out at those around them. Besides violence, there is escapism: drug offenses among school students, particularly the use of stimulants, are not uncommon despite strict drug laws (Shotaro 1998).

The Japanese are troubled by what they perceive to be the underlying causes of these problems. Most Japanese do not consider the pressures of their society to be the problem, but rather the increasing inability to force individuals to submit to those pressures. The blame for increasing juvenile delinquency is divided between family and school. A conversation with Professor Aiba, a former probation officer who has taught courses concerned with the problems of juvenile delinquency at a college in Hokkaido, helped to shed light on juvenile violence. She said that her own youngsters were thirteen and fourteen years of age and that they frequently informed her of what was happening in their school. Typically, she said, there would be a minor precipitating factor. The offending youngsters might take another child to a lavatory area and "hit and kick" him. She viewed it as a kind of scapegoating in response to the intense pressure of school and felt that educational competition had increased in the past ten years and that the hierarchical ranking of both secondary schools and universities was even more sharply perceived. This increased pressure, combined with a "low frustration tolerance" due to excessively indulgent parents, resulted in juvenile crime. When I asked her if problems with juveniles foreshadowed increases in adult crime, she strongly protested. "It's true that Japanese people love their children and indulge them, but we don't think they will be cold-blooded. The main fault is indulging them, not neglecting them." Professor Aiba noted that schools in the Sapporo area had very few counselors and school psychologists and that, unlike the situation in the United States, practically no psychotherapists (either psychiatrists or psychologists) were available to offer treatment. Like other scholars and criminal justice professionals with whom I talked, she was convinced that if teachers were stricter, violence in schools could be reduced.

My own visits to several junior high schools resulted in one particularly illuminating comment from an administrator in Sapporo: "The big problem psychologically is that they feel they have no purpose for the future. Some have no idea what they wish to do occupationally." There have been reports that in some schools, where disorder and lack of discipline are particularly acute, some teachers seek refuge in the teachers' room as soon as class is over. Their approach seems to be "see, hear, and speak no evil," and they do nothing to stem the violence.

Dropping Out and Truancy

More young people seem to be dropping out of school, and Howard French's observations and interviews with youngsters in several of

Tokyo's entertainment districts reveal their thinking. Two fifteen-year-olds, "sporting bleached blond hair, chalky makeup and pink highlights" were making a night of it in the Shibuya section of Tokyo. As both teenagers acknowledged, they were not just doing this on a weekend night, but virtually every night—they had both dropped out of school claiming boredom. Dropping out, drinking, drugs, and more teen sex have all increased in the 1990s in Japan's largest cities. Dropping out and higher truancy rates appear to be the product of weakening morality and lax discipline in at least some Japanese households. The law requires that students complete only junior high school. In 1999, among ten million students of junior and high school age, 120,000 dropped out, a 20 percent increase from 1997. Again, it seems that young people who are unable to compete academically do not see any career possibilities in Japanese society (French 2000).

Truancy rates can be viewed as symptomatic of youngsters' problems. The truancy rates among elementary and junior high school students jumped 21.1 percent in 1998 from 1997 to a new high of 127,694 students absent from school for more than thirty days. This resulted in an increase of 22,228 students compared with the previous year. It meant that 1 in 295 elementary school students, and 1 in 43 junior high school students were truant during 1998. Teachers claimed that the traditional idea that "everyone has to attend" has weakened and that fewer teachers are pressuring students to attend school if they are inclined to stay away. In a survey conducted by Japan's Ministry of Education, the following reasons were cited by students for not attending school (*Asahi Evening News* 1999).

> "emotional confusion," a vague sense of worry about going to school, 26.5%
> "lethargy," 21.5%
> "playing delinquency," 10.8%

Juvenile Counseling Centers

As a counseling psychologist who once worked with federal offenders in a pre-release counseling center in Brooklyn, New York, I was particularly interested in learning about Japan's juvenile counseling centers. I made arrangements to visit the headquarters of the Metropolitan Police Department (M.P.D.) counseling service in the Kasumigaseki section of Tokyo and four branches in Shinjuku, Setagaya, Sugamo, and Asakusa. There are seven centers operated by the M.P.D. Some prefectural and municipal police agencies in other parts of Japan also offer counseling services for juveniles, but the M.P.D.'s operation is the most elaborate. Among the counseling services offered by police, which often prove to be the first step in referring a problem, are the hot lines, or crisis lines, that have been established at police stations throughout Japan. Police juvenile consultation services take a number of different forms. These counseling and consultation services are staffed by specialists, who, the police agency claims have expertise in psychology and teaching. In addition to the telephone hot line called "Young Telephone Corner," which has existed for more than thirty years, the police installed a fax line in the late 1990s to make it easier for individuals to contact the juvenile consultants. In 1997, the police accepted 103,252 cases for consultation, up 143 (0.1 percent) from the previous year (National Police Agency 1998). Contacts from parents numbered 78,249 or 75.8 percent of the total. Typically, the youths themselves sought counseling for problems at school, while the parents' concerns were related to delinquent behavior.

Interviewing the director of the "Young Telephone Corner" in Tokyo, I was informed that the service started in 1972 with a great deal of publicity. It is the only one in Japan that operates twenty-four hours a day. Information and the center's telephone number are disseminated mainly through the schools, but it is frequently parents who call, and the problem most often has to do with a crime that has already been committed. The parents are generally upset and seeking advice. Calls from young people are generally not about suicide or other life-threatening situations, but more often involve family or school problems. The staff member I observed at Tokyo's "Young Telephone Corner" had at least seven years of street experience in working with juveniles. There were seven staff members, two of whom were civilians with degrees in psychology, while the others were out-of-uniform police officers. No doctoral level psychologists or psychiatrists were involved in this operation. Asked about trends in the calls, the director remarked that there had been a slight increase in calls related to family violence. As in most counseling services, referrals were made to other agencies when it was deemed appropriate, as, for example, in the case of medical or sexual problems.

A manual for staff members entitled "Techniques of Counseling" illustrated the approach that is used. At the outset the manual cautioned, "Counselors do not make a record of smoking or drinking violations or of two people riding on a motorcycle" (technically, all of the above are illegal for people under twenty). The manual went on to encourage an emotional involvement with the client as opposed to a "businesslike" approach, but it added that since counseling has a lot to do with the relationship between human beings, the counselor should be personally secure and offer an objective point of view, a statement that might appear in any American text on counseling.

Each juvenile counseling center served four or five police stations. Shinjuku personnel indicated that their main function was to go into the streets of the Shinjuku area (a particularly popular entertainment district) to offer guidance to youth. These activities would include observing youngsters who were loitering, frequenting "game centers," or drinking and smoking. Often, civilian volunteers join the plainclothes police on these patrols. The police assigned to this duty include both male and female officers.

I accompanied some of these staff members early one afternoon. They were quite easily able to identify youths in the above categories, and of course during school hours the presence of minors is particularly noticeable. By engaging him in informal conversation, the officers try to learn whether a youngster is a runaway. If they confirm that he is, they hold the youngster until he is picked up by a parent or guardian. In cases where there is a potential danger to the young person in releasing him to the parent, the staff member might recommend family counseling. As long as the minor has not broken the criminal code, the service must be offered strictly on a voluntary basis. As in the United States, the biggest problem confronting the counselor is that those persons—parents and children alike—who are in the greatest need of help are the ones least likely to seek it.

When family members do become involved in counseling, they usually come once or twice a week for six months. One family that came to the Shinjuku center had been coming for over six years. One counselor noted that most youngsters they encounter are not bona fide runaways, but are merely "hanging around."

A growing self-interest on the part of both parents and children was often pointed out by staff members as a problem. During a discussion with counselors at the Sugamo center, one of the staff made the following observation:

> Earlier, if a boy was taken into custody, other members of his group would come to inquire, but today, with greater individuality, the peer group is

less supportive. Superficially, there is group membership, as in dress, but young people don't form such close bonds.

Another, older counselor spoke of the erosion of parental authority:

The authority of the father is declining. Even if one of his children is acting badly, the father seems unable to act. The mother is more reluctant than she used to be to firmly direct and supervise the education of the child. She seems more willing to shift this responsibility. It's not always that she seeks more time for herself, but that she is somehow less conscious of her responsibilities. Most importantly, the parents are so concerned with the academic credentials of their children that they neglect to develop relationships with their offspring.

There were two counselors at the Sugamo center. The other ten personnel attached to this center were all police officers who went out in the streets offering guidance and giving "cautions." "Cautions" are not recorded and therefore have no legal ramifications. I sat in on a number of counseling sessions at the Asakusa center. The program was started in 1963, and the staff seemed proud of the fact that their's was the first branch to be established.

One case involved a thirteen-year-old junior high school student who refused to attend school. He frequently fought with his friends and visited "game centers," returning home late at night. Though he had six sisters living at home, his counselor was convinced that he received little attention from family members: "the mother could not recall ever having caressed the boy."

Observing the session between this boy and his counselor, I was impressed with the rapport she had established. Despite cultural differences, I readily sensed the warmth and empathy this woman exuded. After ten minutes of conversation, she left for a few moments and returned with some big chunks of clay. As they each started to shape the material, they talked. The boy mentioned that he would be attending a residential school in Shizuoka Prefecture, but he said that he would still like to come every day and visit her. When the boy mentioned that he had been thinking of saving his money, the counselor supported this idea, saying, "Yes, that is better than spending it at 'game centers.'" The boy's behavior toward the counselor resembled that of a child toward its mother, and I was struck by his apparent docility.

The counselor inquired, "How is your father? Does he hit you?" To which the child responded, "No." The counselor said, "Perhaps it is because you are behaving better." The session continued with a discussion of his relationship with his friends and his frequent school absences. At the end of the session, the boy asked whether he could visit her the next day, but the counselor scheduled him for the following week. The youngster had received counseling six times at ten-day intervals. The counselor had no professional training, but she did have thirty-two years of experience working with juveniles. She noted that the boy was typical of many that were counseled at the Asakusa center: "not relating well at home or at school, timid, and with underlying feelings of inferiority."

Another case involved several members of a family with severe financial problems. The couple had married when the wife was eighteen and worked in a cabaret. The husband made a cash payment for her release from employment. The marriage had started stably, but after a number of years the woman began to drink, and marital fights followed. She eventually attempted suicide, and a year after the attempt, she died in an apparently accidental fire that destroyed the family home. It was believed to have been started by her cigarette.

Of the children raised in this environment, the elder of the two daughters was sixteen and had graduated from junior high school, but was unemployed and often spent the night with her boyfriend. The other sister, at fourteen, seemed to be influenced by her elder sister and had recently stayed away from home for a week. The son, thirteen years of age, had joined a group of *bōsōzoku* and spent most of his time riding his motorcycle. At school, he was physically violent with his classmates and often yelled at his teachers, although he seemed responsive to the supervision of one of them.

While sexually promiscuous young women occasionally receive counseling at the juvenile counseling centers, prostitutes in Japan are usually over twenty years old and thus do not fall under the juvenile code.

Alcohol and Drug Abuse among Teens

Alcoholism has remained a hidden problem in Japan. The scale of the problem is still very much unknown, as the government and treatment agencies have never been involved in a wide-scale attack on the problem. Little publicity is given to the problem of alcoholism. Unlike treatment in the United States where there are numerous chapters of Alcoholics Anonymous and private hospitals and clinics that treat substance abuse, Japanese efforts remain low-profile and relatively few in number. Without using the term alcoholic, one Japanese writer stated that "the number of problem drinkers in Japan has reached an alarming 2.2 million." The author added that a national survey conducted by Kurihama National Hospital of 14,000 high school students found that 80 percent claimed to drink regularly. This survey, conducted in 1992, represented a tenfold increase compared to a decade earlier. A parallel survey of 3,000 junior high school students revealed that 11 percent of boys and 5 percent of girls drank more often than once a week (Meiko 1995).

In the early 1980s a Japanese professor friend at Yale University once remarked to the author that "everything gets done over drinks" in Japan. Indeed, it is commonplace for Japanese workers to go out and drink after work, often staggering home from an evening at a private club or restaurant. Because of the conformity pressure to drink with colleagues and business associates it is not uncommon for Japanese executives to remark that they have to "dry out" on weekends because so many evenings are taken up with imbibing.

For high school students drinking has always existed, but historically it was limited to parties or festivals. Now it is no longer an illicit pleasure confined to special occasions. Meiko (1995), an authority on the subject and the author of *Kittchin Dorinkazu* (Kitchen Drinkers), stated that binge drinking and "chug-a-lug" (an American invention popular fifty years ago) have become more commonplace among youth beginning in the 1990s. Officially the legal age for drinking is twenty, but the law does not require liquor stores or drinking establishments to check IDs before selling alcohol—the law was enacted more than seventy-seven years ago. After midnight, Japan's entertainment districts are often filled with both adults and teenagers too drunk to find their way to the nearest subway. Some are crouched over vomiting while others just lie down anywhere and hope to be rescued by a friend. According to Tokyo emergency services, 9,597 people were hospitalized with alcohol poisoning in 1993, a 19 percent increase from 1988 (Meiko 1995). April and December typically are the busiest months for ambulance drivers. April is the time of year when both universities and companies welcome new members, and alcohol plays a prominent part at these social affairs.

Alcohol is easily available to juveniles in Japan. The ever-present vending machine—more than 200,000 now dispense alcoholic beverages—provide easy access up until 11 P.M. to anyone who can deposit yen. At a World Health Organization meeting in Tokyo in 1991, Japan

Figure 10.3 **Juvenile Violators of the Stimulant Drugs Control Law and Those Cleared by Police, 1970–1997**

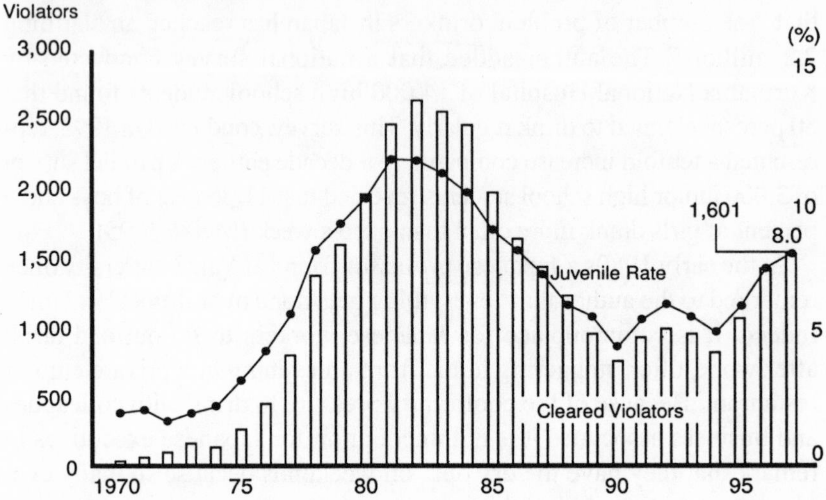

Violators

Source: Ministry of Justice 1998.

was the only country identified where alcohol could be obtained from vending machines (Meiko 1995).

Since the WHO conference various Japanese governmental tax and welfare agencies have recommended that vending machine sales of alcoholic beverages be terminated, but final agreement and actual removal had not taken place by 1999. While vending machines suggest easy access to alcohol to virtually anyone, fashionable television commercials target young people as well as the established adult audience.

Drug abuse among young people in Japan has a very different character from that in the United States. It is not only that there is far less substance abuse, but that the choice of illegal drugs is very different. Stimulant drug use, including paint thinner, is perhaps the most widely abused drug by juveniles. Figure 10.3 reveals the trend in the number of juvenile violators and those cleared by police over the period of 1970 through 1997 (Ministry of Justice 1998). As the data show, juvenile offenders in this category declined from a peak of 2,769 in 1982 to 832 in 1994. It then increased somewhat to 1,601 by 1997.

Shifting to the wider picture of drug abuse and arrests by police for adults as well as juveniles, Table 10.1 provides a picture for stimulant

Table 10.1

Police Arrests for Various Drug Law Violations, 1955–1997

	Stimulant drugs	Marijuana	Narcotic	Opium
1955	32,140	52	1,753	181
1960	476	10	1,987	315
1965	735	259	1,090	902
1970	1,682	733	245	230
1975	8,422	909	232	140
1980	20,200	1,433	158	264
1985	23,344	1,273	138	443
1990	15,267	1,620	240	111
1995	17,364	1,555	334	172
1996	19,666	1,306	275	141
1997	19,937	1,175	238	161

Source: Ministry of Justice 1998.

drugs, marijuana, opium, and other narcotics. Historically, members of gangs engaged in drug smuggling accounted for more than half of all arrests, but individual citizens, including many young people, have been involved in a larger share of the arrests in the past decade. For all individuals, including juveniles, stimulant drug offenses have shifted from over 20,000 in 1980 to a low of 15,267 by 1990 before climbing again to 19,937 by 1997 (Ministry of Justice 1998).

As in the United States, popular singers and entertainers are among the drug abusers. One popular singer, Noriyuku Makihara was arrested on suspicion of concealing stimulant drugs at his home (*Japan Times* August 31, 1999). A friend of the singer, Shuichi Okumara aged twenty-three, admitted that the pair had used amphetamines for a year. They were found in possession of one gram of stimulants when police raided Makihara's house on a tip. Makihara admitted that he had asked his friend to buy the drugs for 40,000 yen (U.S.$400) from a foreigner in the Shinjuku section of Tokyo.

While illicit drug use is greater in the United States overall than in Japan, drug use had declined substantially among American teenagers by 1998. Among youths aged 12 to 17, 9.9 percent used illegal drugs at least once a month in 1998, but this was down from 11.4 percent in 1997 according to the U.S. Department of Health and Human Services. For Americans of all ages, those using illegal drugs numbered 13.6 million or 6.2 percent of the population. This was down from 13.9 million in 1997 (*Japan Times* August 20, 1999).

One Japanese scholar who has profiled the changes in drug abuse among Japanese youth is Mizutani Osamu (1998), who is also a high school social studies teacher in Yokohama. Osamu stated that he spent seven years observing and talking with young drug users in the fashionable urban areas around Yokohama. He authored a 1998 book entitled *Drug Sedai* (*Drug Generation*). He claimed that there was a shift around the time of Japan's bubble economy or the late 1980s. Osamu stated that the new breed of drug abuser was not always a product of a troubled home (as in earlier periods), but rather reflected a general despair concerning the future in Japanese society. As with the earlier mentioned school dropouts and truants, youngsters have been drawn to trendy entertainment areas of cities and their all-night binges reflect an insecurity associated with future employment prospects. The author identified the weakening of the lifetime employment system— a "disposable workplace"—as undermining the future prospects of youth. Many that he interviewed were loquacious and sensitive, but also lonely and disconnected from mainstream Japanese society. Most of the increase in drug use was in the form of stimulants and marijuana. Osamu tracked the current wave of drug abuse to around 1994— the year in which pocket pagers and cell phones became popular with teenagers. A booming trade in bogus phone cards erupted at around this time in Japan and the culprits were both *boryokudan* members as well as illegal immigrants. In addition to the phony phone cards, organized crime also marketed "speed" and amphetamines. By 1996, according to the author, in order to pay for illegal drugs, young girls began to work for massage parlors and other businesses related to pornography and sex. On the other hand, boys began hustling drugs at schools to pay for their drug habits. A bit later, in 1997, there was another phase in which pushers moved from high schools to junior high schools. In conclusion, the author returned to focus on Japanese family life in which he viewed parents as neglecting their duty in nurturing their offspring. Too often, both parents are employed and were not available to both communicate and discipline their children (Osamu 1998).

The Family Court

Family courts were established in 1949 and their branches exist in the same locations as district courts throughout Japan. Also local offices of the family courts are located at the sites of seventy-seven summary courts. The family court system includes within its organization around 200 judges and 150 assistant judges. Assistant judges are newly appointed from the ranks of those who first passed the national bar examination and then completed two years at the Legal Research and Training Institute. They are usually among the top graduates. They are allowed to sit only with a three-judge court. Predictably, these courts are the courts of first instance in all matters involving disputes and conflicts concerning families, juveniles, and domestic affairs that have legal significance. They employ two vehicles: determination and conciliation (Supreme Court of Japan 1998).

Determination proceedings, for example, deal with declarations of incompetence, permission to adopt a minor, appointment and removal of a guardian, probate of wills, matters relating to support, and partition of estates. A variety of matters involving domestic affairs such as divorce, separation, mediation, and partition of an estate also come under the family court's umbrella.

Of particular interest in this chapter is the role of the family court as it relates to juveniles. All criminal matters involving juveniles (aged twenty and under) must first come before a family court. This court, like its counterpart in other countries can take a variety of actions. After an investigation and hearing, usually conducted by a probation officer, the court may take educational or corrective measures, but most are directed toward the goal of rehabilitation. As mentioned earlier, in very serious cases, the family court may turn a juvenile over to a prosecutor for processing in a traditional criminal proceeding for adults. In this latter instance this is only done if the individual is sixteen years old or older and the offense is punishable by imprisonment or death.

Family court proceedings are currently handled by a single judge, but one of the proposed reforms (mentioned earlier) would allow panels of three judges to adjudicate very serious cases.

Conclusion

The growth of urbanization brought in its wake major changes in social, economic, and family institutions. The current wave of juvenile delinquency appears to be linked to the spread of affluence and its consequences: educational pressures, lack of parental nurturing, the growth of individualism, and the erosion of traditional family values. Any number of scholars and police personnel have pointed to the lack of purpose and the "self-indulgence" of Japanese youth. But Japanese society has not, as yet, developed a tolerance for self-indulgence, and those who cannot "fit in" experience despair, the symptoms of which have been identified in this chapter. One major symptom of underlying depression and low self-esteem is drug abuse.

11

The Police and the Community

Family Counseling

Family counseling, both formal and informal, is offered to citizens by the police. This counseling is closely linked to crime prevention, both in the theory and practice of Japanese policing. United States police agencies have not typically organized crime-prevention services into separate units, reflecting the fact that crime prevention by police has not been a well-developed concept in the United States, but starting with the emergence of "community policing" in the 1990s, it is often incorporated in that approach by many departments. In Japan, officers engaged in crime prevention perform a variety of duties including family counseling, which I would like to consider first by virtue of its differences from what are normally thought of as crime-prevention activities.

In addition to police officers who offer counseling, each of Tokyo's ninety-five police stations has a "family affairs" staff person assigned to it. The "family affairs" officers and crime-prevention personnel usually counsel citizens who bring their problems to the police station. However, a considerable amount of informal counseling is also done by patrol officers at the *kōban*.

Before discussing the specific forms of counseling offered by police, a word seems in order about how the Japanese generally view counseling and its more sophisticated cousin, psychotherapy. According to Hattori (personal communication 1999), over the past twenty years commencing around 1980, psychiatrists and psychologists have begun to

197

open private clinics for the treatment of individuals suffering from emotional problems. Although small in total numbers they are gradually expanding. Earlier, the stigma of mental illness, as in the United States, prevented individuals from seeking therapeutic help from practitioners in clinics or in private practice. Only in very severe cases did a family member bring a relative to a psychiatric hospital.

However, individuals in low-profile positions, such as workers at "nonestablished" companies, have been more willing in recent years to seek out treatment than they would have been earlier. According to Hattori, a manager at a high-profile company such as Toyota might be reluctant to seek help because, if discovered, he might be shifted to a less important position within the corporation.

In 1980 when the author interviewed Dr. Haruo Akimoto, director of Tokyo Metropolitan Matsuzawa (Psychiatric) Hospital, he reported that there were only twenty or thirty psychiatrists in private practice in Tokyo and not more than one hundred existed in all of Japan. Furthermore, conversations with other Japanese psychologists brought out the fact that some of those psychiatrists were probably not psychotherapists (offering verbal, or "talk," therapy) but were medication-oriented practitioners—a view confirmed by Dr. Shizuo Machizawain in 1999.

In a newspaper interview in Japan, Machizawain, a psychiatrist, stated that treatment of those suffering from depression and other mental illnesses was primarily in the form of medication. Dr. Machizawain had been hired by NEC and other major Japanese firms to consult with distraught employees—many suffering as a result of job loss or underemployment brought on by Japan's lengthy recession in the 1990s. In general, he noted that psychiatric care in Japan was limited to administering antidepressant medication and advising patients to try to take time off—the latter advice rarely taken because of the pressures of rising unemployment (Strom 1999).

Reminiscent of the United States perhaps thirty years ago, some practitioners are licensed and some are not. Also, perhaps parallel to the United States in an earlier time, social workers have yet to become established as private practitioners in the mental health field. Today, in the United States, they outnumber psychologists and psychiatrists as licensed practitioners. Historically it is evident that in Japan there has been no history of seeking relief from emotional problems through seeing practitioners such as psychiatrists, psychologists, and social workers.

No police officer, either in the United States or in Japan, would pretend to offer formal psychotherapy, but, as practiced in the United States, counseling on family or personal problems clearly bears a relationship to the more sophisticated treatment offered by professional psychiatrists.

Trained as a professional counseling psychologist, I was particularly interested in the counseling offered by police. When I asked about the training of officers who offered counseling, including those at the Family Counseling Office, I invariably received a puzzled look. Similar to the situation with the professions of psychiatry, psychology, and social work, personal counseling does not have a tradition such as guidance and counseling in the United States. For example most probation officers in Japan are not thought of as counselors nor trained as such, but rather they think of themselves as administrators. While American probation officers are often overwhelmed with vast numbers of offender clients, thereby effectively preventing them from counseling their clients, they counsel when time permits and their original role incorporated the counseling function. Counselor education programs do not exist in Japan, and therefore it is not surprising that the police officers who engage in counseling are not formally trained. While counseling by these individuals may result in a therapeutic benefit, their approach has been designed more often merely to mediate a dispute.

As in the United States, police are asked to intervene in domestic or family disputes. Despite the availability and convenience of an emergency telephone line, Japanese family members are still reluctant to call for police assistance when trouble breaks out, although officers report a gradual change in this attitude. One patrol sergeant at a Seijo *kōban* commented on the incidence of "family fight" calls in his jurisdiction, an upper-middle-class neighborhood:

> Family fights for this *kōban* area average one every two weeks, and far more often than not (perhaps ten to one) we deal with this problem at people's homes, as opposed to their coming in. Before we had the emergency telephone system—perhaps forty years ago—people were reporting fights far less frequently than now. Also, a feeling of shame was a bigger factor forty years ago. People were more reluctant to call in the police. Values have changed, and there is greater concern for one's rights.

In addition to mediating in family fights, Japanese police counsel citizens on financial, civil, and neighborhood matters more than American police do. While professional counseling as indicated above is fairly rare, there is in its place a long history of the police officer working as a helpful mediator in disputes.

As the chief of the Motofuji police station in Tokyo observed, "Husband–wife problems are sometimes resolved by the third party who had arranged the marriage, and when people do come to the police, they do not usually come for advice on matters of divorce or sex." Two examples he mentioned as typical of problems brought to the station for police assistance: (a) a mother came in worried about her daughter. They had moved to a new residence, and disputes with the neighbors had erupted in the building. This seemed related to the fact that they had received a very cool reception from the neighbors; (b) a conflict over payment of rent between a landlord and tenants flared. Tenants refused to pay the recently raised monthly rent, and the owner responded by shutting off the water. All parties were called and the police helped to settle the matter. The chief added that most people are still reluctant to bring such problems to court and that this is also a reflection of the reluctance to litigate on the part of the Japanese people.

Police policymakers view the handling of family problems as possibly preventing more serious acts and even criminal offenses, and strongly encourage officers to be helpful to citizens with these concerns. The existence of juvenile counseling centers, along with the Tokyo Family Counseling Office of the M.P.D., offers concrete evidence of their concern for this problem. The *White Paper on Police* of 1998 (National Police Agency of Japan) stressed the importance of police "listening to troubles attentively." This is in marked contrast with the policies and attitudes of many United States police departments.

Having personally tried to promote "crisis intervention" training for police in both the United States and Canada for more than thirty years as a psychologist and criminal justice educator, I have had a great deal of exposure to police attitudes on this subject. Many individual police officers as well as administrators and policymakers regard family disputes as non–police work that they are required to do because social agencies cannot handle it or are not available twenty-four hours a day. Despite the fact that many police officers have lost their lives over the years while intervening in domestic disputes (Parker, Meier, and Monahan 1989), American police departments still provide little training to handle these potentially explosive situations. The comments of individual American officers range from "I answer the call and get the hell out as fast as I can" to "I can't spend time on these calls to help people because my sergeant is on the radio telling me to get back on the street." Whether it is a reflection of insecurity about this ability to handle people who are emotionally upset or because departmental priorities place other problem areas ahead of domestic crisis intervention, the result is the same—American police are very reluctant participants in these encounters. Of course, the physical hazard cannot be discounted in explaining this reluctance.

The Japanese *White Paper on Police* (National Police Agency of Japan 1998) provided data on the types of problems and overall incidence of counseling for the year 1997. Overall, during 1997, police counseled citizens a total of 215,342 times, up 6,625 (3.2%) from 1996. The various kinds of problems handled and the way these cases were disposed of is revealed in Table 11.1

The coordinating agency for the counseling work of the police is the Tokyo Family Counseling Office, which is next door to the headquarters of the Juvenile Counseling Center in the Kasumigaseki section of Tokyo. The administrator with whom I spoke proudly announced that the office had been in existence since 1920 and had counseled over 3 million people. She told me that in many of the ninety-five police stations under the M.P.D.'s jurisdiction, special rooms were set aside to provide space for counseling.

Suicide

During late 1999 I was returning to the International Christian University campus in Mitaka, Japan, when my Chuo line express train abruptly stopped around 9 P.M, at a station midway to my destination. The train remained at the platform with the doors open for more than one and a half hours. I had never experienced such a major disruption in train travel, as the large majority of Japanese trains are highly efficient and run precisely on time. After listening to periodic announcements over the intercom, I finally asked a fellow passenger for an explanation. He just shrugged and said, "probably an accident." Later that evening an academic colleague back on campus suggested it might have been a suicide. Unknown to me at the time, the Chuo line had been nicknamed the "Chuo-cide" line because its tracks are a favorite site for suicides due to the high speed of this Japan Railways East train. The company that operates the line charges families a fee depending on how badly the rail traffic is delayed. Shockingly, the rise in this line's number of suicides reflected the escalating number of suicides in Japan over the past few years.

Table 11.1

Types of Problems and Disposition of Counseling Cases by Police, 1997

Types of problems/classification	Number of requests	Percent
Total number	215,342	100.0
Family problems		
Personal affairs	35,109	16.3
Marriage, divorce	4,438	2.0
Poverty	7,399	3.4
Others	14,002	6.5
Civil affairs		
Money lending and borrowing	11,622	5.4
Land and house	6,045	2.8
Transaction of articles	2,620	1.2
Others	14,610	6.8
Crime prevention		
Prevention of danger and crime	39,747	18.5
Others	40,184	18.7
Others	39,566	18.4

Disposition	Total number	Settled	Advice, guidance given	Referred to other police sections	Referred to other agencies	Suspended	Continued
Number of cases	215,342	70,912	104,062	5,025	8,486	19,974	6,883
Percent of cases	100.0	32.9	48.3	2.3	4.0	9.3	3.2

Source: National Police Agency 1999.

In the fiscal year that ended March 31, 1999, thirty-three individuals were killed on this rail line compared with twenty-five in 1998 (Strom 1999). Officially, the JR East line calls the deaths accidents because it claims it cannot distinguish between a suicide and a person (perhaps drunk) who mistakenly wandered onto the tracks. But for most observers there is little question as to the classification.

In 1998, approximately ninety people a day committed suicide in Japan, a 34.7 percent rise over the previous year, according to statistics provided by the National Police Agency. Not only the stress from the economic recession, but the shame and fear of layoffs appear to have played a powerful role. Often depression served as a mediating event.

A recently published book by Satoshi Kamata, entitled *Kazoku-ga Jisatsu-ni Oikomare ru Toki* (When a Family Member Is Driven to Suicide), makes the case that the ethics of Japanese workers, which drove them to achieve economic glory in the postwar world, also have been a strong factor in the narrowly focused workaholic behavior that has resulted in mental illness, depression, and suicide in recent times (Fukae, 1999). The author, a prominent journalist, profiled a number of cases that supported this view and seemed to fit a pattern as a subset in the 31,734 recorded suicides in 1998. These numbers included 22,338 males and 9,396 females. In the case of men, the number of suicides had jumped by more than 8,000 from the previous year (Fukae 1999).

The work cited the case of a fifty-four-year-old man named Hirano who had owned a waterworks firm and who had burned himself to death to protest the demands made by a client firm that had required him to undertake projects without pay. In another case, a triple suicide by Masaaki Kobayashi, aged fifty-one, Masaru Sudo, forty-nine, and Yoshimi Shoji, forty-nine—all presidents of auto-appliance subcontracting firms—reflected a suicide pact designed to repay their firms' debts through death benefits (Fukae 1999).

Japan scholars and psychologists have observed that suicide carries little of the stigma that is tied to it in Western nations. In art, history, and literature suicides are often presented as noble or honorable forms of protest or as matters of conscience (Strom 1999). While the suicide rate in the United States was 11.1 per 100,000 population in 1997, it was 19.3 for the same year in Japan, but, as mentioned above, it jumped significantly in Japan starting in 1998. Overall rates have gone up every year since 1990, except for one year, since the economic bubble burst. Figure 11.1 shows the pattern of suicides for men and women in Japan

Figure 11.1 **Suicide Rates among Japanese Citizens, 1950–1998**

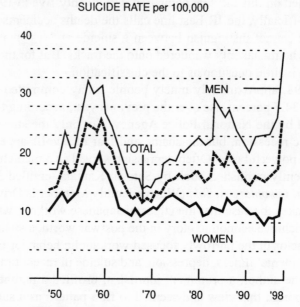

SUICIDE RATE per 100,000

Source: National Police Agency 1999.

for the past fifty years or so. While the line for men spiked in 1998, it showed only a modest increase for women during the same year, and in general the rate for women has shown a slight decline since 1975.

Some of the statistical trends that help to confirm the theory that the economic woes and recession have taken their toll is that suicide rates sharply escalated by 44.6 percent among men aged forty to fifty-nine during this recessionary period. Surprisingly though, younger men in their twenties have not been immune to increases in suicide; their rate jumped by 40 percent during 1998. Historically, young adult males become *shalin* (literally members of society) as they enter the workforce. As Yukiko Nishihara, who has run a suicide prevention line for more than twenty years, noted, "young people are feeling very hopeless about the future" (Strom 1999). She added, "Even if you graduate from one of the best universities, you cannot always find a job."

Finally, and perhaps most startling of all, the largest increase—53.1 percent—has occurred among youngsters aged from ten to nineteen. Not surprisingly, these children of harried and stressed out adults are also experiencing the anguish associated with the high demands and

Table 11.2

Suicide by Age, 1997

Age group	Total		Male	Female
19 and under	469	(1.7)	331	138
20–29	2,534	(13.3)	1,730	804
30–39	2,767	(17.2)	1,971	796
40–49	4,200	(22.1)	3,148	1,052
50–59	5,422	(31.6)	3,969	1,453
60 and over	8,747	(31.9)	5,046	3,701
Unknown	252	(–)	221	32
Total	24,391	(19.3)	16,416	7,975

Source: National Police Agency 1998.
Note: Numbers in parentheses are per 100,000 population.

economic dislocation currently permeating Japanese society. The data
for 1997, as displayed in Table 11.2 show that those aged over fifty have
the highest rates of suicide, but as noted above, the numbers spiked
higher starting in 1998. Table 11.3 gives a picture of the causes and
motives of suicides in 1997, but once again this picture has changed
somewhat since 1998 when suicide rates ratcheted up.

Finally, Table 11.4 (p. 207) shows the leading causes of death in
Japan as ranked by the Ministry of Health and Welfare, and suicide is
sixth on the overall list (*Japan Almanac* 2000). A brief comparative
view of the American situation reveals a very different picture. For
example, due to the ready availability of guns, and despite declines in
homicides in the United States in the 1990s, more individuals committed suicide with guns compared to homicides. In 1997, guns were
used in 17,566 suicides while they were used in 13,522 homicides. A
prominent American psychiatrist, Dr. Kay Redfield Jamison, concluded
that from 90 to 95 percent of suicides were people who had a diagnos-
able psychiatric illness and that the number of young people who committed suicide had tripled since the 1950s. Also, and consistent with
the omnipresent availability of guns in the United States, more than
60 percent of those who commit suicide do so with guns. Furthermore,
Jamison's research showed that having a gun in the home increased
the risk of suicide. This picture is consistent with reports I have received over the years from police officer students who have claimed
that easy access to a gun has contributed to the high rate of suicide
among urban police officers. Another report on this topic by Dr. Garen

Table 11.3

Causes and Motives for Suicides, 1997

Classification	Total	Family problems	Illnesses, etc.	Household finances	Business problems	Problems between the sexes	School problems	Mental disorders, alcohol dependency, etc.	Others	Unknown
Total (persons)	24,391	2,104	9,058	3,556	1,230	631	203	4,601	1,395	1,613
Percent	100.0	8.6	37.1	14.6	5.0	2.6	0.8	18.9	5.7	6.6
Male	16,416	1,252	5,465	3,203	1,154	395	165	2,519	963	1,300
Percent	100.0	7.6	33.3	19.5	7.0	2.4	1.0	15.3	5.9	8.0
Female	7,975	852	3,593	353	76	236	38	2,082	432	313
Percent	100.0	10.7	45.1	4.4	1.0	3.0	0.5	26.1	5.4	3.9

Source: National Police Agency 1998.

Table 11.4

Leading Causes of Death in Japan, 1998

| | Number of deaths | | |
Cause of death	Total	Male	Female
Cancer	283,827	172,255	111,572
Heart disease	142,998	71,072	71,926
Cerebrovascular disease	137,767	65,505	72,262
Pneumonia	79,894	42,634	37,260
Accidents	38,897	24,971	13,926
Suicide	31,734	22,338	9,396
Renal insufficiency	16,602	7,715	8,887
Liver disease	16,094	11,147	4,947

Source: Ministry of Health and Welfare 1999.

Wintemute supports this view by noting that the risk of suicide has remained twice as high for handgun purchasers in California compared to the general population (Butterfield October 17, 1999). In summary owning a gun, or having immediate access to a gun, is correlated with a higher incidence of suicide.

**Living on the Edge—Day Workers, the Homeless,
Prostitutes, and Social Welfare Recipients**

Not much has been written about the marginalized people in Japan—*burakumin* (social outcasts), day laborers, the homeless, and so forth, but Stevens's (1997) work entitled, *On the Margins of Japanese Society* provides an insightful portrait of those people that are shunned and "invisible" to average Japanese. *Yoseba*, or day laborers, are described as a "floating reserve" in that they are a backup force of workers that have to struggle to find work every day. They suffer obvious insecurity and are often picked up in the morning and herded like cattle on to vans or buses to be transported to areas where they are employed for the day. Some are *burakumin* who have been treated as outcasts for more than a century. Certain areas in Japan's big cities have sectors in which day laborers and the homeless can be found. Sanya in Tokyo and Kamagasaki in Osaka are typical. In Stevens's anthropological study of *kotobuki*, an "inner-city" district of Yokohama, the author described the plight of marginalized individuals in contemporary Japanese society:

> In Japanese society social marginality in this case is defined as belonging
> to an ambiguous group. Ambiguity is defined as dangerous and socially
> undesirable . . . marginal categories are created to label and control the dis-
> order. . . . A steady job, stable family life and Japanese citizenship are con-
> sidered necessary for establishing a mainstream identity in Japanese
> society. (1997, p.16)

The author goes on to observe that day laborers and the homeless do
not fit into socially acceptable categories, or belong to groups, or have
affiliations—they are considered loners and outsiders by the rest of society. Also included among the marginalized are gangsters, prostitutes,
traveling gamblers, the disabled, and Japanese–Koreans who operate various businesses. Some of the handicapped, those on welfare, and the impoverished elderly are also thrust into this amorphous limbo. The socially
marginalized have trouble networking because they are cut off from
economic resources (Stevens 1997). Most are uneducated, of course, in
a society that places a very high premium on academic achievement.
Chronic illness, alcoholism, and drug addiction help to fuel the situation
that forces individuals into poverty and isolation. In this context *yakuza*
(gangsters) sometimes act as labor brokers, demanding protection money
from *pachinko* (pinball) businesses, and operate other illegal business
such as loan-sharking.

Much as in the field of probation and parole, which I studied in Japan
in the early 1980s, volunteers are often in the front lines of efforts to
address social problems. In the social welfare system in Japan this is
also characteristic. The government plays a role, but volunteers play the
most important role in the counseling and support of social welfare recipients. As Stevens noted, in contrast to the mobile lifestyle of *yoseba*
(the marginalized) the successful welfare recipient must meet some basic social rules—conformity to a "stable residence, moderate lifestyle,
dependency on others and forfeiture of privacy in exchange for mutual
support." In general, because it is so humiliating, Japanese resort to social welfare only as a last resort.

Southeast Asian women—often from Thailand and the Philippines—
have become part of the Japanese sex industry, and organized crime is
often involved in this seedy business. Police acknowledge that prostitution exists but appear to close their eyes to it. Only in recent years was it
declared illegal, and officers complain that the cover of the Turkish baths,
the principal outlet, makes it difficult to apprehend violators. In one
conversation, an officer confided that he knew some single officers who

enjoyed visiting Turkish baths during the off-duty hours. Data on prostitution, gathered by social scientists at the National Research Institute of Police Science indicated that the average age of Turkish bath prostitutes is twenty to twenty-two years, while streetwalkers tended to be a little older. Furthermore, the former group have better incomes and appear to exercise more choice in deciding to engage in prostitution (i.e., they seemed attracted to it rather than forced into it by economic hardship). For example, Turkish bath prostitutes gave the following reasons: "to get much more money for their future life" and "to get a high standard of living," but streetwalkers cited "poverty," "broken home," and "running away from home." The researchers concluded that Turkish bath prostitutes were drawn to this way of life for the income, while social conditions appeared to be a factor in encouraging streetwalkers to take up prostitution.

Unlike some areas of the world where AIDS has reached epidemic proportions, there has been a relatively small number of cases in Japan. According to the *Japan Almanac* (2000), the first case of AIDS in Japan was confirmed in 1985, and by the end of 1998, the total number of cases had reached 1,917. Of those, 631 cases were believed to have resulted when the parties had been infected by blood clotting agents contaminated with the AIDS virus.

Crime Prevention

Various features of crime prevention have been described elsewhere, but the topic deserves to be examined in terms of the way services are integrated and how crime prevention operates within the Japanese police system. While traditionally neighborhood associations were active in crime-prevention work, the multilayered crime-prevention associations of contemporary Japan are more sophisticated and highly organized. While Japanese police agencies make major contributions to crime prevention, much of the work is done by volunteers at the community level. Walter Ames's point was well taken that crime prevention should be considered as just one of the ways in which Japanese have historically engaged in voluntary community service. He stated:

> Volunteerism covers a wide range of areas, from voluntary welfare-case workers (*minseiin*) and voluntary probation officers (*hogoshi*) to the myriad of citizen support groups that surround the police. Similar types

of persons are engaged in all the various volunteer activities, and often
the same persons hold several positions simultaneously in different voluntary service organizations. They are mostly elderly men, often over
sixty, and usually they either are self-employed shop or small-factory
owners or are retired. Unlike office or factory workers, they have free
time to spare for engaging in community service activities. (Ames 1981)

Senior Superintendent Mitsuo Uehara, of the National Police Agency,
was helpful to me not only in providing a thorough briefing on crime-
prevention activities in Japan, but in arranging numerous visits with
crime-prevention associations (*bohan kyokai*) and the counseling services discussed earlier in this chapter.

As the public relations police literature has observed (e.g., *Police of Japan*), "urbanization has given rise to many crime-inducing factors: namely
a weakening sense of community among residents, greater anonymity, and
more 'blind spots' in the urban space" (National Police Agency of Japan
1998). The police agencies have had various programs and associations in
place for many years in their effort to mobilize and encourage citizens to
assist in crime prevention. Some endeavors are national in scope while
others are local. They include the familiar block-watch patrols, sponsorship
of crime-prevention meetings, and the distribution of literature.

Nationwide, approximately 440,000 households are designated as
crime-prevention liaison stations. They serve the purpose of generating
reports of incidents and accidents, sponsoring discussions on relevant
issues, and delivering publications. The police sponsor a "National Community Safety Campaign" annually—before 1995 it was called the "National Crime Prevention Campaign," but its purpose was broadened to
include activities designed to prevent accidents and disasters. By December 1996, the number of security companies had increased to a total
of 8,669, and included 377,140 security guards. Many security personnel are retired police officers. A similar practice that occurs in the United
States. Under the Private Security Business Law in Japan, police officials provide security firms with advice and consultation.

Not surprisingly, local associations in smaller, traditional, middle-
class neighborhoods are stronger than those in larger communities with
more transient populations. Crime-prevention authorities are mindful
of the role that housewives can play and actively encourage their participation. In contrast, some sections of Tokyo or other large cities, such
as Osaka, have neighborhoods with weak social networks. Areas where
associations are weak are, as previously mentioned, those with a rapid

turnover, usually of young couples who live in the increasing number of high-rise apartment complexes. Wealthier Japanese neighborhoods, such as those in the Seijo police station area, also have weaker neighborhood crime-prevention networks. A visit to that neighborhood and conversations with several home owners reminded me of life in an affluent suburban American community, especially with respect to the loose neighborhood ties.

The work with local associations is not the only concern of national crime-prevention policymakers. They are also wisely interested in city planning and the architectural design of large-scale condominiums and skyscrapers. They express concern about the increasing number of hallways and "dead-end" areas in these complexes that do little to discourage crime. In planning future malls, underground parking facilities, parks, and other projects, policymakers are taking into account surveys of citizen concerns.

Visits to local crime-prevention associations yielded interesting information on activities at the grassroots level. In the Tokyo Metropolitan Police Department, individual specialists at each of the ninety-five stations receive direction and guidance on policy matters from the central office. Increased funding can be diverted into certain areas if the need arises.

Local crime-prevention association members I met at the Manseibashi police station in Tokyo said that breaking and entering and the defacing of walls were the two major concerns. The members were older businessmen who lived in this busy commercial neighborhood. I asked about their activities to combat these problems. Mr. Tsuchida, their president, offered a brief history of the focus of their work over the years.

> Working with this group for over forty years, I've seen changes in the pattern of activities. We were stimulated to establish this association right after the Second World War, when crime was high. Mainly, we patrolled the streets. Later, in the early 1970s, there were many leftists and students causing problems and we again emphasized walking patrols. Usually, we offer crime-prevention information (e.g., on locks) to residents, shop owners, and others—there are 1,200 buildings to cover, including many shops and businesses, within this jurisdiction. As members, we sometimes help police officers out on "big" cases by using community contacts. Sometimes we bring in snacks to officers required to work long hours on a particular case. Also, I should mention that we try to encourage citizens to report crimes immediately.

Another member of the association remarked that professional criminals were usually the culprits in the most recent rash of breaking and entering.

Members of a local crime-prevention association in Kobe, in the central part of Japan, voiced concern about the activities of gangsters. This older port city has traditionally been a center of gangster activity, with the *Yamaguchi* group being the most infamous. The spokesman and most of his fellow members were older men, averaging perhaps sixty years of age. A perspective was offered by the Shinto priest who was their leader.

> Having lived here for fifty years, I've experienced Kobe before, during, and after the war. Many citizens come to my shrine, and they tell me what's on their minds. Organized crime is concentrated here, with many gangs operating in the heart of Kobe. They concentrate mainly on gambling, loan sharking, prostitution, and drugs. It is difficult to dislodge them because they are clever and have legitimate businesses as a front.

Association members also described their general activities. They emphasized that their main function was to provide police with information on all forms of criminal activity in their area—drug-selling, suspicious individuals, fights, and so forth. The Shinto priest echoed the earlier statement of a police officer when he said, "We want to be the eyes and ears of the community."

There are many bars, cabarets, and nightclubs sandwiched together in this highly commercialized center of Kobe. "Game centers," amusement parlors, and pornography vending machines attract junior high school children. As in the juvenile counseling centers in Tokyo, police officers and vounteers collaborate to offer "guidance" to juveniles. One man, who was retired, coordinated the work of 100 adult volunteers who sought out youngsters frequenting these establishments. "We approach them rather sensitively and softly, informing them that this is not the place for them, and we try to persuade them to avoid future visits. We don't wish to embarrass them publicly, but if these young people repeatedly return to these places, the police will be advised. This might result in a plainclothes officer bringing a youngster to a *kōban*, where a card will be filled out and his parents contacted."

Crime prevention was a major topic of conversation with the chief of the Motofuji police station during my field research in Tokyo. He noted that in addition to offering crime-prevention information to citizens and counseling to families, crime-prevention officers take custody of lost children, the emotionally disturbed, and the senile. In the case of an emotionally disturbed person, the station might receive an emergency call and, after taking the person into protective custody for twenty-four hours, refer the person to a psychiatric hospital. Though these procedures are effective in removing individuals from an environment in which they might harm themselves or others, there was some concern among legal scholars about the broad authority of police to detain and hospitalize mentally ill persons.

"Trying to assist individual citizens in ways that actually prevent crime and working extensively with crime-prevention associations are the two major objectives of the crime-prevention section," the Motofuji chief observed. He outlined some of his future concerns:

> It's true that the transience of people in neighborhoods, along with the growth of individuality as an attitude toward life, has decreased the willingness of people to report crimes, but it means we must try to build even stronger cooperation among citizens. It means an even greater expansion of the service aspects of policing. An example of how this pays off is the case of a taxi driver who helped solve a murder. The taxi driver came forth with some critical information, and it was accidentally discovered that he had previously been   helped by a police officer. The driver claimed that he had been so impressed by the assistance offered to him that it had contributed to his desire to help police on this homicide case.

In the 1990s the National Police Agency changed terminology, and activities that had often been described as crime prevention have been relabeled "community safety," although the basic functions remain the same. Often the work of officers in this field is very mundane—public relations campaigns where citizens are urged to "take the key and lock the doors" whenever leaving vehicles. Concerning the theft of motorcycles and bicycles, police are encouraging the locking of wheels and the use of handlebar locks to prevent thefts (National Police Agency 1998). In 1998 the police were encouraging citizens to employ alarm buzzers as a measure to prevent purse snatching.

Private Security

Over the past thirty years there has been significant growth in the private security field. The first company was established in 1962. The work of these firms includes security at nuclear power plants, the transportation of large amounts of money, and guard work at construction sites. It also includes safeguarding private residences, security at airports, and controlling crowds at event sites. Retired police officers often find employment in this field.

Lately mechanized and electronic security has played a larger role, particularly in the commercial sector involving banks and financial institutions. The use of TV monitors, emergency alarms, and cameras is widespread. In 1975 there were 1,682 security firms, but by 1997 the number had risen to 9,122. Similarly, the number of security guards increased from 71,333 to 392,624 over the same time period.

Changes in Public Opinion toward the Police

This section reveals changes in the opinions of private citizens toward the police that emerged from conversations with individuals, public opinion survey data, and newspaper commentary. The information was gathered over a twenty-year period from 1980 to 2000.

First some opinions and information gathered in 1980 from private citizens at the time of my original research study; this is a sampling of the responses of members of the general public to my inquiries about their reactions to the police.

A man in his mid-thirties, whom I met by chance in a Tokyo library touched on several familiar themes:

> Before World War II, the Japanese police had a great deal of power and they exercised it. They engaged in thought control directed primarily at socialists and communists. As a result of the U.S. Occupation, freedom of thought was introduced, and the police were reorganized after the war was over. Nowadays, Japanese police behavior appears hesitant or deferential, but as soon as they are given a reason for needing their power, they will show it. When the reason exists they become like a bear or tiger! I feel a bit fearful of the police even though I have committed no offense.

When I pressed this man for a more exact explanation of his "bit fearful," he gave the answer I had heard many times. "When I was a child, my parents said to me, 'If you misbehave, a policeman will come and catch you.' In short, Japanese citizens are frightened at the prospect of jail, and the police have the power to put them in. I cannot understand it exactly, but police are a symbol of fear."

I was introduced by a probation officer to the general secretary of a YMCA in Yokohama, and our conversation started when he offered a few historical notes. He observed that the strong hierarchical structure of imperial prewar Japan had changed under the new constitution, but the deeper authoritarian roots remained. He felt that the police reflected this shift; while officers are friendly on the surface, deep down, underneath their facade of friendliness, they are authoritarian.

> People do believe that the police can maintain peace and order and that they can be relied upon. Older people perceive the police as representatives of authority and feel that they cannot resist their requests. In the countryside, the policeman was a very important person in the community historically and is today as well. The wife continues to share some of his duties in rural locations. The officer still is very service-minded, doing counseling—he's kind of a father figure.

In the sixties, he said, police and students engaged in battles in the streets and on campuses, but the atmosphere became increasingly less political in the seventies. "Today young people are enjoying the affluent society—they're more conservative and there are few encounters between them and the police. It's a kind of benign relationship." He recalled an incident with police when he was a youngster growing up in the late 1930s:

> When I was in fourth or fifth grade, I was at home by myself. I was tending the fire for the Japanese bath when it got out of control. I yelled "fire!" and many people came to the house and helped me put it out. After my father returned from the bank (my father was an executive of a bank and highly respected), he was called to the police station. It was a very bad experience for him. He was held responsible for my behavior. His one comment was, "I was treated like a criminal. I've never felt that way before."

During field research in Hokkaido in 1981, I asked the adult students of an English class in Sapporo, "How do you feel about police officers?"

Twenty-eight-year-old male: "When I drive and am stopped for speeding, the police are too lenient, but I generally have a good impression. They make society safer."

Twenty-six-year-old woman: "Socially Japan is orderly and it's a safe society. We have a good relationship with the police and I am proud of them."

Forty-year-old woman: "I believe the Japanese police are more sensitive than they were earlier, when I was a child. They have a friendly attitude toward children today."

Twenty-five-year-old woman: "The police don't act as strongly as they used to. Now, if you break a law, you will not be disciplined."

Older woman: "Under most circumstances the police are very reliable (for example, when I need directions), and, to tell you the truth, I feel they are kind and friendly. But inside they like having power—not physically but politically. Therefore, when I ask for help at the *kōban*, they are kind, but when I was caught for speeding, they were very rude. Thus, they change easily."

Thirty-five-year-old male: "I think the police have become friendlier, but, as another student said, I was brought up to be afraid of the police—if I do something wrong, 'the police will catch me.' Most of us feel that there is something to be afraid of. The police have power and if possible I wish to avoid them. We need them to control crime and keep order, but I don't like policemen or their system."

Twenty-year-old female: "We can't separate the law from policemen. If citizens didn't break the law and could keep order, we would be all safe, but it is not so. I am young, and my teenage friends and I sometimes have problems—smoking, dating after midnight, driving, and so on. We're stopped sometimes, and I can't feel friendly toward the police. When my friend was driving and was stopped by an officer, he was treated harshly. The police have a strong character and they are effective—particularly in obtaining information in an investigation."

Twenty-five-year-old male: "In our daily lives the police protect us. If someone attacks me, I will immediately call for police help and receive it instantly. I am confident I will get a quick response. However, let me give you a different type of example. I have an American friend and I visited his residence, which is near the Soviet Consulate. As we left his house we were stopped by the police and asked 'What are you doing here so late?' And he was asked, 'What do you have in your bag?' Another time I went to the Korean Consulate to pick up a passport, and I was also asked about my purpose—the officer was fair, but it was uncomfortable. When I have been in Tokyo and asked for help or directions, I have always received excellent information and assistance."

Thirty-year-old woman: "I think the Japanese people support their police and trust them to help in an emergency such as an earthquake. They're also polite."

Twenty-two-year-old man: "I had a relative who was a policeman but who is now retired. He was very strict, but he had a tough job—he was a section chief. My opinion generally is that the police are helpful and they act friendly, but I can't trust them myself. Perhaps it's the authority. They must have authority to do the job."

Comments from Scholars and Criminal Justice Professionals

Interviews, both formal and informal, with justice officials and scholars supplemented the data from other sources, including the public opinion surveys.

One court official offered this evaluation of the police:

> The police have a mission to prevent crime, but the salary is not very high. They receive awards based on the number of arrests they make. For example, a special badge or certificate is awarded to those who excel. In a democratic society there is freedom of thought and expression, but in the Japanese police organization individuals are asked to be faithful and loyal to the police agency. The police have no labor unions; if an officer is sympathetic to socialism or the Communist Party, he will have to resign from police work. Freedom of expression is an impossibility within the police organization. Instead, an officer forms a close friendship with fellow policemen. The public regards an officer as a friend in a time of trouble, but if people are demonstrating, they feel that the police are against them. During demonstrations, the police occasionally arrest citizens for minor violations.

A conversation with two legal scholars at a Tokyo university yielded the following comments: "Japanese police place too much emphasis on political activities—like student radicals and demonstrations by citizens. Rather, they should focus more on common crimes, such as burglary." The second scholar stated that he had "no basic criticism of the police," but he went on to describe one instance in which he went to ask the police about a lost article. He was surprised and annoyed that they questioned him extensively about his occupation and working hours.

A criminal law professor at Kobe University echoed the earlier concern regarding police behavior on politically related matters.

The police don't respect the rights of labor unions as much as they should, and this is also true for the public election laws. Furthermore, they don't fully back up the notion of equal protection when it comes to political parties such as the Communist Party. There are also problems with the procedures for criminal investigation, particularly in voluntary situations where no warrant has been issued.

He offered several examples of cases that had been decided by the Japanese Supreme Court in the early eighties in which the police had gone too far, in his opinion, in manipulating and coercing witnesses into cooperating and giving self-incriminating evidence. As in the United States, there are Japanese proponents of stronger "search and seizure" laws, but there are also scholars and critics who wish to see greater safeguards for the procedural rights of citizens. In general, he felt that police officers are highly competent but "perhaps too much so." Sensitive to the legal dimension, he questioned how well low-ranking officers were trained in the law.

As in the United States, law professors frequently have a different perspective on law enforcement than do the police themselves. Scholars have the luxury of being distant from daily encounters between the police and citizens, while the police are where the action is. One dean of a Japanese law school, remarking on the "routine visits" of the police, expressed skepticism concerning their avowed purpose. While conceding that the police generally were effective in the crime-prevention facet of their job during their visits to homes and commercial establishments, he was concerned about how far they might go in their desire to learn about suspicious activity in the neighborhood. This mixture of "routine visit" and not-so-routine criminal investigation would quickly raise the issues of invasion of privacy and violation of rights in the United States. One can imagine the uproar that the American Civil Liberties Union would create if the police were to make visits to all homes twice a year and, in the course of the visit, make subtle inquiries about neighborhood activity.

One former American Midwestern police officer, who enjoyed the friendship of a number of Japanese policemen, had somewhat mixed feelings about the police agency generally. He had resided in Japan for several years and was most familiar with officers in the Japanese riot control police units. Like most foreigners, he was impressed by the fact that the police are not treated as much like "outsiders" as they are in

America and that they enjoyed a strong esprit de corps. But he expressed annoyance at the behavior of Japanese officers who stopped him on the street.

> Relationships with foreigners are not good here. When an officer approaches me, I'm apt to be treated badly—you can get harassed easily and frequently. An officer will stop me and not say, "Hello," but rather, "Show me your passport." At least half a dozen times I've had my sword case with me and I've been stopped. When you might expect the older policemen to be indifferent, they are the most helpful.

While the "sword case" might offer some explanation for the police's behavior, the foreigner's annoyance can be attributed to the fact that Americans are generally accustomed to greater freedom of movement and expression.

A probation officer in Hyogo Prefecture said she generally found the police effective and respected, but expressed concern over the riot control police, particularly in their work with street demonstrators. "The police in the *kōban* are friendly, but the riot police are too zealous in their control of young people who are demosntrating." She felt that police practice overkill in the numbers they put on the street. "I saw fifteen or less university students walking around in the street, but more than twenty police had been mobilized."

Public Opinion and Survey Data 1970s and 1980s

Public opinion in Japan has undergone some remarkable shifts over the years from pre–World War II days to the new millennium. First, a look at some survey data gathered in the 1970s and 1980s: In 1968, researchers at the National Research Institute of Police Science surveyed 478 people in Tokyo. One of their most interesting findings concerned responses to the question, "Do you have any fear of policemen?" While just 19 people said "very much"; 112 indicated an in-between, or "average," rating; and 197 said "very slight"; another 128 responded "not at all." Seventeen responses were not included in the analysis. Among those surveyed, teenagers had the most negative and uncooperative attitude, while white-collar workers and owners of small businesses were the most positive and cooperative. Additional information on adults that was provided by surveys conducted by the Prime Minister's Office in 1979 suggested that citizens had a consistently positive attitude toward the police. In response to a question "Do you feel friendly toward the *kōban* policeman?" 40 percent stated "friendly"; 44 percent stated "somewhat friendly"; and 7 percent stated "not friendly." An additional 9 percent claimed "don't know."

In a discussion in 1980 with a police social science researcher, Kanehiro Hoshino (of the National Research Institute of Police Science), concerning his research on public attitudes toward the police, he noted that "there is widespread trust in police, but generally citizens do not wish to be close to them." He continued:

> There are discrepancies in the attitudes of citizens toward the police. For example, for minor offenders, such as a "Peeping Tom," people want an arrest, but police will usually only give a warning. Another discrepancy might be the enforcement of an election law violation. Citizens would permit this violation, but the police do not. Of course, citizens are not always happy with the strict enforcement of traffic laws, but the police usually enforce them consistently, provided the manpower is available. Generally, the public believes that the police do not rigorously enforce laws with regard to top-level managers, politicians, and others. They gain support for their views from the Japanese press.

During the 1970s work by Hoshino shed light on citizens' attitudes toward crime. Hoshino prepared a series of interrelated papers, published as *Reports of the National Research Institute of Police Science* (1975, 1976, and 1977). The program surveyed 8,160 citizens in 350 communities (with 329 police stations) and found that the fear of crime was significantly related to the closeness of the relationship between police and citizens. Not surprisingly, in communities where citizens perceived a closer relationship, there was more reporting of crime and citizens believed more police patrols, detectives, and police boxes contributed to a reduced fear of crime. In discussing his research, Hoshino noted that a closer relationship between police and citizens not only affected fear of crime, but seemed to be related to lower crime rates as well. To what extent this relationship actually reduced crime is unclear, but a correlation does seem to have existed. Also, there was a positive effect on the crime rate when the policemen who work in a community lived there.

Reports in the United States on "community policing" efforts around the same time revealed somewhat similar benefits from closer police–citizen ties. In one of the early studies of foot patrols, conducted in Newark,

New Jersey (Wilson and Kelling 1982), it was found that residents of the neighborhoods patrolled on foot felt more secure than persons in other areas. They tended to believe that crime had been reduced and seemed to take fewer steps to protect themselves (e.g., "staying at home with the doors locked"). While Wilson and Kelling admitted that actual crime rates appeared not to have been reduced as a result of the experimental foot patrols, they pointed out that the order-keeping behavior of police helped to create a better quality of neighborhood life, since officers were able to act as a control on drunks, derelicts, and suspicious-looking strangers. Sometimes the officers were enforcing the law, but just as often they were "taking informed or extralegal steps to help protect what the neighborhood had decided was the appropriate level of public order." Many subsequent studies, conducted throughout the United States through 2000, have continued to find citizen support for "community policing" endeavors that emphasize problem solving and extensive use of foot patrols aimed at improving relationships in the community. In some instances crime rates have also declined. Below is the now classic description of the "Broken Windows" theory of crime set forth by Wilson and Kelling (1982):

> A stable neighborhood of families who care for their homes, mind each other's children, and confidently frown on unwanted intruders can change, in a few months, to an inhospitable and frightening jungle. A piece of property is abandoned, weeds grow up, a window is smashed. Adults stop scolding rowdy children; the children, emboldened, become more rowdy. Families move out, unattached adults move in. Teenagers gather in front of the corner store. The merchant asks them to move; they refuse. Fights occur. Litter accumulates. People start drinking in front of the grocery; in time, an inebriate slumps to the sidewalk and is allowed to sleep it off. Pedestrians are approached by panhandlers. At this point, it is not inevitable that serious crime will flourish or violent attacks on strangers will occur. But many residents will think that crime, especially violent crime, is on the rise and they will modify their behavior accordingly.

Comments and Survey Data in 2000

Fast-forward to the year 2000 and surveys, along with citizen reports, provide a different picture of Japanese attitudes toward the police—a significant erosion of the generally positive attitudes of the previous thirty-year period. Much of the change that has been documented in recent public opinion polls and comments from citizens has been linked to a series of botched investigations, corruption scandals, extortion cases, false reports, drug abuse, and sexual assaults—all involving police. This series of blunders and misuse of authority has had a significant impact on public attitudes (Sims 2000).

In one case, a second grader was stabbed in a school yard in front of playmates, yet the police botched the investigation of the culprit and he escaped from six police investigators during an interrogation. He then apparently killed himself by leaping from the roof of a high-rise building. One of the author's scholar friends at International Christian University noted that in the late 1990s there were almost daily accounts in the press of police problems. One of the recent scandals that focused nationwide attention on the police took place in Kanagawa Prefecture. In this instance, police concealed a fellow officer's illegal drug use. They also were found to have obtained semi-nude photographs of a female officer that they used to extort money from her. Also in Kanagawa Prefecture, officers were discovered to have physically abused younger colleagues with beatings and gunplay.

In a crime in Hokkaido Prefecture, a sergeant was convicted and sentenced to four years of imprisonment as a result of raping and molesting female convicts. Apparently, he was able to indulge in these crimes while sending his partner to other areas of the police station while he sneaked into the detention center unobserved (Sims 2000).

In Niigata Prefecture two senior police officers were forced to resign after a series of mistakes involving the case of a nineteen-year-old woman who had been held hostage for nine years. Despite being aware of the unusual nature of the case, on the night the young woman was rescued, the chief was elsewhere wining and dining with a National Police Agency official. Later, the same chief approved a plan to issue a false news release in an effort to give credit to the Niigata police, although the woman was actually discovered by a health official (Sims 2000).

Police officials acknowledged that these scandals and inept investigations have created a public less willing to cooperate with them in investigations. A number of citizens have criticized and scolded officers on the spot when opportunities have presented themselves. For example when they have been stopped for traffic violations (Sims 2000).

Public opinion poll data collected by *Yominuri Shimbun*, a major newspaper, has documented the disaffection with police. The newspaper reported that 60 percent of those surveyed said their trust in the police had declined in recent years, while over 40 percent stated that they did not trust the police at all. An elderly Kyoto resident claimed that "when I was young, we had faith in the police and we could be proud of them because they stood for something. Today the police are a shame and an embarrassment for all of Japan" (Sims 2000).

In response to the criticism and disapproval that have been heaped on the police, the National Police Personnel Division has undertaken a series of reforms that they hope will stem the tide. These reforms include better oversight and supervision of police operations and changes in police education. It remains to be seen whether these measures will have any impact on future police behavior.

This section ends with a brief report on public opinion survey data collected in 1997 on the subject of human rights as they relate to policing and justice (Prime Minister's Office 1998). In a nationwide stratified random sample, the survey of 3,000 adults was conducted in July of 1997. The following information was elicited from citizens:

- In response to a question as to whether the interviewee's rights had been violated, 1.5 percent cited "improper treatment by police," 3.1 percent cited "violence, threat, extortion," 1.5 percent said they had been "falsely charged with a crime or regulatory violation," and 2.3 percent claimed they had been "stalked by a particular person."

- In a follow-up question as to how the parties responded, most "did nothing" or "resolved the matter myself." A small number (13.8%) spoke to friends or colleagues, while just 1.9 percent consulted with police.

- In a third related question, "If you felt your human rights were being violated, what would you do?" just 4.1 percent would consult with police, whereas the vast majority would "consult with friends" (40.5%) or "complain directly to the offending party" (20.3%).

Dissidents, Radicals, and the Police

During the turbulent sixties, the police and students clashed, both on campuses and in the streets. The intrusion of the police onto the Tokyo University campus was particularly noteworthy since that institution is

considered preeminent in all of Japan. Visiting with a psychology professor and several of his graduate students on the Tokyo University campus, I asked how members of the academic community viewed police
involvement in these matters. It was perplexing to hear the professor
begin his answer with a brief review of the history of the Japanese army.
I later came to realize that this type of thinking was a holdover from the
prewar period, when it was not uncommon for Japanese to associate
police with members of the military establishment despite the fact that
they were separate forces. Given the painful history of confrontation
between students and police in the sixties, the professor noted:

> If a policeman were to walk on campus today, he would be surrounded
> immediately by students questioning him as to his purpose. The univer-
> sity has an agreement with the police department that sets down strictly
> the rules governing on-campus activity of the police—it must involve a
> serious crime and involve the pursuit of an individual offender.

While many campuses reverberated with unrest throughout Japan
during this period, in particular it was the grievances of Tokyo University medical students that spawned the battles on that campus. In one
incident, eighty students occupied the Central Administration Building
on June 15, 1968, whereupon the president of the university called for
police help. On June 17, one thousand riot police in combat dress stormed
the building only to discover that it had been evacuated by the students,
who had gotten wind of the action.

The United States involvement in Vietnam was a rallying point for
many students and leftists, but that faded with the end of the conflict.
During that era, leftist radicals could muster thousands of chanting followers for military-style demonstrations and confrontations with police, but campuses have been relatively quiet through the 1990s.

Two surviving factions of the student movement, the *Chukakuha* and
Kakumaruha groups engaged in a violent series of internecine battles in
the early 1980s. In one episode of their ongoing conflict, members of
the *Chukakuha* used steel pipes and hammers to beat to death members
of the rival *Kakumaruha*. Police investigators claimed that the attack
was so carefully planned that the assailants cut neighborhood telephone
lines so that local residents were unable to phone police.

Clifford (1976) reported on similar conflicts between these rival factions in the 1970s and commented on their history. Both *Chukakuha* and

Kakumaruha groups were spinoffs of the earlier Unified National Committee for the Revolutionary Communist League (*Kakukyodo*):

> *Kakukyodo* had been founded by a group among whom were Kanichi Kuroda, the leader of *Kakumaruha*, and Nobuyoshi Honda, former leader of *Chukakuha*, who had been murdered by *Kakumaruha* members on March 4, 1975, at a Saitama prefecture hideout. Both groups were anti-Stalinists, revering Trotsky and Mao Tse-tung. (Clifford 1976)

One group claimed that there was not yet a climate for revolution, while the other group insisted on maintaining a violent revolutionary mood. Infighting continued among more than a dozen political groups during the late 1960s and early 1970s. Compared with the remarkably high rate of arrest in typical homicides, police had difficulty in making arrests in these cases. The role of security police increased around 1975 when Prime Minister Miki was attacked by a right-wing radical. Security police have been subsequently assigned to guard government leaders.

A different perspective on police behavior toward dissidents was offered by the radicals themselves, some of whom I interviewed in Hokkaido. One former Hokkaido University professor who participated in a number of demonstrations over the years, including those directed against the United States involvement in Vietnam, offered the following opinions:

> *Question*: Under what circumstances have you found yourself engaged in demonstrations and what was the role of the police?
> *Answer*: I participated on a number of occasions in anti–Vietnam War demonstrations held around 1967. They were organized about once a month and included from ten to thirty people in the early days. I was a professor at that time. Demonstrators included students and workers; most were young people. At first, the police were friendly—just a few observed as we demonstrated with placards and a public address system. However, they always gathered information on the participants. As the demonstrations continued, we began to hear from the police comments like, "We know where each of you lives."
>
> Certain participants, particularly younger ones, were invited by plain-clothes officers to meet in coffee shops and were asked, "What do you know about these political activities?" For the most part, people were not affiliated with organizations. I myself had to go to a police box to get a demonstration permit.

In addition to demonstrations directed at the Vietnam War, there were also those concerning the renewal of the U.S.–Japan Security Treaty, and student protests against university administrators. Some of these demonstrations were large, involving thousands of people—perhaps half were college students. On one occasion, I received a telephone call from a police officer, and he inquired, "How many people came to this demonstration?" But by then the demonstrators were numerous and spread out. The police did not prevent this, but they observed that it was illegal. At that time, one or two persons were arrested for doing a snake dance and physical contact was made. Students didn't use their hands, merely had body contact. Neither did the police use clubs; they only pushed.

Later, when the university campus was closed, things got ugly, and both sides were more violent. Stones and Molotov cocktails were thrown, and the police responded with water canons, tear gas, and clubs. Several people were hospitalized as a result. Members of the younger generation seemed to be sympathetic to our cause, but I don't know about older people. Riot police do not react personally; they are highly disciplined. They only obey orders from their commander, and it's true that students try to provoke the police by verbal abuse.

The dangerous aspects of police activities are not the open confrontations but rather the work of plainclothes officers working behind the scenes. Most demonstrators were anxious about the plainclothes officers. People sometimes hate them. These officers try to get the addresses of people and try to penetrate the "new left" or other activist groups such as those demonstrating on pollution or consumer issues. Police consider all antigovernment political activity as subversive. Police are psychologically repressive, not physically repressive.

Since the 1990s, however, a different set of priorities has confronted the Japanese police. For example, in 1997 rightists campaigned actively over the territorial issues linked to Takeshima Island and the Senkaku Islands. Specifically, South Korea constructed a pier and ship berthing facilities on Takeshima Island, which aroused Japanese demonstrators to demand that South Korea withdraw immediately from the island (National Police Agency 1998). During this era dissident rightists hurled flaming bottles in the vicinity of the South Korean Consulate in Osaka. Activists from Taiwan and Hong Kong demonstrated around the Senkaku Island group in the East China Sea protesting Japan's assertion of ownership of the islands. Also, rightists collaborated with organized crime groups and *sokaiya* racketeers (extortionists who prey on corporations) in demanding cash from businesses, threatening to target the firms if they did not pay off. Their activities were focused on illegal fund raising. The National Police Agency claimed that approximately 70 percent of the offenses linked to illicit fund-raising were associated with these alliances of rightists, organized crime, and *sokaiya*.

Police have also been placed on alert from time to time for years in Okinawa, as there have been periodic protests against the U.S. Security Treaty and the U.S. military presence on this island. In 1997 these demonstrations numbered 4,560 and included a total of 460,000 participants. Although rare, crimes in recent years committed by American military personnel against Japanese civilians living in Okinawa have created an uproar, and there have been increasingly strident demands that the American military base be withdrawn.

Tension created by farmers and dissident groups opposed to the state's determination to expand runways at Narita Airport has also persisted for more than twenty years, with many attempts at negotiating agreements between the parties having failed. The *Chukakuha* (revolutionary) faction resurfaced in 1998 and became involved in at least seven attacks against government facilities including a police station. In the latter case a "Committee of the Revolutionary Communist League" fired a projectile into the Narita police station on September 22, 1998 (National Police Agency 1998).

Japanese have always been sensitive to nuclear issues dating from the nuclear bombs unleashed on Hiroshima and Nagasaki to end World War II. Therefore it is not surprising that citizens would be cautious and sensitive about the use of nuclear energy for civilian purposes. Still, overall the government had been reasonably successful in dampening down tensions and anxieties over the safety of nuclear energy in recent years. However, in 1997 alone, a core group helped generate 490 anti-nuclear demonstrations, which included 33,200 persons, throughout the nation.

Disaster struck in the form of a series of missteps by workers at a nuclear energy facility in late 1999, causing an uproar in Japan. The event badly burned some workers and several had died by mid-2000. The deaths and the release of radiation triggered apologies from the prime minister, helping to fuel the apprehensions of citizens. As of this writing the future of the nuclear energy industry in Japan remains in doubt.

The *Aum Shinrikyo* Sect

The major terrorist activity of the 1990s, which is continuing into the new millenium, was clearly the activities of the *Aum Shinrikyo* cult or sect. The noted legal scholar, Yasuhiro Okudaira, placed the sect's lethal attack on Japanese citizens in context:

> During the early days of 1995, it looked as if Japan was under some curse. On January 7, the Kobe area was struck by an earthquake of great magnitude, killing more than 5,500 people and injuring thousands more as well as causing property damage on an enormous scale. And on March 20, highly poisonous sarin gas was released in various places throughout the Tokyo subway system, depriving twelve people of their lives and causing injuries to hundreds more. Ten days after the subway incident, on March 30, Koji Kunimatsu, inspector general of the National Police Bureau, was the victim of an unknown, would-be assassin. All of these unusual events took place in rapid succession within a very short time. (1996)
>
> In the light of the widely held belief that the Tokyo metropolis, despite its dense population and high level of industrial activity, was one of the safest cities in the world, the sarin incident in the Tokyo subway system greatly shocked people throughout the world. It became all too clear that any populous place in the world could be a target of attack by fierce and indiscriminate terrorists. (p. 127)

The *Aum Shinrikyo* sect (translated as Supreme Truth Sect), headed by guru Shoko Asahara had released lethal poison gas into subway cars in Tokyo during the morning rush hour on March 20, 1995. The intent was to kill massive numbers of citizens and create pandemonium. The latter mission was clearly accomplished, but the number of deaths and injuries (around 5,000) would have been far greater if members of the cult hadn't bungled the operation. The incident provoked a nationwide investigation on the part of the police and widespread fear that such a "safe" society could be so vulnerable. For years the cult had been rumored to have engaged in a variety of crimes including abductions, illegal confinements, firearms violations, kidnapping for ransom, and swindling people in addition to plotting and committing murder (Okudaira 1996).

Before discussing the criminal justice system's response to the criminal activities of *Aum*, a brief historical sketch of the cult and its leader seems appropriate. Psychiatrist Robert J. Lifton's (1999) book, *Destroying the World to Save It: Aum Shinrikyo, Apocalyptic Violence and the New Global Terrorism* provided an in-depth look at the cult and its historical beginnings. The author noted that Shoko Asahara was originally named Chizuo Matsumoto; he was a respected yoga practitioner in the

1980s before his transformation. The practitioner and teacher (*sensei*) became the bearded charismatic cult leader with long flowing hair somewhat later. In *Aum* he preached sexual abstinence while maintaining that superhuman powers could be achieved by spiritual means. He recruited talented young scientists as well as many lay people, young and old, to his flock. Security experts claimed that almost 200 of the 1,400 *Aum* monks were university students or graduates (Miller 1998). His persuasive powers seduced a variety of people, many of them wealthy, who turned over all their financial resources to his totalistic community. Similar to many other cults, *Aum* practiced principles associated with brainwashing in which members are required to be obedient and in which they are "mystically manipulated" (Lifton 1999). Later, after cult members had been arrested for the deadly attack, they claimed that they had been unable to defy the guru's order to kill.

The backdrop for *Aum*'s appeal lay in the megalomaniac guru's prophetic fantasy of an Armageddon. According to psychiatrist Lifton (1999), there have been prophets and gurus from the beginning of recorded history who have predicted the end of the world. With vast resources and thousands of followers Shoko Asahara set out to bring about the apocalypse. He drew on the "poor man's atomic bomb" (chemical and biological weapons).

In interviews with *Aum* defectors and some current members Lifton attempted to probe the reasons why cults such as *Aum* could successfully recruit intelligent and talented people to the fold. One person, while condemning the violence, stated he was drawn to the cult's fervent critique of and hostility toward contemporary Japanese society and, in a more positive view, to its spiritual explorations and search for personal meaning. Many Japanese citizens, as well as critics of the society, have pointed to the emptiness of the materialistic nature of modern Japan. Many early media portrayals of Asahara and *Aum* tended to separate the leader and his flock from the rest of society by portraying them as evil and monstrous. Others, according to Lifton (1999), noted the alienation of young people from society and the absence of meaning in their lives. Recall that most Japanese are not strong religious adherents and that Buddhism and Shintoism are only nominally practiced and present convenient vehicles for weddings and funerals. In general, modern industrial Japan can be described as secular.

Over the past five years it appears that at least some Japanese have come to recognize that *Aum* and other cults have emerged from Japanese soil and that they are not an isolated aberration with no links to mainstream society. Moshavi (1999) reported on some other cults that have alarmed police authorities. One group named *Ho-no-hana Sam pogyo*, was reported to be charging people tens of thousands of dollars to tell their fortunes by reading the soles of their feet. In another case, police discovered a corpse in a hotel room linked to the cult, "Life Space." The victim had been dead for four months. In a bizarre twist, the cult's guru claimed that the man was still alive. Some Japanese observers claim that they are not surprised at the various cults and sects that have surfaced, given the materialism and lack of spiritual enrichment in contemporary Japanese society (Moshavi 1999). Officially, the number of registered religious groups has increased by 15 percent over the past decade to more than 6,500. But as a result of *Aum Shinrikyo*'s criminal activities, the Japanese public has become more wary of other cults' activities, which have increasingly been scrutinized by the Japanese media. In an interview on August 28, 1999, a translator of books on spirituality, Yesuko Yamakawa, noted that "after the bubble economy burst, we began to look for something more in this world." One group that is being monitored, *Kenshakai*, is targeting high school and university students; its membership has recently tripled to 670,000.

By 2000, some members of *Aum* had been convicted along with the leader, Shoko Asahara, in the sarin gas attack and other members were still under investigation. One former member, Masato Yokoyama, was sentenced to death in Tokyo District Court. The Japanese government has been under great public pressure to outlaw the sect, but Diet members have had to step gingerly around the matter to observe constitutional safeguards on freedom of expression. The police have pushed the envelope, according to constitutional scholar Okudaira, in their desire to get as much evidence as possible against the cult and its vast membership. They have engaged in a practice known as *bekken taiho*, in which the police invoke an arrest warrant on the grounds of the nominal cause of a minor crime in order to obtain clues and evidence of a suspected more serious offense.

Historically, there was almost no freedom of religion in prewar Japan, but after the war the occupation powers demanded that the government abolish state Shinto as a state religion and guarantee freedom of religious expression (Okudaira 1996). The government has been successful in seizing some of *Aum*'s financial assets to compensate victims. In October of 1998, the sum of 960 million yen was awarded to around two thousand claimants. In a development in January of 2000, Tatsuko Muraoka, who replaced Asahara as the leader of *Aum*, offered apologies and additional financial compensation of U.S.$186,900 (Stoddard 2000). Skeptics claimed that the belated apologies and compensation were directly related to the Japanese government's new legal initiative designed to curtail and weaken *Aum*'s influence. Additional developments included the cult changing its name to *Aleph* and its agreement to not recruit new members. None of this was sufficient to prevent new legislation from being passed by the Diet. Although the group is not identified by name in this legislation passed in 2000, the law effectively gives governmental authorities broad powers to monitor and curtail the activities of organizations that have committed indiscriminate mass murder and whose leaders hold strong influence over its members. Although membership in the cult had declined significantly to a few hundred in the wake of the sarin gas attack, by the late 1990s membership had again surged, reaching 2000 plus by the end of 1999. At its peak, and prior to its bankruptcy, the cult had an estimated membership of over 10,000. After the police managed to close most of *Aum*'s extensive facilities, including its head office, branch offices, and training halls, members continued to meet in apartments and condominiums (National Police Agency 1998). The final chapter on *Aum* has yet to be written, but its viability as an organization capable of unleashing havoc on Japanese society has been effectively gutted.

Organized Crime

The *yakuza* or *boryokudan* (organized crime gangs) have already been mentioned, but I would like to look at them more closely. The term *yakuza*, which has had a more romantic patriotic connotation, is no longer used by the police, and law enforcement authorities almost exclusively refer to organized crime groups as *boryokudan*. Historically, studies conducted in the 1970s by Kanehiro Hoshino, Fumio Mugishima, and Ayako Tsurumi of the National Research Institute of Police Science shed light on the activities of organized crime. One of those studies (Hoshino 1973) provided a picture of *Yamaguchi-gumi* as depicted by members of "local" and "semi-national" gangs. The *Yamaguchi-gumi*, considered the most infamous and largest gang in Japan, has often been compared with the Mafia in the United States. Interviews with rival gang members revealed that the *Yamaguchi-gumi* had a feudalistic class system that involved a network of local groups organized in a pyramid structure. All the group bosses were subject to a single *oyabun* (head of the family). This system offered cohesiveness and strict, arbitrary control of the behavior of individual members. Hoshino stated that traditional values of *giri* (obligation, duty) and *ninjo* (empathy, humaneness) were weakening, but aggression, exclusiveness, and fatalism continue to characterize major gang activities.

Pseudo-kinship relationships have remained popular among Japanese gang members, and more than half of those studied maintained "brotherly" kinship ties. A ritual exchange of the sake cup in front of an altar and pledges of loyalty help cement ties. Members must obey every order of their boss. Often, a "blood oath" binds them to a code of behavior that is not easily broken. Gang members believe that this contributes to morale.

Despite the facade of honor and even patriotism (some groups have names such as Japanese Nationalist Organization and the Great Japanese Peace Association), they have continued to bleed Japanese society and drain resources much as similar groups do in the United States.

At the end of 1998, there were an estimated 43,500 full-time members of *boryokudan* in Japan. Table 11.5 provides information on the various *boryokudan* groups, revealing that the *Yamaguchi-gumi* group (headquartered in Kobe City) is the largest with an estimated membership of 18,300. According to police records organized crime membership peaked in Japan in 1963 with around 184,000 members (National Police Agency of Japan 1998). Since that time membership has eroded, primarily through the impact of the so-called anti-*boryokudan* law, which specifically targeted organized crime's activities. It was amended a number of times in the 1990s, providing a further bulwark against the destructive tentacles of *boryokudan*'s endeavors. Interestingly, these groups have also paid the price of the recession of the 1990s—their illicit revenues have been seriously reduced. Furthermore, civil suits have also weakened crime organizations and their revenues. One of the amendments to the "anti-*boryokudan* law" specifically targeted "front" businesses, those legal businesses that serve as a cover for the *boryokudan*'s illegal activities—racketeering, stimulant drug sales, trafficking in firearms, gambling, and prostitution. In addition, one element of the law prohibits those groups designated as *boryokudan* from coercing juveniles into joining their entities. In the government's endeavors to weaken or shut down organized crime groups, police actively support local businesses and communities, through door-to-door

Table 11.5

Boryokudan **Membership in Japan, 1997**

Name of *Boryokudan*	Main office	Strength
Godaime Yamaguchi-gumi	Hyogo (Kobe City)	18,300
Inagawa-kai	Tokyo	5,600
Sumiyoshi-kai	Tokyo	6,700
Nidaime Kudorengo Kusano-ikka	Fukuoka	530
Sandaime Kyokuryu-kai	Okinawa	310
Okinawa Kyokuryu-kai	Okinawa	470
Godaime Aizu Kotetsu	Kyoto	1,300
Yondaime Kyosei-kai	Hiroshima	300
Rokudaime Goda-ikka	Yamaguchi	210
Yondaime Kozakura-ikka	Kagoshima	140
Sandaime Asano-gumi	Okayama	130
Nidaime Dojin-kai	Fukuoka	500
Sinwa-kai	Kagawa	80
Soai-kai	Chiba	400
Sandaime Yamano-kai	Kumamoto	100
Nidaime Kyodo-kai	Hiroshima	200
Sandaime Taishu-kai	Fukuoka	120
Rokudaime Sakaume-gumi	Osaka	340
Kyokuto Sakurai Soke Rengo-kai	Shizuoka	370
Kyokuto-kai	Tokyo	2,000
Azuma-gumi	Osaka	180
Matsuba-kai	Tokyo	1,700
Kokusui-kai	Tokyo	540

Source: National Police Agency of Japan 1998.

campaigns (particularly focused on "entertainment" businesses). As noted in the *White Paper on Police* (National Police Agency 1998), a total of 220 organized crime groups (including 1,390 individuals) were dissolved or disintegrated in 1997. Of those, 157 were affiliated with the largest crime groups—*Yamaguchi-gumi, Inagawa-kai,* and *Sumiyoshi-kai.* In general, the authorities claim that since 1993 there has been a steady decline in the number of *boryokudan* groups at the rate of around 220 per year. Citizen groups have sometimes banded together to successfully shut down or force out local *yakuza* groups. In one case, in Amagasaki City, citizens shut down a protection and extortion racket.

Table 11.6 provides a picture of the arrests of both "regular" and "associate" members of organized crime from 1988 through 1997. The numbers in parentheses show the percentages of arrests among the largest three groups identified above. The type of offenses for which

Table 11.6

Arrests of Regular and Associate *Boryokudan* Members, 1988–1997

Classification	1988	1989	1990	1991	1992	1993	1994	1995	1996	1997
Total arrests from all *Boryokudan* forces	40,401	35,972	34,599	31,257	32,850	33,970	33,436	33,011	33,270	32,109
Yamaguchi-gumi	11,396	11,200	11,926	12,484	15,021	13,207	14,046	14,274	14,512	14,715
Inagawa-kai	5,724	5,192	5,601	4,729	4,917	5,668	5,140	4,570	4,413	4,559
Sumiyoshi-kai	4,479	4,485	3,988	3,651	3,923	4,797	4,530	4,317	4,345	4,118
Three groups combined	21,599	20,877	21,515	20,864	23,861	23,672	23,716	23,161	23,644	23,392
	(53.5)	(58.0)	(62.2)	(66.7)	(72.6)	(69.7)	(70.9)	(70.2)	(71.1)	(72.9)

Source: National Police Agency 1998.
Note: Numbers in parentheses show the percentages of arrests among the three major crime groups.

organized crime members were arrested included the violation of the Stimulants Control Law, which topped the list at 24.3 percent of the total of offenses. This was followed by assaults (14.3%), extortion (8.2%), and gambling (5.4%).

One leader of *Yamaguchi-gumi* was shot and killed with a handgun in a Kobe hotel in 1997. An innocent bystander, a physician, was also accidentally killed in the encounter. And much like the United States with its rival organized crime groups, in Japan a series of rival gangland activities ensued in which a series of thirty-five shooting incidents followed the Kobe murder. As has been noted throughout this book, there are relatively few firearm incidents in Japan, but a significant number of those can be placed at the doorstep of *boryokudan*. In 1997, there were six rivalry conflicts, which included fifty-three separate incidents of internecine warfare and in which 70 percent involved the use of guns. The police seized 761 handguns from *boryokudan* clans in 1997 (National Police Agency 1998).

While relatively small in number, the police agency, in cooperation with various prefectural governments have successfully lured over 3,500 members of *boryokudan* from their former lives of crime. They have provided jobs and other forms of social assistance.

The following represent several of the more recent serious incidents involving *boryokudan* in Japan in the 1999–2000 period. First, in their effort to get a foothold in Tokyo's pornographic video-shop businesses, Kobe-based *Yamaguchi-gumi* penetrated this field by intimidating the illegal shop owners into paying protection money. The police claimed that in their raids that they confiscated 45,000 videos, 11,000 magazines, and video equipment valued at 300 million yen (approximately U.S.$2,700,000) (*Asahi Shimbun* 1999).

In Kobe, the Ring Ring House, the site of a telephone dating (prostitution) service, was firebombed in March of 2000, raising fears of more gangland warfare. The club, in a fashionable district of Kobe, had been the setting for clients to arrange meetings with prostitutes. This firebombing had the imprint of a *Yamaguchi-gumi* turf battle, according to police officials. Police said that the mob faced a shrinking piece of the financial pie—much like the rest of Japan in the 1990s—and that the loss of income played a pivotal role in the violent struggles between groups. Specifically, the affiliated crime groups have been under pressure to pay monthly premiums to the parent organization and, given the recession, have struggled to meet the monthly financial demands.

In an effort to survive financially, some groups have tried to expand into new areas such as waste management and the furnishing of low-cost labor pools to the construction industry (Sims 2000).

Reflecting society generally, *boryokudan* leaders no longer command the discipline of underlings as they did earlier. Rules posted at *Yamaguchi-gumi* headquarters that state that members should not use or sell narcotics such as marijuana and stimulants or engage in behavior that disrupts the neighborhood are often ignored.

Finally, the question of whether a new wiretapping law will be a critical tool in law enforcement's fight against organized crime remains in doubt. While the police had long claimed that the law would aid in their prosecution of *boryokudan* crimes, some detectives feared that it would push illegal gang activity further underground (Johnston 1999). Journalists who have reported on the mob stated that top organized crime figures had already assumed that police were listening to their conversations and that mob leaders had developed countermeasures such as using fax transmission. Furthermore, wiretapping of cellular phone conversations presents technical problems depending on what kind of signal is being used. For example, while digital cellular phones operate better, they are easier to tap (Johnston 1999).

In conclusion, today's gang members can leave gang life more easily than in previous years. Researcher Kanehiro Hoshino of the National Research Institute of Police Science remarked that, "earlier gang members might suffer the loss of a finger joint or might even be lynched, but today secession is much easier (Hoshino 1974).

12

Conclusion

Despite the blemishes on the record of the Japanese police in the late 1990s, I continue to hold the police agency in high regard. No system in the world is without its flaws, and while the National Police Agency and its sister prefectural police agencies may have let their guard down, I expect that the handful of police abuses and blunders will be corrected. I do not believe that these abuses and missteps, regardless of their widespread, well-publicized notoriety, are symptomatic of a systemic breakdown. In general throughout my writing I have both explicitly and implicitly made clear my high regard for both the police system itself and its parallel criminal justice institutions. They will regain the confidence of the Japanese public over time.

In moving into the new millennium, however, the police will face some severe challenges, as will police agencies all over the world. The fact that the Japanese system is fundamentally a national system will aid in this endeavor. I will have more to say about this feature a bit later.

Of course one of the moving forces in globalization is the Internet. Use in Japan has skyrocketed, and one of the most interesting repercussions has been the elevation of individualism in a society with strong roots in group-oriented behavior. The collectivist mentality has weakened, but other sectors have been strengthened.

One change that has been helped by the Internet has to do with the role of women. Most women have long suffered a second-class citizenship, as previously noted, and nowhere has this been more evident than in the workplace. Historically, they have been stymied by a system that has kept them in inconsequential jobs. By the end of 1998, some 25.6 percent of the 14 million Japanese using the Internet were women, up 17.8 percent from the year before (Strom 2000). The *Japan Almanac* (2000) tracked the number of "Internet hosts" and noted that it has risen dramatically in recent years. The following numbers were offered (per 10,000 computers): 1993 (2.3); 1995 (9.7); 1997 (73.4); and 1999 (168.8).

Women, forced out of traditional businesses and corporate offices at the time of marriage or childbirth, are now able to work at home either in their own enterprises or for someone else by telecommuting to their jobs. Freed from the bureaucratic shackles of an encrusted system of regulations, red tape, and rigid seniority, both males and females can generate business more easily through the Internet. Farming in Japan is a classic example. Historically, small farmers, forced to go through middlemen and governmental red tape, saw their profits evaporate. Now they can sell directly to customers.

As Professor Jiro Kokuryo of Keio University noted, "It [the Internet] is changing people's point of view and empowering them to challenge traditional ways of doing things" (Strom 2000). Traditional behavior patterns such as face-to-face business meetings over sake are also at risk as more individuals will cut deals through e-mail communication or accomplish business transactions through faxes and cell phones. Face-to-face relationships will no longer be at the heart of the business deal. All of this has repercussions for the justice system. Expanding individuality and the flip side, the erosion of group behavior (which has already been underway for decades), will take a further leap forward with greater Internet use. This in turn, will weaken traditional interpersonal bonds among Japanese citizens. I have always thought of the word "brotherliness" in describing the relationships of Japanese with one another, and while a bit strong, there is a ring of truth to it. However, it seems inevitable that these ties will continue to weaken in the face of globalization and the Internet. In turn, these developments may accelerate the number of divorces in Japan and, with the weakening of family life, increased levels of juvenile delinquency may follow, unless other social control mechanisms emerge to offset the changes in family life.

Lessons from Japan

Japan's system of crime control and policing are markedly different from America's, primarily because of vast cultural differences. Still, I am hopeful that the United States can take advantage of certain facets and characteristics of the Japanese system that are adaptable to our own. Possibilities for learning from this system are rather obvious, and therefore I have no intention of presenting an exhaustive list of them. Furthermore, the usual caveat about vast differences in culture making some reforms impossible to achieve is eminently applicable here. Having said that, I am prepared to offer some general recommendations. Let me hasten to note, however, that while the ideas that follow are based on my research, at times I have strayed well beyond the data presented in my discussion. Moreover, I have not attempted a lengthy justification of what follows, since it is intended principally to stimulate thinking on the subject, not to present a definitive solution.

The police system of the United States is much like an eight-cylinder car chugging along on six cylinders. Crime is still widespread, even with declines over the recent decade. We currently have a fragmented patchwork of inefficient, marginally trained, and poorly equipped police forces. Far too frequently, a person can become a police officer if he or she has the right political connection or a relative "in the right place." Morale is low, in part because of bickering between police managers and unions, but also because of the discouragement that talented officers experience within a system that has no mechanism to allow them to advance at a rate equal to their worth. Of all the complaints I have heard from hundreds of police officers I have taught over past decades, none is more serious than this; it often compels intelligent and creative officers to leave police work. Some view a college degree in criminal justice not as a means of advancing within their police agency but as a ticket out. In too many departments there is no professional personnel system that allows the top individuals to advance. Instead, favoritism prevails. While fewer in number, stories still exist of high school–educated police chiefs who discourage and even harass subordinates who seek to improve themselves by obtaining college degrees. While a small number of police departments require a college degree to enter the force, most do not. In most departments, educational background has little relevance; indeed, it is not unusual to hear of a master's degree recipient taking the prescribed recruit training class alongside high school graduates.

As mentioned earlier, in Japan college-educated men and women complete an extensive course of training at the outset of their careers, while high school graduates complete an even longer course of training. More and more college-educated personnel are actively sought, and increasingly—perhaps because of the economic recession of the 1990s—apply for jobs in the police field. The United States has no equivalent of England's Bramshill Police College or Japan's National Police Academy, which allow for upward movement based on advanced training and selection. For example, an officer in England from a local police constabulary can enter a course designed for newly appointed sergeants. After satisfactorily completing the one-year course, he or she can be assured of a promotion to the position of inspector. In the Netherlands, as well, college-educated individuals who are able to pass a stringent set of examinations can start their careers at a rank commensurate with a second lieutenant position in our military forces. Officer candidate school allows an American college graduate who can successfully pass the physical and mental exams to start his or her career in the military as a commissioned officer, but we do not have a parallel system for police work. The United States does not have anything approaching the "elite" system of Japan, whereby top university graduates can enter the police field as "management trainees," with appropriate rank and salary. In Japan, riding the "fast track," they can feel assured of regular promotions and lifetime job security.

The FBI Academy near Washington, D.C., in addition to training FBI personnel, does offer some training courses to police officers, but its capacity is limited. Some local police departments periodically select an officer or two to attend a specialized course, but the choice of who is selected may be politically biased. The training at the FBI Academy has a reputation for high professional standards, but because numbers are severely limited, most officers never set foot inside its doors. The first recommendation is that the United States establish a national police college that would provide both advanced academic, as well as professional, training. This is a tall order because our system has thousands of separate police agencies with varying standards of selection and promotion. Still, we could establish some national selection criteria, including an examination, along with minimal rank and allow top applicants to attend a national police college. Much like the graduates of our national military academies, such as West Point and the Naval Academy, the graduates would be the corps of our future police managers. Highly trained, sharing experiences and backgrounds in the academy, and perhaps, as in Japan, rotated in various assignments around the nation, they would strengthen our system of law enforcement. A parallel suggestion follows.

While it is heresy to suggest it in a nation that views its police establishment as a necessary evil, the second recommendation—a major one—is that Americans should attempt to overcome their strong emotional biases against a national police force and consider at least a quasi-national system. A system that has national standards for selection, training, and promotion has many virtues, including established entrance requirements for recruits. While it would be unfair to suggest that the charges of physical abuse occasionally leveled against American officers could be eliminated by higher selection standards, I do feel that such a move would bear fruit in this sensitive area. Police departments should now thoroughly screen applicants according to psychological criteria. Many do, but many still do not. Some police departments, such as those in New York City and Los Angeles, employ full-time personnel psychologists (as does the Tokyo Metropolitan Police Department), but the practice needs to be standardized. This could be facilitated by a national administration. The states and municipalities could be given some input in budget and other decision making as the prefectures are in Japan.

The need for high standards, both physical and psychological, is particularly pressing, as American officers are under much greater stress and pressure than many of their counterparts in other countries. The physical abuse mentioned above is in part a response to this, although that is often an excuse. Americans offer much less respect to police than do the Japanese, and the police officer–citizen relationship in the United States is complicated by racism, poor working conditions, and in some cases weak supervision. Incidents of violence between police officers and citizens in the United States can also be attributed in part to the low level of physical fitness among American police. While Japanese police are required to maintain physical fitness through kendo or judo, it is common to see overweight, out-of-condition officers patrolling the streets in American cities. Officers who are out of shape are more insecure than those in good physical condition. Thus they are more likely to be drawn into physical confrontations with citizens. Physical and psychological standards of selection need to be tightened.

In addition to controlling intellectual, psychological, and physical standards for officers, a quasi-national system of policing would do much to remedy the current chaotic state of affairs whereby town policing functions overlap with those of county and state police. A unified system, even just at the state level, would be more efficient and more economical. The investigation of crime would be vastly improved. Jealousies that are rampant between police and local FBI offices would be greatly reduced, if not eliminated. If the public had a better image of police, the officers would in turn have higher self-respect. Furthermore, they would feel less pressure to "moonlight" at other jobs. Indeed, states could make it illegal, as the Japanese government does, for officers to take outside employment, thereby reducing the ineffectiveness of officers who exhaust themselves in their efforts to hold down two jobs.

The proposed quasi-national system, loosely linking various states, would not change the financial mechanism substantially. There would continue to be considerable local autonomy in terms of funding and budgeting. In both Japan and Great Britain, local police forces are funded up to 50 percent by local governments.

Public safety commissions staffed by local citizens could act as a buffer to control and oversee police operations. Undue local political influence on the policies of these regional police forces would be minimized. Either the FBI could be broadened to assume a larger role in setting standards and policies for police on a national level, or a new national police agency could be created. Because a cadre of professional police managers could be rotated periodically throughout the different states, there would be a tremendous reduction in police corruption— which is still far too common in the United States. Over the years, many of my students, who include working police officers, have admitted that political connections are often influential in hiring as well as promotions in many departments. A professional managerial approach would supplant today's archaic police bureaucracies, where political influence rather than qualifications, often determines who becomes chief. This would reduce the need for the special investigatory commissions that have often been required to root out corruption and police abuse of power. In 2000, despite energetic attempts at thwarting an outside investigation, the Los Angeles Police Department and the Los Angeles County district attorney finally had to yield to an FBI investigation of the department. It was triggered by widespread abuse in the so-called Ramparts unit that had been charged with investigating gang violence. Just a few years before, the Christopher Commission, led by former secretary of state Warren Christopher, had suggested a major overhaul of the Los Angeles Police Department in the wake of the Rodney King beating. However, those reforms were never fully implemented and the LAPD has continued to suffer as a result. I am sure that some Americans would resist the strengthening and professionalizing of the police because they fear police power, but this is, I think, a misunderstanding. Merely because police agencies would be linked to an integrated, national structure would be no reason for them to take on a strong authoritarian character. As in Japan, a vital, unfettered press and the electronic media would serve as one of the checks on police abuse of power. Actually, in America, with its deeper democratic values, the risk of police abuse of power is even less.

We do not have to go as far as Japan or Great Britain to find a model for an integrated police force—Canada has a system that has worked effectively. With a few exceptions, such as the Ontario Provincial Police and the Quebec Provincial Police, the Royal Canadian Mounted Police (RCMP) has provided police services throughout much of Canada. There have been occasional problems in Canada's quasi-national police force, but they have been dealt with and it has been retained. Chapman (1978) sketched the historical evolution of the Canadian police and noted that eight of Canada's provinces maintained their "contracts" with the RCMP for police services. In Alberta province, where I lived and trained police for two years, the force was made up entirely of RCMP, with the exception of the police in Edmonton and Calgary, the two major cities. Other Canadian cities such as Montreal and Vancouver also have their own police agencies, but the RCMP's Criminal Intelligence Service Canada has a computer-linked operation that ties in practically all of Canada's police forces. An organization such as the RCMP attracts more applicants and applicants of better quality than small, independent, local departments ever could. Occasionally, the media have alleged scandalous behavior or abuse of authority on the part of the RCMP, there appears to be proportionately less corruption among Canadian police than among American.

Again, to be fair to American police officers, a Los Angeles Police Department patrol officer transferred to one of Japan's police boxes for a year, would probably undergo a dramatic change. Faced with a far less stressful environment and a much more approachable public, the American officer would become considerably more relaxed, friendly, and helpful. The stress of urban police work in the United States, as well as further reduction in crime, could be achieved with an even greater emphasis on neighborhood- or community-based policing. The advantages of a system that places a premium on local neighborhood policing, using mini-stations (kōban) as a vehicle, is powerfully demonstrated in Japan. This appears to be one of the very best mechanisms for improving ties between police and citizens and thereby reducing crime. A quasi-national system could facilitate these changes to an even greater extent than they have already taken place in the United States. The Japanese example makes it apparent how important this system is, regardless of its cost. Only through a national system would it be possible to implement such a revolutionary change in American police practices.

A quasi-national police system would allow a far more effective use of manpower, and the financial benefits might make it possible to establish a greater local police patrol presence without reducing the crime-fighting power of "street crime" undercover units, detectives, and so on. Manpower could be allocated according to need, with the cost spread throughout the nation proportionally. Fewer administrators, at least theoretically, would be required.

Obviously, in many small towns and rural communities in the United States there is often a good working relationship between police and citizens. For all practical purposes, small-town policing in Japan and the United States may not be so radically different, but in municipal and state policing major beneficial changes could be accomplished. As Japan has demonstrated, it is not necessary to sacrifice a strong service-oriented police at the community level to gain an efficient national system.

The next recommendation is to establish counseling centers for families and juveniles and to expand crime prevention activities. Because these services are linked I will discuss them together. While police officers in small towns currently engage in some informal counseling of citizens, most American departments shun this type of work. I feel that a change of approach in this area would help to foster a better overall relationship between police and citizens in the United States. Not surprisingly, many officers and some chiefs, who would consider it "social work," would resist this change. A national approach could accomplish such a goal. Crime-prevention work, along with counseling, provides an excellent basis for deepening the police–community relationship.

Japan's success in crime control is due primarily to the type of society it is rather than its police force, and it would be ridiculous to predict a massive reduction in crime in the United States based on an integrated system of law enforcement of the type I am advocating. Some changes, however, could be effected, even in our very different society, with positive results.

Gun control, for example, is another of my recommendations. While a stronger federal gun control law could make a serious dent in felonious crime, without a quasi-national police force it would be difficult to implement the law. Illegal guns move from states with few restraints to those with stronger laws.

Many features of the Japanese police system could not be transplanted easily. America's heterogeneous population, with its varied ethnic and racial groups, will never become a homogeneous society such as Japan's with its shared heritage and system of values. More accustomed to authoritarianism, the Japanese allow police to penetrate far more deeply into the community. The American Civil Liberties Union and many other organizations would be outraged if police officers started visiting every American household and commercial establishment. Traditional Japanese values of loyalty and obedience and the sense of responsibility people feel for one another also contribute to the lower crime rates and help to maintain ties between police and citizens. As Japanese society continues to become more urban and impersonal, those values will continue to be tested. As mentioned earlier, the expansion of Internet use in Japan is changing the way people work and live.

While the Internet and other technological advancements are heartening, the flip side is that these same tools are providing opportunities for cheaper and deadlier means for criminals and terrorists to create mayhem. These developments make both Japan and the United States more vulnerable to worldwide networks of drug trafficking, organized crime, assaults on computer networks, and other criminal endeavors.

References

Ames, W. *Police and Community in Japan*. Berkeley: University of California Press, 1981.

Amnesty International, "Japan: Abusive Punishments in Japanese Prisons" (pamphlet), New York: Amnesty International, 1998.

Asahi Evening News. "Truancy Rate Jumps by Record 21% to Hit New High," August 13, 1999, p. 4.

———. "Yamaguchi-gumi Muscling in On Tokyo's Kabuki-Cho," August 22, 1999, p. 1.

Asakura, T. "Canadian Software Puts Face on Crime," *Japan Times*, September 1, 1999, p. 2.

Associated Press. "Young Cons Proliferate," *New Haven Register*, February 28, 2000, p. A2.

Astill, J. "Brit Tells of False Arrest, Brutality," *Japan Times*, August 28, 1999, p. 3.

Auerbach, J. "A Plague of Lawyers," *Harper's Magazine*, 253, October 1976.

Bando, S. "Japanese Women Yesterday and Today," *About Japan Series*. Tokyo: Foreign Press Center, 1996.

Bayley, D.H. *Forces of Order: Police Behavior in Japan and the United States*. Berkeley: University of California Press, 1976.

———. *Forces of Order: Policing Modern Japan*. Berkeley: University of California Press, 1991.

Beer, L. *Freedom of Expression in Japan: A Study in Comparative Law, Politics, and Society*. Tokyo and New York: Kodansha International Ltd., 1984.

Benedict, R. *The Chrysanthemum and the Sword*. Tokyo and Rutland, VT: Charles E. Tuttle, 1954.

Berkowitz, L. "How Guns Control Us," *Psychology Today*, June 1981.

Bisignani, J. *Japan Handbook*. Chico, CA: Moon Publications, 1993.

Borchard, E. *Convicting the Innocent: Errors of Criminal Justice*. New Haven, CT: Yale University Press, 1932.

Butterfield, F. "Guns Used More for Suicide than Homicide," *New York Times*, October 17, 1999, p. A18.

———. "F.B.I. Study Finds Gun Use in Violent Crimes Declining," *New York Times*, October 18, 1999, p. A19.

Chapman, B. "The Canadian Police." *Police Studies*, March 1978, pp. 62–72.

Chwialkowski, P. "Japanese Policing—An American Invention," *Policing: An International Journal of Police Strategies and Management* 21, no. 4, 1998.

Clifford, W. *Crime Control in Japan*. Lexington, MA: Lexington Books, 1976.

Cohen, T., and H. Passin, eds. *Remaking Japan: The American Occupation as New Deal*. New York: Free Press, 1987.

Crichton, M. *Rising Sun*. New York: Alfred Knopf, 1992.

Currie, E. *Crime and Punishment in America*. New York: Metropolitan Books, Henry Holt and Company, 1998.

Daily Yomiuri. "Cell Phones Pose Problems for Wiretap Law," September 9, 1999.

Dore, R. *City Life in Japan*. Berkeley: University of California Press, 1958.

———. *Shinohata: A Portrait of a Japanese Village*. New York: Pantheon Books, 1978.

Foreign Press Center, "Juvenile Crime," Tokyo: Foreign Press Center, 1998.

———. "Facts and Figures of Japan." Tokyo: Foreign Press Center, 1999.

French, H. "Disdainful of Foreigners, the Japanese Blame Them for Crime," *New York Times*, September 30, 1999, p. A17.

———. "Japan's Troubling Trend: Rising Teen-Age Crime," *New York Times*, October 12, 1999.

———. "T.V. Star Loses Marriage, Privacy, and Her Job Too," *New York Times*, October 27, 1999, p. A4.

———. "Japanese Only Takes Body Blow in Court," *New York Times*, November 15, 1999, p.1.

———. "Exam Wars, Prepping and Other Nursery Crimes," *New York Times*, December 7, 1999, p. A4.

———. "Tokyo Dropouts' Vocation: Painting the Town," *New York Times*, March 4, 2000, p. A1.

Fujiwara, T. "Criminal Justice System in Japan (II): Criminal Investigations." Unpublished paper for the United Nations Asia and Far East Institute for the Prevention of Crime and Treatment of Offenders, Tokyo, Japan, Fall 1980.

Fukae, M. "Killed in the Line of Duty," *Asahi Evening News*, August 3, 1999, p. 3.

Gibney, F. *Japan: The Fragile Superpower*. New York: W.W. Norton, 1975, p. 82.

Gordon, A. "Scaring the Salary Man Isn't the Japanese Way," *New York Times*, October 30, 1999, p. A15.

Hall, J. *Japan: From Prehistory to Modern Times*. New York: Delacorte, 1970.

Hattori, K, personal communication with chief probation officer, Yokohama, Japan, September 11, 1999.

Herbert, B. "Addicted to Violence," *New York Times*, editorial page, April 22, 1999.

Herbert, W. *Foreign Workers and Law Enforcement in Japan*, London and New York: Kegan Paul International, 1996.

Hirano, R. "The Accused and Society: Some Aspects of Japanese Criminal Law." In A. Von Mehren, ed. *Law in Japan: The Legal Order in a Changing Society*, Cambridge, MA: Harvard University Press, 1963, p. 290.

Horiuchi, K. *Japan: Criminal Justice Profiles of Asia,* Fuchu, Japan: United Nations Asia Far East Institute for the Prevention of Crime and Treatment of Offenders, 1995.

Hoshi, E. "Parent-Child Relations and Parental Discipline in Delinquents' Families: A Comparative Study between Delinquents and Non-Delinquents on Perceived Interpersonal Relations within the Family." *Reports of the National Research Institute of Police Science* 19, no. 1, September 1978.

Hoshino, K. "Crime, Victimization, Suicide and Accidental Death as a Result of Running Away from Home" (p. 154) and "Family Relationships and Running Away from Home" (p. 144). *Reports of the National Research Institute of Police Science* 14, no. 1, 1973.

———. "The Analysis of Descriptions of *Yamaguchi-gumi* by Members of Organized Criminal Gangs." *Reports of the National Research Institute of Police Science* 14, no. 1, 1973.

———. "Process of Secession from Organized Criminal Gangs." *Reports of the National Research Institute of Police Science* 15, no. 1, 1974.

———. "A Measurement of the Level of Public Safety from Crime (II)." *Reports of the National Research Institute of Police Science* 16, no. 2, 1975.

———. "Police Activities to Raise the Level of Public Safety from Crime." *Reports of the National Research Institute of Police Science* 17, no. 1, 1976.

———. "Police Activities to Raise the Level of Public Safety from Crime: The Satisfaction Point of Public Safety Examined by the Delphi Method." *Reports of the National Research Institute of Police Science* 18, no. 2, 1977.

———. "Victims of Organized Crime and the Process of Victimization." *Reports of the National Research Institute of Police Science* 21, no. 1, 1980.

Ike, N. *Japanese Politics: Patron-Client Democracy.* New York: Alfred Knopf, 1972.

Ishida, T. *Heiwa no Seijigaku.* Tokyo: Iwanami, 1968.

Japan Almanac 2000. Tokyo: Asahi Shimbun Publishing Co., 2000.

Japan Society. "The Role of Public Prosecutors in Criminal Justice: Prosecutorial Discretion in Japan and the United States." A Seminar Report, *Public Affairs Series* 14, New York, September 15, 1980, p. 5.

Japan Times. "Lessons from the Tragedy," editorial page, December 1, 1980.

———. "Normal Kids Hitting Teachers: New Violent Trend among Students Soar," August 14, 1999, p. 2.

———. "Chinese Security Minister in Japan to Talk Crime," August 20, 1999, p. 2.

———. "Fewer U.S. Teens Taking Drugs," August 20, 1999, p. 5.

———. "The Slow Road to Gender Equality," editorial page, August 28, 1999.

———. "Makihara Arrested after Drug Raid on Tokyo Home," August 31, 1999, p. 2.

———. "Prison Ruled Despite Illegal Detainment," September 5, 1999, p. 2.

———. "Man Kills One in Stabbing Spree," September 9, 1999, p. 2.

———. "Known Illegal Foreigners on Decline," September 26, 1999, p. 2.

———. "Man Kills 3, Injures 12 in Stabbing Spree," September 30, 1999, p. 1.

Johnston, E. "Will Wiretap Law Catch Mob Off Guard," *Japan Times*, August 21, 1999, p. 3.

Kamiya, S. "Korean Resident's Long Campaign Is a Victory for Foreigners Here." *Japan Times*, July 29, 1999, p. 3.

Kamm, H. "In Tokyo, a Raucous Honky-Tonk Area That Has No Crime," *New York Times*, July 22, 1981.

Kanetake-Oura, B. *Fifty Years of New Japan*. London: Smith Elder, 1910.

Kanji, N. *Sakoku' no susume.* Gaikokujin rodosha ga. Nihon o horobosu. Tokyo: Kobunsha (Kappa bijinesu), 1989.

Kaplan, D., and Dubro, A. *Yakuza: The Explosive Account of Japan's Criminal Underworld*. Reading, MA: Addison-Wesley, 1986.

Kawashima, T. "Dispute Resolution in Contemporary Japan." In A. Von Mehren, ed., *Law in Japan: The Legal Order in a Changing Society*, Cambridge, MA: Harvard University Press, 1963, p. 43.

———. "The Status of the Individual and the Notion of Law, Right, and Social Order in Japan." In Charles A. Moore, ed., *The Japanese Mind: Essentials of Japanese Philosophy and Culture*, Honolulu: East-West Center Press, 1967, p. 264.

Keishicho. *Metropolitan Police Department*. Tokyo, 1980.

Kennedy, R. "In Police Pay, New York City's Top Ranking Is History." *New York Times*, February 1, 1997, p. A1.

Kirk, D. "The Shame of Japanese Justice." *Asahi Evening News (London Observer Service)*, February 2, 1981.

Kitagawa, Z. "Method of Solving Legal Disputes in Japan." In *Materials on Legal Institutions in Japan*, 1–49, Multilith, 1974, p. 78.

Koschmann, J. Victor. "Soft Rule and Expressive Protest." In J. Victor Koschmann, ed., *Authority and the Individual in Japan*. Tokyo: University of Tokyo Press, 1978.

Koshi, G.M. *The Japanese Legal Advisor: Crimes and Punishments*. Tokyo and Rutland, VT: Charles E. Tuttle, 1970.

Kuno, O. "The Meiji State, Minponshugi, and Ultranationalism." In J. Victor Koschmann, ed., *Authority and the Individual in Japan*. Tokyo: University of Tokyo Press, 1978, p. 61.

Lacey, M. "Teen-Age Birth Rate in U.S. Falls Again," *New York Times*, October 27, 1999, p. A16.

Larivee, J. "Helping Prisoners after Their Release," *Boston Globe*, December 4, 1999, p. A19.

Lifton, R. *Destroying the World to Save It: Aum Shinrikyo, Apocalyptic Violence, and the New Global Terrorism*, New York: Metropolitan Books, 1999.

Loftus, E. *Eyewitness Testimony*. Cambridge, MA: Harvard University Press, 1979.

McKay, R. "Japan: Streets without Crimes, Disputes without Lawyers." Manuscript, Aspen Institute Program on Justice, Society and the Individual, 1978.

Magnier, M. "A Bit More Equal: Women Inch Ahead in Japan," *International Herald Tribune*, September 2, 1999, p. 5.

Matsumoto, S. "The Roots of Political Disillusionment: 'Public and Private' in Japan." In J. Victor Koschmann, *Authority and the Individual in Japan*. Tokyo: University of Tokyo Press, 1978.

Meiko, H. "Intoxicated Youth," *Japan Quarterly*, April–June, 1995.

Meyerson, A. "Legal Profession in Japan: A Small Guild," *Asian Wall Street Journal*, February 17, 1981, p. 4.

Miller, J. "Some in Japan Fear Authors of Subway Attack Are Regaining Ground," *New York Times*, October 11, 1998, p. 12.

Ministry of Justice. *White Paper on Crime, 1998*. Tokyo: Research and Training Institute, Ministry of Justice, 1998.

―――. "Problems of Juvenile Delinquency in Japan" (Reported by Director Tabita, Juvenile Division, Criminal Affairs Bureau). Tokyo: Research and Training Institute, 1980.

Mitchell, R. *Thought Control in Prewar Japan*. Ithaca, New York: Cornell University Press, 1976, p. 192.

Moore, C., ed. *The Japanese Mind: Essentials of Japanese Philosophy and Culture*. Honolulu: East-West Center Press, 1967.

Moshavi, S. "In Japan, Worry As Cults Flourish Amid Wave of Faith," *Boston Globe*, December 30, 1999, p. A11.

Mugishima, F., and Hoshino, K. "A Study of Murder Committed by Members of Organized Criminal Gangs." *Reports of the National Research Institute of Police Science* 17, no. 2, 1976.

Munehiro, H. Personal interview on the subject of international crime, National Police Agency Headquarters, August 28, 1999, Tokyo, Japan.

Murata, K. "Savage In-Fighting ('Uchigeba') among Radical Groups Goes on Relentlessly." *Japan Times*, November 7, 1980.

Nagashima, A. "The Accused and Society: The Administration of Criminal Justice in Japan." In A. Von Mehren, ed., *Law in Japan: The Legal Order in a Changing Society*, Cambridge, MA: Harvard University Press, 1963, p. 299.

Nakane, C. *Japanese Society*. Berkeley: University of California Press, 1970.

Nakasato, Y., and Tamura, M. "A Study on Stimulant Abuses in Japan and a Study on Non-Medical Use of Dangerous Drugs in Adolescents." *Reports of the National Research Institute of Police Science* 15, no. 1, June 1974.

National Police Academy, "Community Policing in Japan." Tokyo: International Research and Training Institute for Criminal Investigation, National Police Academy, Japan: International Cooperation Agency, 1998.

National Police Agency, *National Police Academy*. Tokyo: National Police Agency of Japan, 1980.

―――. *The Police of Japan*. 1998. Tokyo: International Cooperation Division, National Police Agency of Japan, 1998.

―――. *White Paper on Police. 1998*. Tokyo: National Police Agency of Japan, 1999.

National State of Japan. "Crime Prevention and the Quality of Life." Statement prepared for the Sixth United Nations Congress on the Prevention of Crime and the Treatment of Offenders, 1980.

Newsweek. "Japanese Graffiti," October 12, 1981, p. 58.

Nishimura, H., and Matsumoto, T. "Analysis of Attitudes towards Police." *Reports of the National Research Institute of Police Science* 9, no. 1, 1968.

Niyekawa, A. "Authoritarianism in an Authoritarian Culture: The Case of Japan." *The International Journal of Social Psychiatry*, XII, no. 4, 1966, pp. 283–88.

Okudaira, Y. "Political Censorship in Japan from 1931 to 1945." Unpublished manuscript, Institute of Legal Research, University of Pennsylvania, Philadelphia, 1962.

―――. "Some Preparatory Notes for the Study of the Peace Preservation Law in Prewar Japan." *Annals of the Institute of Social Science*, Tokyo: University of Tokyo Press, 1973.

―――. "Current Controversies on the Control of Religious Organizations in Japan." *Columbia Journal of Asian Law* 10, no. 1, Spring 1996.

Osamu, M. "Youth under Siege in a World of Drugs." *Japan Quarterly*, October–December 1998.

Ouchi, W. *Theory Z: How American Business Can Meet the Japanese Challenge.* New York: Avon, 1981.

Parker, L. *Legal Psychology: Eyewitness Testimony, Jury Behavior.* Springfield, IL: Charles C. Thomas, 1980.

———. *Parole and the Community Based Treatment of Offenders in Japan and the United States,* New Haven, CT: University of New Haven Press, 1986.

———. "What U.S. Can Do to Lessen Crime." *Japan Times,* January 18, 1981. Op. Ed. page.

———. Meier, R.D., and L.H. Monahan. *Interpersonal Psychology for Law Enforcement and Corrections.* St. Paul, MN: West, 1989.

Perry, J.C. *Beneath the Eagle's Wings: Americans in Occupied Japan.* New York: Dodd, Mead, 1980.

Prime Minister's Office. "Public Opinion Surveys." Tokyo: Foreign Press Center, 1998.

Rokumoto, K. "Legal Problems and the Use of Law in Tokyo and London—Preliminary Study in International Comparison." *Zeitschrift fur Soziologie* 7, August 1978, pp. 228–50.

Rout, L. "Rural Justice: Old-Fashioned Sheriff of Grant Country, South Dakota, Doubles As a Friend," *Wall Street Journal,* August 10, 1981, p. 1.

Sakamoto, T. "Young High-Fliers Face Challenging Future with Clipped Wings." *Asaki Evening News,* August 13, 1999, p. 5.

Scott-Stokes, H. "In Japan, Crime Is Rare and Reaction Swift." *New York Times,* April 12, 1981, p. E7.

Shaw, G. "Inmate Total Nears Two Million," *Boston Globe,* December 29, 1999, p. A16.

Sherman, L. *The Quality of Police Education.* San Francisco, CA: Jossey-Bass, 1976.

Shotaro, T. "When Student Violence Erupts," *Japan Quarterly,* July–September 1998.

Shreiber, M. "Juvenile Crime in the 1990s," *Japan Quarterly,* April–June 1997.

Sims, C. "Misdeeds by Once-Honored Police Dismay the Japanese," *New York Times,* March 7, 2000, p. A3.

———. "Feeling Pinch, Japan's Mobs Struggle for Control," *New York Times,* April 2, 2000, p. 6.

Statistics Bureau. *Statistics Handbook of Japan.* Tokyo: Prime Minister's Office, 1980.

Stevens, C. *On the Margins of Japanese Society.* London and New York: Routledge, 1997.

Stoddard, S. "Japan Cult Offers Funds to Victims of Its Subway Raid," *Boston Globe,* January 30, 2000, p. 5.

Strom, S. "In Japan, Mired in Recession, Suicides Soar," *New York Times,* July 15, 1999, p. A1.

———. "Use of the Internet Quietly Transforms Way Japanese Live," *New York Times,* May 14, 2000, p. 1.

Sugai, S. "The Japanese Police System." In R. Ward, ed., *Five Studies in Japanese Politics.* Center for Japanese Studies, Occasional Papers, no. 7. Ann Arbor: University of Michigan Press, 1957.

Supreme Court of Japan, *Justice in Japan.* Tokyo: General Secretariat of the Supreme Court of Japan, 1998.

Takahashi, Y., Nishimura, H., and Suzuki, S. "A Social Psychological Study on

Prostitution (II): The Comparison between the Streetwalker and the Turkish Bath Prostitute." *Reports of the National Research Institute of Police Science* 16, no. 2, December 1975.

Tamura, M. and Mugishima, F. "Survey on the Groups of Violent Drivers (I & II)." *Reports of the National Research Institute of Police Science* 16, no. 2, December 1975.

Tanabe, T. "The Processes of Litigation: An Experiment with the Adversary System." In A. Von Mehren, ed., *Law in Japan: The Legal Order in a Changing Society*, Cambridge, MA: Harvard University Press, 1963, p. 77.

Tanaka, H., ed. *The Japanese Legal System: Introductory Cases and Materials.* Tokyo: University of Tokyo Press, 1976.

Terrill, R. *World Criminal Justice Systems: A Survey*, Cincinnati, OH: Anderson Publishing, 1999.

New York Times, "Killer's Parents Agree to Pay Kobe Families," January 21, 2000, p. A12.

Tipton, E. *Japanese Police State: The Tokko in Interwar Japan.* Honolulu: University of Hawaii Press, 1990.

Toffler, A., and H. Toffler. "Sifting Facts from Fiction about 1, *Japan Times*, February 22, 1981, p. 8.

Tokyo Metropolitan Police Department, "Metropolitan Police Department," pamphlet, Tokyo: Tokyo Metropolitan Police, 1998.

Tsuchiya, S. "Crime Trends and Crime Prevention Strategies." Paper written for the United Nations Asia and Far East Institute for the Prevention of Crime and Treatment of Offenders, Tokyo, Japan, October 1980.

Uchiyama, A. "A Study on the Factors of Delinquency among Primary School Children." *Reports of the National Research Institute of Police Science* 20, no. 1, September 1979.

UNAFEI (United Nations Asia Far East Institute). "The Criminal Justice System in Japan: Prosecution," Asia Far East Institute for the Prevention of Crime and Treatment of Offenders, *Resource Material Series, No. 53*, Fuchu, Japan: United Nations, 1998.

U.S. Bureau of the Census. *Statistical Abstract of the United States.* Washington, DC: U.S. Government Printing Office, 1980.

U.S. Department of Justice. *Bureau of Justice Statistics: Local Police Departments, 1997.* Washington, DC: U.S. Government Printing Office, 1999.

———. *F.B.I. Uniform Crime Reports—Crime in the United States, 1998*, Washington, DC: U.S. Government Printing Office, 1999.

———. *Criminal Victimization in the U.S. National Crime Survey Report 1998.* Washington, DC: U.S. Government Printing Office, September 1999.

———. *Crime in the United States: Uniform Crime Reports, 1997*, Washington, DC: U.S. Government Printing Office, 1997.

Vogel, E. *Japan As Number One: Lessons for America.* Cambridge, MA: Harvard University Press, 1980.

Von Mehren, A., ed. *Law in Japan: The Legal Order in a Changing Society.* Cambridge, MA: Harvard University Press, 1963.

Wagatsuma, H. "Minority Status and Delinquency in Japan." In George De Vos, ed., *Socialization for Achievement: Essays on the Cultural Psychology of the Japanese.* Berkeley: University of California Press, 1973.

Wall, P. *Eyewitness Identification in Criminal Cases*. Springfield, IL: Charles C. Thomas, 1965.

Westney, E. "The Emulation of Western Organizations in Meiji Japan: The Case of Paris Prefecture Police and the Keishi-Cho." *Journal of Japanese Studies*, 8, no. 2, 1982.

Wicker, T. "Attica: Settled but Not Healed," *New York Times*, January 7, 2000, op-ed page.

Wilson, J. *Varities of Police Behavior*. Cambridge, MA: Harvard University Press, 1974.

Wilson, J.Q., and G. Kelling. "The Police and Neighborhood Safety." *Atlantic Monthly*, March 1982.

Index

A

Administration. *See* National Police
  Agency
AIDS, 209
Akimoto, Haruo, 198
Alcoholism, 190–192
Alien Registration Law, 174
American Occupation Force, 29–30,
  146
America's Most Wanted, 62
Ames, Walter, 6, 15, 17, 72, 74–75,
  128, 209–210
Amnesty International, 153–154
Acquittal rates, 147
Arrest warrant, 136
Asahara, Shoko (Chizuo
  Matsumoto), 228–229,
  230
Asakura, T., 62
Astill, J., 124, 125
Attitudes
  toward legal system, 15
  of police, 69–80, 101–103,
    104–105, 112
  of police administrators, 80–89

Attitudes *(continued)*
  toward police, 9, 58, 71, 98–99,
    214–217, 219–223
  toward psychotherapy, 197–198
Auerbach, J., 15
Aum Shinrikyo sect, 227–231

B

Bail decision, 137
Bando, S., 54, 178
Bayley, David, 6, 30, 63, 67, 76, 82
Bicycle theft, 51–52, 109
Borchard, E., 61
Bortz, Ana, 175
Brazilians in Japan, 159, 175
"Broken Windows" theory of crime,
  221
Bullying cases, 181–182
Business
  alcohol abuse in, 191
  conflict resolution in, 14–15
  downsizing, 55–56
  financial crime in, 129, 130
  psychological counseling in, 198
  security firms, 210, 213–214

Business *(continued)*
   suicides in, 203
Butterfield, F., 45, 207

C

Canada, national police system in,
   243
Chapman, B., 243
Chinese in Japan, 159–160, 163,
   165, 167, 171
Chiu Xiong Yin, 163
Choi (Korean pianist), 174–175
Christopher, Warren, 242
Chukakuha group, 224–225, 227
Chwialkowski, P., 30
Citizen attitudes, toward police, 9,
   58, 71, 98–99, 214–217,
   219–223
Citizen cooperation, with police,
   57–59, 77
Citizens groups, anti-crime, 25–26,
   88, 209–213, 233
Citizens' rights, during criminal
   investigation, 64, 79, 113, 218,
   223
Clearance rates, 125
Clifford, W., 6, 134, 149, 224–225
Cohen, T., 30
Colleges and universities
   law programs in, 16
   police station at, 65–66
   student demonstrations in, 65, 66,
      75, 215, 223–224
Community-based treatment, 156
Community-police relations
   benefits of community policing,
      220–221
   crime prevention activities, 98,
      115–118, 213
   and crime prevention associations,
      25–26, 88, 209–213

Community-police relations
   (continued)
   family counseling service, 13,
      197–201, 202
   juvenile counseling service,
      186–190, 212
   with rural police boxes, 92, 95–99,
      104
   telephone lines (*Jumin* Corner), 98
   and victims of crime, 109
Computer-related crime, 129–130
Confessions, 124–125, 141
Conflict resolution, 8, 12–18
Conformity, 8, 126
Constitution of 1947, 146
Convictions, 140, 141, 142–143, 152
Correctional system
   community-based treatment, 156
   probation and parole, 154,
      156–157, 199
   See also Prison system
Corruption, police, 78, 222
Courts
   convictions, 140, 141, 142–143,
      144, 152
   and detention, 124, 136
   disposition of cases (1988–1997),
      137–140
   district court, 146, 150–151
   and eyewitness identifications, 62
   Family Court, 146, 149, 194–195
   sentencing, 144–145, 152, 164
   Summary Court, 146, 149,
      150–151, 195
   Supreme Court, 146, 218
   trial length, 150–151
   trial proceedings, 60, 147–149
Crichton, Michael, 3
Crime
   academic pressure as cause of,
      122–123
   "Broken Windows" theory of, 221

Crime *(continued)*
citizens' attitudes toward, 220–221
computer-related/high-tech,
129–130
and data accuracy, 4–5
financial, 129, 130
by foreigners, 108, 159–160,
164–175
larceny, 5, 109, 125, 166
organized, 109–111, 113, 161, 212,
231–236
police, 78, 222
reporting of, 128
robberies, 5, 45, 108–109, 132, 165
and sex industry, 161, 194,
208–209, 235
and victims' rights, 113–114, 119
white-collar, 83, 108, 129
See also Crime rate; Drug offenses;
Homicide; Juvenile
delinquency; Violent crime
Crime prevention associations,
25–26, 88, 209–213, 233
Crime rate, 59, 109, 125
and police presence, 80
reasons for low rate, 7–11,
126–127
vs U.S., 3–6
Criminal investigation
botched, 222
citizen cooperation with, 57–59, 77
citizens' rights during, 64, 79, 113,
218, 223
and confessions, 124–125, 141
detention during, 124, 136, 149,
163–164
and eyewitness accounts, 60–62,
111
of foreigners, 124–125, 163–165
"hot pursuit" issue in, 114, 119
and informants, 128–129
and interrogation, 80

Criminal investigation *(continued)*
methods of, 128
prosecutors' role in, 60, 134–137
undercover operations, 114, 137
and wiretapping, 137, 236
and written evidence, 137
Criminal Procedure Code of 1890,
12
Cults and sects, 227–231
Currie, Elliott, 45

D

"Dad hunting," 182
Daimyo, 18
Death, causes of, 207
Defense lawyers, 124, 136, 147, 164
Destroying the World To Save It
(Lifton), 228–229
Detention, pre-trial, 124, 136, 149,
163–164
Disaster relief, 80, 88
Discipline problems, police, 76–77,
83
Dissidents and radicals, police
behavior toward, 224–227
District courts, 146, 150–151
Divorce rate, 126, 177
Domestic disputes, 45–46, 59–60,
64–65, 109, 199
Dore, R., 97
Drug Generation (Osamu), 194
Drug offenses
by entertainers, 193
by foreigners, 167, 173, 174
by juveniles, 186, 192–194
by organized crime groups,
109–110, 232, 235
by police, 222
and Safety Bureau, 82–83
Drunkenness, 140, 191
Dubro, A., 161

E

Earthquakes, 80, 88, 228
Economy, 7, 10–11, 55–56, 113
Education
 drop outs/truants, 185–186
 of police administrators, 16, 81–82
 police entrance requirements, 34,
  239
 stressful effects of academic
  pressure, 122–123
 violence in schools, 184–185
Eichenberger, Robert, 29
Emergency calls, 45–52, 59–60,
 120
Employment. *See* Labor force
Energy
 nuclear, 227
 supply, 7
Entrance standards, police, 34, 239
European Economic Community, 7
Eyewitness testimony, 60–62, 111

F

FACES, 62
Facial likeness composites, 62
Family
 academic pressures on, 123
 counseling, 13, 188–189, 197–201,
  202, 244
 and domestic disputes, 45–46,
  59–60, 64–65, 109, 199
 instability, 87–88, 126–127, 194,
  238
 police work tradition in, 75
 responsibility, 7, 126
 routine police visits to, 46–49, 63,
  97–98, 106, 218
 working mothers, 177–178
Family Court, 146, 149, 183,
 194–195

Federal Bureau of Investigation
 (FBI) Academy, 240
 crime data of, 4, 45, 128, 177
Filipinos in Japan, 162, 163–164
Firearms. *See* Guns
Firearms and Swords Control Law,
 110
Food supply, 7
Foot and bicycle patrols, 60,
 220–221
Forces of Order (Bayley), 76
Foreigners in Japan
 and citizenship, 108, 159
 crime by, 108, 159–160, 164–175
 detention of, 124–125, 163–164
 illegal immigrants, 160–162, 170
 Japanese willingness to assist,
  120
 nationalities of, 159–160
 population of, 159, 164
 prejudice against, 158–159, 160,
  162–163, 175
 routine police questioning of,
  63–64, 219
 in sex industry, 161, 208
French, H., 55, 123, 162–163,
 175, 177, 185–186
Fuchu Prison, 153, 155
Fukae, M., 203
Fukuoka Prefectural Police, 78

G

Gender Equality Law, 54
Ghosn, Carlos, 10
Gibney, F., 13
Gordon, A., 10
Group membership. *See* Social
 groups
Guns
 control, 9, 45, 110, 244–245
 in homicides, 44–45, 205

Guns *(continued)*
  and organized crime groups, 110,
    235
  police use of, 49–50, 73, 108
  in suicides, 205–206, 207

H

Hagihara, Keizo, 181
Halfway-house facilities, 156
Handgun Control, 45
Hase, Jun, 182
Hattori, Ken, 182–183
Herbert, W., 158, 159, 160, 161, 162,
    163, 164
High-tech crime, 129–130
Hirano, R., 18
Hokkaido Prefectural Police, 72,
    91–105
Homelessness, 207–208
Homicide
  and academic pressures, 123
  clearance rate, 125
  gun use in, 44–45, 205
  by juveniles, 182–184
  Kobe murders, 182
  by organized crime, 110, 235
  random, 131, 222
  rate, 5, 6, 45
Homosexuality, 140
Ho-no-hana Sam pogyo cult, 230
Horiuchi, K., 136, 137, 140, 147
Hoshino, Kanehiro, 132, 220, 231,
    232, 236

I

Iguchi, Katsuhiko, 124
Ike, N., 20
Illegal immigrants, 160–162, 170
Immigration Control Act, 160
Immigration policy, 162

Informants, 128–129
Intelligence gathering, 105–106
Internet
  pornography, 129
  women's use of, 237–238
Interquest, 62
Interrogation, 80, 164
Investigation. *See* Criminal
    investigation
Ishida, T., 20
Ishikawa, Hiroyoshi, 163

J

Jamison, Kay Redfield, 205
Japan, strengths and weaknesses of,
    6–7
Japan Culture Council, 15
Japanese Bar Association, 164
Japanese Police State (Tipton), 28
Japan as Number One (Vogel), 7
Japan Society, 134, 144
Judges
  bail grant by, 137
  detention requests to, 136
  panels, 146
  sentencing of foreigners, 164
  in summary procedure, 140
Judicial and Legal Training Institute,
    16, 82, 83, 195
Judo, 35, 60, 73
Justice Policy Institute, 149
Justice system. *See* Legal system
Juvenile delinquency, 80, 84, 238
  academic pressures as cause of,
    87–88
  and alcohol abuse, 191–192
  bullying cases, 181–182
  "dad hunting," 182
  defined, 176–177
  and drug abuse, 192–194
  in family court, 194–195

Juvenile delinquency *(continued)*
  Kobe murders, 182
  motorcycle gangs *(bōsōzoku)*,
      180–181, 190
  offense categories, 109, 177, 178
  prosecution of, 182–184
  rise in, 177–180
  in rural community, 104–105
  school violence, 181, 184–185
Juveniles
  counseling centers for, 186–190,
      200, 212, 244
  pregnancy of, 127
  suicide of, 204–205

K

Kakumaruha group, 224–225
Kamata, Satoshi, 203
Kamm, Henry, 50–51
Kanetake-Oura, B., 21, 24–25
Kanji, Nishio, 162
Kaplan, D., 161
Kawashima, T., 12, 13–14, 17
Kelling, G., 221
Kendo, 35, 60
Kenshakai cult, 230
Kirk, Donald, 141
Kitagawa, Z., 14
Kitchen Drinkers (Meiko), 191
Kobayashi, Masaaki, 203
Koreans in Japan, 108, 159, 174–175
Koschmann, J. Victor, 20
Kunimatsu, Koji, 228
Kuno, O., 20
Kuroda, Ayumi, 55

L

Labor force
  day workers, 207–208
  downsizing, 55–56

Labor force *(continued)*
  future prospects of, 194
  gender discrimination in, 54–55
  illegal foreign workers, 160–161
  unemployment, 10, 55
  women in, 54, 126–127, 177–178,
      238
  and workaholic behavior, 203
Lacey, M., 127
Larceny, 5, 109, 125, 166
Larivee, J., 156
Lawyers
  defense, 124, 136, 147, 163, 164
  education of, 16
  nonlicensed, 16–17
  numbers of, 17
  public prosecutor, 60, 134–141,
      144
Legal system
  Constitution of 1947, 146
  foreigners in, 124–25
  and gender discrimination, 54–55
  lack of litigation, 8, 12–18
  of Meiji period, 12, 26–27, 135
  prosecutors' role in, 60, 134–137,
      140–141, 144
  See also Correctional system;
      Courts; Judges; Lawyers;
      Prison system
Lifton, Robert J., 228–229
Lineups, 61
Loftus, E., 61
Los Angeles Police Department
      (L.A.P.D.), 242
Lost items, 98

M

MacArthur, Douglas, 30, 146
Machizawain, Shizuo, 198
Magnier, M., 54
Maki, Y., 165, 167

Makihara, Noriyuku, 193
Marriage rate, 126
Matsumoto, S., 20–21
Meier, R.D., 200
Meiji period
  authoritarianism of, 19–20, 27–28
  legal system in, 12, 26–27, 135
  modernization program of, 19
  neighborhood associations in, 25, 26
  police services in, 20–25, 28–29, 31
  prison system in, 149
  radical leftist suppression in, 26–27
Meiko, H., 191
Mitchell, R., 26, 27–28
Miwa lock maker, 162
Monahan, L.H., 200
Morihara, Hideki, 124–125
Moshavi, S., 230
Motorcycle gangs (*bosozoku*), 180–181, 190
Mugishima, Fumio, 231
Munehiro, H., 165, 174
Muraoka, Tatsuko, 231
Murder. *See* Homicide

N

Nader, Ralph, 15
Nagashima, A., 140
National Community Safety Campaign, 210
National Crime Survey (U.S.), 128
National Guard (U.S.), 74–75
National Police Agency, 30, 46
  attitudes toward work, 80–89
  crime data of, 4–5
  and foreign criminality, 164–165, 174
  lawyers in, 16, 80
  in Meiji period, 23

National Police Agency *(continued)*
  organizational chart of, 90
  promotion in, 81
  reassignments/transfers in, 85–87, 105, 106
  recruitment to, 80–81, 82
  Safety Bureau, 82–83
  training program of, 35–36, 82
  victims' rights policy of, 113–114, 119
National police system, 241–244
National Public Safety Commission, 30, 31, 32
National Public Service Exam, 80–81
National Research Institute of Police Science, 59, 132, 219, 231
Neighborhood associations, 25–26, 88, 209–213
Nishihara, Yukiko, 204
Nishimura, Haruo, 132
Nissan, 10
Nonprosecution, 137, 138–139, 140
Nuclear energy, demonstrations against, 227

O

Okayama Prefectural Police, 72, 105–121
Okinawa, anti-American demonstrations in, 227
Okudaira, Y., 26, 27, 28, 230
Okudaira, Yasuhiro, 228
On The Margins of Japanese Society (Stevens), 207
Organizational structure
  National Police Agency, 90
  police station, 92, 94
  prefectural, 92, 93
Organized crime, 109–111, 113, 161, 212, 231–236

Osaka Bar Association, 164
Osamu, Mizutani, 194
O'Toole, Stephen, 124
Ouchi, William, 85–86

P

Parental Leave Law of 1992, 54
Parker, L., 8, 61, 149, 156, 200
Peace Preservation Law, 26–27,
    29
Penal Code of 1880, 12
Perry, J.C., 29, 30
Perry, Matthew, 158
Phone cards, bogus, 194
Photo arrays, 61, 111
Police
    attitudes toward work, 69–89,
        101–103, 104–105, 112
    and Aum Shinrikyo sect,
        227–231
    citizen opinion of, 9, 58, 71,
        98–99, 214–217, 219–223
    clearance rates of, 125
    and community. See
        Community-police relations
    and courts, 60
    crime/corruption, 78, 222
    discipline problems among, 76–77,
        83
    and dissident/radical groups,
        224–227
    entrance standards for, 34, 239
    investigation. See Criminal
        investigation
    in Meiji period, 20–25, 28–29, 31
    numbers of, 32
    occupational choice of, 70–74, 75,
        77
    postwar reorganization of, 29–31
    prefectural organization, 92, 93
    professionalism of, 33–34

Police *(continued)*
    professional/scholarly evaluations
        of, 217–219
    promotion of, 81, 82, 240
    railway, 121
    rank structure of, 32–33, 43,
        80–81
    recruitment of, 34–35, 72–73,
        112, 239–240
    reforms, 223
    retirement of, 71, 112–113
    riot, 74–75
    salaries, 37, 81, 120
    samurai as, 18–19
    and student demonstrations, 65,
        66, 75, 215, 223–224
    training of, 35–36, 60, 82, 84
    and women's employment, 52,
        54, 84, 96, 108, 114
    See also National Police Agency;
        United States, police in
Police boxes, rural (*chūzaisho*),
    21, 42
    attitude toward work, 101–103,
        104–105
    community relations of, 92,
        95–99, 104
    daily routine in, 103–104,
        119–120
    firearms use in, 108
    physical setup of, 96
    recruitment for, 100–101
    and routine family visits, 97–98,
        106
    types of crime, 99–100, 104,
        120
Police boxes, urban (*kōban*),
    39–40
    conflict resolution services of,
        13
    criticism of system, 84, 88–89
    daily routine in, 53

Police boxes, urban (*kōban*)
(*continued*)
emergency calls to, 45–46, 59–60
firearms use in, 49–50, 73
foot and bicycle patrols of, 60
goals of, 65
in Meiji period, 21, 23–24
mobile, 97
national standardization of,
40–43
routine family visits, 46–49, 63,
218
routine questioning of citizens,
63–64
in skid row district, 66–68
traffic enforcement by, 66, 79
and violent crime, 44–45
working conditions in, 42–43
work schedules of, 42
Police of Japan, The, 30
Police Law of 1954, 30–31
Population, homogeneous, 7
Pornography, 129, 194, 212
Prison system
conditions and treatment in,
153–154
incarceration rate, 149, 153
pre-trial detention, 124, 136,
149, 163
recidivism rate, 153
regulations, 153, 155
Probation and parole, 154, 156,
199
Professionalism of police, 33–34
Promotions, 81, 82, 240
Prosecutor, public, 60, 134–141,
144
Prostitution, 161, 190, 194,
208–209, 235
Protection cells, 154
Psychiatrists, 198
Psychotherapy, 197–198

Public opinion. *See* Attitudes
Public Police Law of 1900, 27

Q

Questioning, routine, 63–64

R

Radical movements, 26–27,
224–227
Railway police, 121
Rank structure, 32–33, 43, 80–81
Rape, 5, 114, 222
Recidivism rate, 153
Reckless, Walter, 76
Recruitment, 34–35, 72–73, 112,
239–240
*Reports of the National Research
Institute of Police Science*,
220
Retirement, 71, 112–113
Ring Ring House, 235
Riot police, 74–75
Rising Sun (Crichton), 3
Robberies, 5, 45, 108–109, 132,
165
Rosal, Manalili, 164
Rout, L., 103
Royal Canadian Mounted Police
(RCMP), 243

S

Safety Bureau, 82–83
Sakamoto, T., 55
Salaries, 37, 81, 120
Samurai, 18–19, 21, 135
Sarin gas attack, 228, 230
School drop outs, 185–186
School violence, 184–185, 222
Security industry, 210, 213–214

Sentencing, 144–145, 152, 164
Seto, Jun'ichi, 183
Sex crimes, 114, 222
Sex industry, 161, 194, 208–209, 235
Shaw, G., 149
Shikito, Public Prosecutor, 134
Shogun, 19
Shoji, Yoshimi, 203
Shoplifting, 109
Shotaro, T., 181, 184
Show-ups, 61, 111
Shreiber, M., 182
Sims, C., 78, 222, 223
Social groups
  collective interest of, 17
  conflict resolution in, 14
  hierarchical nature of, 13–14
  teamwork in, 7
Social values, and crime rate, 7–8
Social welfare system, 208
Social workers, 198
Sterling, Eric, 184
Stevens, C., 207–208
Stoddard, S., 231
Strom, S., 198, 203, 204
Student demonstrations, 65, 66, 75, 215, 223–224
Sudo, Masaru, 203
Sugai, S., 21, 23
Suicide, 109, 182, 201, 203–207
Summary Court, 146, 149, 150–151
Summary procedure, 138–139, 140
Supreme Court, 146, 218
Suzuki, Shingo, 132
Suzuki, Yoshio, 141, 144

T

Takahashi, Yoshiaki, 132
Takaike, Toshiko, 154, 156

Tanabe, T., 12
Tanaka, H., 135
Tanaka, Yasuro, 164
Tanisho, Yasuto, 124
Teachers, violence against, 184–185
Teamwork, 7
Teenagers. *See* Juvenile delinquency; Juveniles
Terrill, R., 149
Terrorism, of *Aum Shinrikyo* sect, 227–231
Tetsuya, Fujimoto, 182
Theory Z (Ouchi), 85–86
Tipton, E., 23, 26, 28, 29
Toffler, Alvin and Heidi, 6–7
Tokugawa Shogunate, 12, 18
Tokuhisa, Haruhiko, 181
Tokyo Association of Chinese Residents, 163
Tokyo Metropolitan Police Department, 38–39
  and crime prevention associations, 211–212
  family counseling by, 200, 201
  and foreign criminality, 167, 170, 172, 174
  history of, 22, 23, 28–29
  recruitment in, 72
  riot police in, 74–75
  station activities in, 39–68
  traffic enforcement in, 79
  women in, 52
Tokyo University
  law program of, 16
  police station at, 65–66
  student demonstrations at, 223–224
Traffic enforcement, 66, 79, 119
Training, 35–36, 60, 82, 84
Trial proceedings, 60, 147–149

Truancy, 185–186
Tsuchiya, S., 140
Tsurumi, Ayako, 231
Turkish bath prostitution, 209

U

Undercover operations, 114, 137
Unemployment, 10, 55
Uniform Crime Reports (FBI), 4, 45,
    128, 177
United Nations Congress on the
    Prevention of Crime and
    Treatment of Offenders, 114
United States
  crime rate in, 5, 6, 45, 125, 126
  crime statistics in, 4
  drug abuse in, 193
  family instability in, 126–127
  incarceration rate in, 149, 153
  juvenile delinquency in, 176–177,
      180, 183–184
  litigation growth in, 15
  Okinawa demonstrations against,
      227
  probation/parole system in, 156
  suicide in, 203
  unreported crime in, 128
  victims' rights in, 113
United States, police in
  clearance rates of, 125
  community relations, 92, 220–221,
      244
  court appearances by, 60
  and domestic disputes, 200–201
  entrance standards for, 34
  and eyewitness testimony, 61
  foot and bicycle patrols of, 60
  lack of standardization, 41–42
  numbers of, 32
  quasi-national system model for,
      241–244

United States, police in *(continued)*
  and routine questioning, 64
  in rural areas, 103
  salary of, 37
  training of, 35, 240
  weaknesses of, 239, 241
Universities. *See* Colleges and
    universities

V

Vagrancy, 64, 140
Valentine, Lewis, 30
Vandalism, 49
Victims' rights, 113–114, 119
Violent crime
  and domestic disputes, 45–46,
      59–60, 64–65
  by foreigners, 166
  gun use in, 44–45, 110, 205
  increase in, 130–132
  by juveniles, 181, 182–185
  organized, 111
  reasons for lack of, 132–134
  See also Homicide
Vogel, Ezra, 7
Von Mehren, A., 135

W

Wall, P., 61
Wealth distribution, 10
Westney, E., 18, 22, 23, 33, 68
*When A Family Member Is Driven
    to Suicide* (Kamata), 203
White-collar crime, 83, 108, 129
White Paper on Crime, 125, 144
White Paper on Police, 54, 110,
    164, 200, 201, 233
Wicker, Tom, 149, 153
Wilson, J.Q., 221
Wintemute, Garen, 205, 207

Wiretapping law, 137, 236
Women
    Internet use by, 237–238
    labor force participation of, 54,
        126–127, 177–178, 238
    police wives, 73, 76, 87, 96,
        119–120
    in police work, 52, 54, 84, 96, 108,
        114
    and workplace discrimination,
        54–55
    See also Family

Workforce. See Labor force
World Conference on Women,
    Beijing, 54
World Health Organization (WHO),
    191–192

Y

Yamaguchi-gumi gang, 110,
    232
Yamakawa, Y., 164
Yokohama Police Department, 22

L. Craig Parker, Jr. is at present professor of criminal justice at the University of New Haven. He received his AB degree from Bates College and his Master's degree in Psychological Services from Springfield College. Prior to being awarded his Ph.D. from the State University of New York at Buffalo, he worked as a counselor in a federal pre-release guidance center for youthful offenders and as a clinical psychologist for the New York State Department of Mental Hygiene. In 1967, he was appointed assistant professor at the University of Wisconsin, where he taught rehabilitation counseling and criminal justice. In 1970, he joined the faculty of the University of Alberta as an associate professor and counseling psychologist. During that period, he provided in-service training for the Royal Canadian Mounted Police and the Edmonton City Police Department. His publications include *Legal Psychology* (1980) and, with L. Monahan and R.D. Meier, *Interpersonal Psychology for Law Enforcement and Correction* (1989). His most recent book was *Finnish Criminal Justice: An American Perspective* (1993).